BOUNCE BACK!

Teacher's Handbook

BOUNCE BACK!

A CLASSROOM RESILIENCY PROGRAM

Teacher's Handbook

Helen McGrath and Toni Noble

PEARSON
Longman

Pearson Education Australia
Unit 4, Level 2
14 Aquatic Drive
Frenchs Forest NSW 2086

www.pearsoned.com.au

Senior Acquisitions Editor: Diane Gee-Clough
Senior Project Editor: Natasha Dupont
Copy Editor: Janice Keynton
Proofreader: Felicity Shea
Cover and internal design by R.T.J. Klinkhamer
Illustrations by Techa Noble
Typeset by Midland Typesetters, Maryborough, Vic.

Printed in Malaysia

2 3 4 5 07 06 05 04

National Library of Australia
Cataloguing-in-Publication data

McGrath, Helen.
Bounce back! : a classroom resilience program : teacher's handbook.

Bibliography.
ISBN 0 7339 9957 3.

1. Resilience (Personality trait) in children. 2. Resilience (Personality trait) in adolescence. I. Noble, Toni. II. Title.

370.153

An imprint of Pearson Education Australia

CONTENTS

What's in this book? *ix*

1 An introduction to the BOUNCE BACK! Resiliency Program *1*

The background of the BOUNCE BACK! Resiliency Program *2*
An overview of the contents of the BOUNCE BACK! Resiliency Program *3*
Content of the three Teacher's Resource Books *3*
The underlying principles of the BOUNCE BACK! Resiliency Program *9*
Frequently asked questions *12*
References *13*

2 The concept of resilience *14*

What is resilience? *14*
The emergence of resiliency *14*
The protective processes and resources that promote resilience *15*
Environments that promote resilience *17*
Personal coping skills that empower young people to act more resiliently *21*
Myths and realities about resilience *24*
In summary *27*
References *28*

3 The big picture of resilience *31*

The world of young people today *31*
What are some of the social and cultural changes young people face today? *31*
Counselling and psychology today *34*
Social welfare today *34*
Resilience and today's educational context *35*
Resilience and issues of bullying, school violence and behaviour management *36*
Resilience and drug education *36*
Resilience and suicide prevention *36*
Resilience and boys' education *36*
Resilience and the teaching of social skills *37*
In summary *37*
References *38*

4 The personal coping skills approach *40*

Optimistic thinking *40*
Maintaining hope in difficult situations *43*
Normalising *44*
Everyday stressors and major stressors *45*
Using humour *45*

Helpful and rational thinking *49*
Help-seeking and self-disclosure *49*
Self-concept, self-esteem and self-efficacy *50*
What schools can do to develop healthy self-esteem *52*
Interpersonal and intrapersonal intelligence and emotional intelligence *52*
Teaching the BOUNCE BACK! acronym *52*
More details about the statements in BOUNCE! and BOUNCE BACK! *53*
How the BOUNCE BACK! acronym addresses specific emotional and behavioural patterns *55*
Creating psychological safety when using the BOUNCE BACK! Resiliency Program *55*
Indicators for referring a student for professional help *60*
References *60*

5 The role of teachers in building resilience *62*

The environmental building blocks of resilience *62*
The important role of schools and teachers in building resilience in young people *62*
Building resilient schools and classrooms *63*
References *74*

6 Leading resilient schools *77*

Understanding that change is a people process *77*
Developing 'school spirit' *78*
Sustaining new programs and using a whole-school approach *79*
Not expecting too much too soon *80*
Not letting a program implementation 'go cold' *81*
Creating opportunities for constructive dissent and problem solving *81*
Developing collaborative partnerships with the local and broader community *82*
In summary *82*
References *82*

7 Building family resilience *84*

Families *84*
Family strengths *85*
Building positive family–school connections *86*
In summary *89*
References *89*

8 Managing school bullying *90*

Begin with a clear definition of what bullying is *91*
Recognise the different forms of bullying behaviour *92*
Have a clear picture as to why some students bully others *94*
Understand why some students *don't* bully others *98*
Understand why some students are more likely to be bullied *99*
The negative effects of being bullied *99*
What schools can do about bullying *101*
Developing an anti-bullying policy *102*
Identification *102*
Preventing bullying *103*

Managing bullying *107*
Schools as safe places where all students feel protected *111*
References *111*

9 Measuring aspects of resilience *113*

The purpose of the measurement instruments *113*
The PEPS: Protective Environmental Processes Scale *115*
PEPS: Protective Environmental Processes Scale—Upper version *116*
PEPS: Result chart—Upper version *118*
PEPS: Protective Environmental Processes Scale—Middle version *119*
PEPS: Result chart—Middle version *121*
The PRASE: Protective Resilient Attitudes and Skills Evaluation *122*
Protective Resilient Attitudes and Skills Evaluation (PRASE)—Upper version *123*
Coping statements in the PRASE—Upper version *127*
Scoring details for PRASE—Upper version *127*
Result sheet for PRASE—Upper version *129*
Protective Resilient Attitudes and Skills Evaluation (PRASE)—Middle version *130*
Coping statements in the PRASE—Middle version *133*
Scoring details for PRASE—Middle version *133*
Result sheet for PRASE—Middle version *135*
Students' perceptions of classroom connectedness (SPOCC) *136*
SPOCC: Students' Perceptions of Classroom Connectedness—Primary *137*
Teachers' Observations of Classroom Connectedness (TOCC) *139*
TOCC: Teachers' Observations of Classroom Connectedness—Primary *140*
Teacher Assessment of Resilience Factors In their Classroom (TARFIC) *140*
TARFIC: Teacher Assessment of Resilience Factors In their Classroom—Primary *141*
TARFIC: Scoring my personal profile—Primary *146*
TARFIC: Teacher Assessment of Resilience Factors In their Classroom—Secondary *147*
TARFIC: Scoring my personal profile—Secondary *150*
Assessing changes in aspects of resilience *151*
Reference *151*

10 Cooperative group strategies *152*

Teaching aids for cooperative learning groups *152*
Group cooperative learning strategies *152*
Whole-class cooperative learning strategies *152*
Teaching aids for cooperative learning groups *153*
Whole-class cooperative activities *160*
Grouping strategies *162*

11 Resources and other teaching strategies *165*

Resources *165*
Other classroom strategies and activities *177*

12 Black line masters *183*

BLM 4:1 BOUCE BACK poster *184*
BLM 4.2 BOUNCE BACK acronym *185*

BLM 4:3 Rules for classroom discussions *186*
BLM 8:1 Survey on bullying *188*
BLM 11:1 A–Z of emotions *189*
BLM 11:2 How to make a ball that bounces *190*
BLM 11:3 Cube pattern *192*
BLM 11:4 Template for electronic matching pairs quiz *193*
BLM 11:5 Instructions for making a moveable responsibility pie chart *194*
BLM 11:6 Templates for making a moveable responsibility pie chart *195*
BLM 11:7 How animals and plants protect and defend themselves *198*
BLM 11:8 How humans protect and defend themselves *202*

What's in this book?

This Teacher's Handbook is divided into the following sections:

Chapter 1—An introduction to the BOUNCE BACK! Resiliency Program

Chapter one provides an overview of the BOUNCE BACK! Resiliency Program and a summary of the ten units of work that appear in the three separate Teacher's Resource Books. One is designed for Junior Primary, one for Middle Primary and one for Upper Primary/Junior Secondary years.

Chapter 2—The concept of resilience

Chapter two looks at the construct of resilience in greater detail. It outlines the protective factors and skills that have been identified by research as the most significant resources in helping young people grow stronger. Myths and realities relating to the concept of resilience are also discussed.

Chapter 3—The big picture of resilience

Chapter three presents the bigger picture of the world in which today's young people live. It also outlines the social, psychological, welfare and educational contexts within which the BOUNCE BACK! Resiliency Program is located.

Chapter 4—The personal coping skills approach

Chapter four details the personal coping skills taught in the BOUNCE BACK! Resiliency Program and outlines their theoretical rationale. These skills have been incorporated into the acronyms of BOUNCE and BOUNCE BACK. The two acronyms form the core of the program and have been designed to assist students to learn and use effective coping skills. Guidelines for creating a class-room environment of psychological safety are also described.

Chapter 5—The role of teachers in building resilience

Chapter five discusses strategies for creating strong levels of school connectedness, peer connectedness, and teacher connectedness: three of the most significant environmental factors to contribute to resilient behaviour in students. From an educator's point of view these are the most accessible of all the protective environmental factors that foster resilience in young people.

Chapter 6—Leading resilient schools

Chapter six draws on the school change literature to review key factors that build whole school connectedness and lead to success in implementing a new program in a school such as BOUNCE BACK.

Chapter 7—Building family resilience

Chapter seven describes the ways to build strong family–school connectedness. This chapter also offers ideas on running parent information sessions on the BOUNCE BACK! Resiliency Program.

Chapter 8—Managing school bullying

Chapter eight explores the issue of school bullying. One of the greatest challenges to student wellbeing is peer persecution. Resilience cannot develop well where there are high levels of school bullying. This chapter looks at strategies for whole-school management of bullying as well as the theory and concepts underpinning the units of work on bullying.

Chapter 9—Measuring aspects of resilience

Chapter nine contains assessment materials which can assist teachers to identify students who are less resilient or in less resilient circumstances, and to assess student learning about resilience. There are also checklists to facilitate reflection and evaluation by teachers and students of how much the classroom environment fosters student resilience.

Chapter 10—Cooperative group strategies

Chapter ten contains details of cooperative learning strategies that have been used extensively across the ten classroom units in each of the three Teacher's Resource Books.

Chapter 11—Resources and other teaching strategies

Chapter eleven provides details of other classroom strategies and teaching resources referred to frequently throughout the ten units in each of the three Teacher's Resource Books.

Author acknowledgements

Thank you

We would like to express our thanks to the following people who all assisted in some way with the development, trialling or writing of the program. Many others also assisted and we apologise if we have left anyone out.

Jamie McGrath; Kate Bott; Techa Noble; Margaret Lewis; David Lewis; Chris Perry; Denise Attwater; Judy Van Pelt; Sandra Metz; Marj Wordsworth; Susie Andrews; Kay Ely; Marg Armstrong; Elizabeth Anders; Kelle Costellano; Pam Blackman; Teresa Bossio; Sue Murray; Robyn Nillson; Pam Mathieson; Brendan Saville; Marg Quon; Kris Arcaro; Debbie Pynenborg; Jenny Hurley; Laureen Walton; Kerry Barratt; Elaine Wilson; April Quinn; Jan Wright; Wendy Bleek; Mark Pescud; Steve Blackwell; Pam Burnau.

The BOUNCE BACK! project has been a huge enterprise over many years. We would especially like to thank our husbands, Robert Attwater and Andrew Noble, for their faith in the project, their patience, their love and their support.

AN INTRODUCTION TO THE BOUNCE BACK! RESILIENCY PROGRAM

For all of us, life is an exciting and often unpredictable journey that provides joys, satisfactions and highlights, but also some difficulties, frustrations, disappointments and hard times. Through meeting life's challenges we grow stronger and gain personal coping skills and a sense of who we are. We become more resilient. When we talk about human resilience we usually mean the capacity of a person to cope with times of adversity and hardship.

Young people have always needed coping skills to deal with life's challenges, but there is an ever-increasing body of evidence from many different disciplines that suggests that the world of today's young people is different from that of previous generations in four significant ways:

> We do not receive wisdom, we must discover it for ourselves, after a journey through the wilderness which no one else can make for us, which no one can spare us, for our wisdom is the point of view from which we come at last to regard the world (Proust, *Remembrance of Things Past* 1951:923).

- Young people are more likely nowadays to encounter a greater range of difficult circumstances, negative events and down times than previous generations.
- They are less well equipped and well situated than previous generations to cope well with these challenges and down times.
- In response to such stressors, they are more likely to turn to maladaptive strategies like overusing drugs and alcohol, behaving in an anti-social way, and suicide.
- There is a relative epidemic of depression among young people that was not apparent in previous generations. The World Health Organisation predicts that depression will be the world's leading cause of disability by 2020. Being depressed makes it even more difficult for some young people to cope with normal but negative life events. However caused, depression itself can also become one of the hardships that a young person has to deal with.

These four factors are looked at in greater detail in Chapter 3.

That's the bad news. The good news is that research has now been able to identify the most significant coping skills and protective life circumstances that help young people to become more resilient. The study of resilience is emerging as a powerful tool in our ongoing battle to prevent youth depression, suicide, self-harm, violence and problematic substance abuse.

Schools can make a major contribution to the development of resilience in students. Next to families, schools are the most effective places in which resilience can be developed. Most coping skills can be taught at school and integrated into the contemporary curriculum. Many of the protective environmental processes can be put into place at school with not too much reorganisation. The BOUNCE BACK! Resiliency Program has been developed as a school-based curriculum program designed to teach students how to become more resilient and to establish environmental contexts and processes that are protective. The program has the following features:

- It is based on research outcomes and sound psychological and educational theory.
- It can be taught to students from their first year of schooling up to Year 8.
- It can inoculate students against the possibility of not coping when faced with future difficulties or adversity, just as vaccinations can inoculate them against the possibility of being adversely affected by exposure to future disease.
- It incorporates practical classroom-friendly activities and strategies that can be integrated with relative ease with current curriculum content and outcomes across all Key Learning Areas.

The background of the BOUNCE BACK! Resiliency Program

An abbreviated version of the BOUNCE BACK! Resiliency Program was trialled in a joint research project between the Drug Education section of the Department of Education in Victoria and the Faculty of Education at Deakin University (McGrath & Anders 2000). Eight teachers were involved in implementing the program in their Year 5 or Year 6 classrooms over 14 weeks. These teachers taught in diverse school communities that included both working-class and middle-class schools, secular and private schools, and rural, inner city and suburban schools.

All the teachers in the study reported that the BOUNCE BACK! Program was user-friendly and easy to implement. At the end of 14 weeks of teaching the program, seven of the eight teachers reported greater confidence in teaching the coping skills that underpin the program. They also reported marked improvements and greater confidence in their ability to counsel their students. They believed their use of the program facilitated better communication with their students, which helped in the students' management of personal issues as well as schoolwork issues. All teachers reported that teaching the program improved their own personal and professional resilience and their capacity to cope with difficult times.

The research also demonstrated that the students in the eight classes were able to learn, understand and recall the BOUNCE BACK! acronym with an average 80% success rate after 14 weeks of the program. At the end of the program, students showed an increase in resilient thinking, especially optimistic and helpful thinking, when asked to solve problems in hypothetical difficult situations. In focus group interviews many students reported using the coping skills in their own lives, including difficult family situations. Some students mentioned they had taught some of the BOUNCE BACK! coping skills to members of their family. During the 14 weeks of the program teachers also observed some students spontaneously using the BOUNCE BACK! statements in real-life stressful situations and in supporting their classmates and friends.

These outcomes suggest that students, their families and their teachers can all gain by their participation in the program. Further research to investigate longer-term outcomes is planned.

There are many anticipated outcomes after consistent implementation across the school of the BOUNCE BACK! Resiliency Program.

In the short term

- The development of a more positive, supportive, prosocial school culture
- Improved student mental health for all students, especially for those who could be considered 'at risk'

- A greater likelihood of students offering effective peer support to friends and classmates
- Improved student learning outcomes as a result of:
  —Increased peer connectedness
  —Increased school connectedness
  —Higher levels of emotional wellbeing
  —Enhanced self-esteem.

In the long term

- Decreased long-term student reliance on drugs and alcohol as a method of coping
- Improved school performance by students in external assessments
- More successful workplace lives for students
- More successful relationships for students
- Stronger families
- Higher levels of teacher resilience and emotional wellbeing
- More effective teacher counselling for students
- More effective goal achievement
- Fewer behaviour problems.

An overview of the contents of the BOUNCE BACK! Resiliency Program

Program materials

There are four books in this program. These are:

Teacher's Handbook for the BOUNCE BACK! Resiliency Program

The contents of this book have been described earlier under the heading 'What's in this book'.

Teacher's Resource Book—Level 1—Junior Primary

This book is suitable for students in the first three years of primary schooling; that is, students aged approximately five to seven years.

Teacher's Resource Book—Level 2—Middle Primary

This book is suitable for students in the third and fourth years of primary schooling; that is, students aged approximately eight to ten years.

Teacher's Resource Book—Level 3—Upper Primary/Junior Secondary

This book is suitable for students in the fifth and sixth years of primary schooling and the first two years of junior secondary; that is, students aged approximately 11 to 14 years.

Content of the three Teacher's Resource Books

Each Teacher's Resource Book contains ten classroom units of work at the appropriate year levels and curriculum outcomes. These are:
- Core values
- Elasticity
- People bouncing back
- Courage
- Looking on the bright side
- Emotions
- Relationships
- Humour
- Bullying

- Success (STAR! In the Junior Primary book, CHAMP! in the Middle Primary book and WINNERS! in the Upper Primary/Junior Secondary book).

The following sections provide a brief description of each unit of work and how the unit teaches young people to be resilient.

Unit 1—Core values

Values are important beliefs about how one should behave. Some schools very clearly communicate their underlying values, whereas in other schools values are implicit rather than explicit. Many schools articulate their values in regards to academic excellence, but are less articulate about prosocial values that underpin how students and staff are expected to interact with and treat each other. One explanation for the phenomenal rise in the popularity of alternative religion-based private schooling across Australia has been that these schools articulate clear prosocial values to parents. A recent article in the *Sydney Morning Herald* explains:

> Parents have been looking for schools that have a strong value base. As our society has grown more diverse, it has been increasingly difficult in large state schools to find a proper value base that can be accepted by atheists, agnostics, Buddhists, Muslims and Christians. (Jacobsen & Wainwright 2001)

A survey of parents of school-aged children by the *Age* newspaper (June 2002) in Victoria found that after 'quality teaching' the most significant attribute of a quality school was seen to be a school's ability to give children a good set of values to live by. Schools with religious affiliations usually articulate prosocial values based on their religious ethos and these values are generally well understood by the school community. Schools without such affiliations may need to consider more explicitly communicating their prosocial values to their school community to facilitate greater parental support.

The core prosocial values of honesty, fairness, support, cooperation, acceptance of differences, respect and friendship are universal values that are linked to the development of resilience. Empathic thinking underpins all these values. These values underpin all religions. Behaving consistently with these prosocial values increases the likelihood that all students will be more accepted and hence gain self-esteem as well as support from others. These values help young people to be connected to their family, peers and teachers. A belief in core values was identified as one of three most prevalent protective factors for young people in Australia today in a recent large-scale study of 9000 young people (Bond et al. 2000). Belonging and feeling supported are critical protective processes in helping students to cope when they experience difficulties, frustrations and hard times. Acting on these prosocial beliefs can increase one's sense of being a decent, successful and worthwhile person, and at the same time provide some support for peers who might need it.

Defining one's values does not, by itself, necessarily transfer into acting in accord with those values. The classroom units of work on core values provide concrete and practical activities to help students understand the importance of the core prosocial values and how these values determine how they behave and relate with others. The unit focuses on activities to teach young people how to behave in ways that reflect the following values:

- Integrity: being honest, fair, responsible and loyal and socially 'just'
- Support: supporting and caring for other people
- Cooperation: cooperating with others
- Acceptance of difference: accepting, respecting, living with and finding the positive side of differences in others
- Respect: respecting the rights of others, and acknowledging your own rights and responsibilities to others in a respectful way
- Friendliness: being friendly and socially responsible, and including others in games and conversations.

Unit 2—Elasticity

This unit introduces the scientific concept of physical resilience or 'bouncing back'. When something is resilient, it is elastic and capable of returning to its original shape after being stretched,

squashed or bent. The elasticity unit serves as an introduction to the unit that follows called 'People bouncing back'. The focus of the elasticity unit is on:
- Investigating and experimenting with elastic forces (e.g. rubber bands, balls bouncing) and stretching (e.g. fabrics, skin)
- Elastic animals (e.g. kangaroos and springboks)
- Springs: how they work and their uses
- Inflatables: where they are and what they are used for (e.g. tyres, balloons)
- Linking scientific resilience to human resilience.

Unit 3—People bouncing back

This unit introduces human resilience, or the capacity of people to bounce back after experiencing hard times. In the Level 1 book, students are introduced to the main acronym of BOUNCE! In the Level 2 and Level 3 books they are introduced to the acronym of BOUNCE BACK! Each acronym acts as a coat hanger for specific coping skills. Teaching students coping skills makes it more likely that they will attain greater emotional wellbeing. Coping skills provide them with cognitions, behaviours and attitudes for making their lives in the classroom and playground happier and more productive; they are also given life skills for coping with any difficult times in their future careers and relationships. The acronyms help them to learn to master the coping statements that underpin the personal skills of resilience. The focus in the unit is on:
- The ways in which 'nature' bounces back (e.g. bush regeneration, skin repair, the immune system)
- People who have 'bounced back' after hardship (e.g. Helen Keller)
- The BOUNCE BACK! acronym and ways of understanding and learning the acronym
- Using helpful thinking (e.g. not overgeneralising, not 'mind-reading', not jumping to conclusions and looking for evidences)
- Normalising negative events rather than personalising them
- Talking to trusted people in order to get a reality check on their thinking and perceptions and seek assistance with problem solving
- Developing skills in taking responsibility or having a 'fair' view of why something went wrong. That means working out how much was due to your own actions, how much was due to the actions of others and how much was due to random factors such as bad luck and timing.

Unit 4—Courage

Courage is needed before one can even contemplate dealing with adverse events or tackling a difficult and threatening task. In this unit, courage is not presented as the absence of fear or distress. Courage is defined as the capacity to face threatening or difficult situations that cause fear or distress, without giving in to those feelings. It is a state of mind that enables us to try to overcome fear with some degree of confidence. Courage is an important life skill that can help young people be more resilient when faced with adversity. The focus in the unit is on:
- Understanding the differences between everyday courage, heroism, thrill seeking, professional risk taking and foolhardiness.
- Understanding that fear is relative. What makes one person scared or nervous may not make another person scared or nervous.
- Developing the skills and perceptions that lead to being more courageous in many areas of one's life.

Unit 5—Looking on the bright side

Optimism has been described by Peterson (2000) as the 'velcro' construct of resilience, to which everything else sticks. A student who thinks optimistically tends to look on the bright side of situations and hope for the best, even when things are not looking good. Being optimistic can empower students and help them to get on top of challenges and manage life's difficulties. Optimism is also a contributing factor to getting along well with others and having good physical health. In contrast, pessimism is linked to a sense of hopelessness and despair and, eventually, depression. The focus in this unit is on:

- Positive tracking, that is, the ability to focus on the positive aspects of a negative situation, however small they may be.
- Positive conversion of negative events and mistakes into opportunities and learning experiences.
- Accepting that bad times are temporary and don't have to spoil other parts of your life.
- Finding hope in difficult times.
- Having confidence in your own ability to solve problems and take positive actions.

Unit 6—Emotions

Correctly recognising and naming their emotions helps students to understand and manage their lives and relationships more effectively and less stressfully. This unit incorporates activities that help young people to identify and understand their feelings and to understand how their thoughts affect their feelings and their behaviour. The main message is that their perception or interpretation of an event helps to determine how they feel, not just the event *per se*. If they are over-aroused and interpret an event in a negative, hopeless or threatening light, then their emotions are likely to be stronger. Stronger emotions may make it more difficult for them to be resilient and bounce back. If they are able to stay calm and find a helpful way to interpret a situation, then they are more able to cope and to problem solve.

Poor management of negative emotions such as anxiety, anger, fear and sadness narrows one's range of thoughts and limits action choices. People who allow their negative emotions to overwhelm them are more likely to act impulsively and be more vulnerable to substance abuse and other acts of self harm. Learning how to express emotions in a positive and assertive way helps people to feel more in control when things are difficult for them. The unit also encourages young people to reflect on what makes them happy and satisfied, a theme that is picked up again in the Success unit. The focus of this unit on emotions is on activities based around the following:

- Understanding that very few events are good or bad in themselves; how you think about something strongly influences how you feel about it.
- Recognising and managing one's own negative emotions such as anger, sadness, worry, disappointment and embarrassment and understanding that you have choices about this.
- Recognising the feelings and intentions of others.
- Responding with empathy to the feelings of others.
- Recognising and enjoying their own positive emotions such as happiness, pride, surprise and excitement.
- Learning how to use positive self-talk and low-key language so that they interpret situations more realistically and helpfully.

Unit 7—Relationships

The two most significant protective environmental factors that promote resilience are feeling connected to peers and feeling connected to family. Students with close relationships cope better with stressors such as failure, bereavement, relationship break-ups, embarrassment and illness. Those supported by close relationships with friends, family or classmates are less vulnerable in the long term to ill health and premature death (Myers 2000). It makes sense to teach young people how to improve their relationships with others. It also makes sense to establish school communities and use class learning strategies that foster the development of strong and positive interpersonal relationships between students.

Having a friend is a very important source of wellbeing for students, as it is for most of us. The Australian Unity Wellbeing Index, released in July 2002, demonstrated that it is relationships with others that have the biggest impact on personal wellbeing. Although all students would like to be well accepted by their peers or be popular, it is their relationships with their friends that are the more important. Having a friend gives a student a sense of self worth; someone who can provide loyalty, support and companionship; someone to bounce ideas off; someone to help with problem solving; and provide an opportunity to receive and give affection. Having a friend also enables a student to practise essential social skills such as conflict resolution, empathic thinking and negotiation. Although many of these skills are also practised in students' everyday classroom and playground interactions, their use in the context of a deeper and more intimate and ongoing relationship enables students to prepare for the more significant relationships they will have later in their lives. Friends provide important emotional support for young people in the social context of today that includes high incidence of relationship and marriage breakdown, the later age of marriage, the greater likelihood that families will be geographically distant, and the pressure of constant change.

Long-term romantic partnerships are the goal of most people in adult life. Married people report being more resilient, happier and more satisfied with life (Myers 2000); the Australian Unity Wellbeing Index (July 2002). However, sustaining a long-term romantic partnership is a great challenge in today's world. It is not easy to do. The social skills that contribute to satisfying friendships and peer relationships are almost identical to the social skills that contribute to satisfying romantic relationships. Among married people, those whose spouse is
• Agreeable (cooperative, positive and able to handle conflict well)
• Conscientious (responsible, hard working and able to achieve goals)
• Emotionally stable (able to manage their emotions) and
• Open to experience (flexible and risk taking)
tend to be more emotionally and sexually satisfied with their relationships than do those who do not have spouses with these qualities (Buss 2000).

The long-term research of John Gottman (1994) has shown that the most satisfying and sustainable romantic relationships are those where both partners have the skills to handle conflict well and focus more on the positives than the negatives in their relationship. He also identified that one of the main reasons many couples found it so hard to deal with conflict effectively was their inability to manage the 'flood' of anxious and angry emotions that overwhelmed them during conflict situations. Relationship skills are not the only factors that contribute to a satisfying and sustainable relationship, but such skills do make a significant difference to the quality of the relationship. The social skills we can teach students at school will contribute to their later success in important adult relationships. This is an additional reason for including this unit on relationships.

In summary, if we teach relationship skills to students:
• In the short term, they will be more likely to be resilient because they will have social support, a sense of social value, and people with whom to cross-check their perceptions about life.
• In the longer term, they will be more likely to:
  —Attract supportive partners
  —Have successful adult friendships which will act as protective factors if they face adverse circumstances
  —Have sustainable romantic relationships which will be protective for themselves as well as for their own children in the next generation
  —Be able to model effective relationship skills for their children.

There are three earlier books by the authors that offer classroom activities that teach social skills. These are:
Friendly Kids, Friendly Classroom. Teaching Social Skills and Confidence in the Classroom
Different Kids, Same Classrooms
Dirty Tricks: Classroom Games for Teaching Social Skills.

They can be found in the references to this chapter. It is not feasible within the scope of this book to incorporate all the material already published in these three books. Instead this unit focuses on aspects that have not been covered extensively in those books. The focus in the 'Relationships' unit is on activities that:

- Develop skills for making and keeping friends
- Develop skills for getting along well with others
- Teach skills for managing conflict
- Provide opportunities for self reflection about one's own current levels of skills in these areas.

Unit 8—Humour

Humour is one of the processes of optimism that significantly contributes to personal resilience. We are able to feel more hopeful and light-hearted when we are laughing. Humour helps us to gain a sense of perspective on our problems because it can throw a little light in an otherwise totally black situation. It reminds us that life goes on. It helps us to cope with what we can't change. Humour can provide an opportunity to release the tension created by strong and uncomfortable emotions such as sorrow, fear and anger. Research consistently demonstrates that laughing results in beneficial physiological changes in our bodies that improve our health and help us to fight illness. This understanding underpins the therapeutic use of humour in medical contexts. Shared laughter is also a unique human bond that helps us to connect with others. Having fun with peers and incorporating humour into classroom activities helps kids to feel more connected with each other, and to stay engaged and on task. Students who are having fun learn more and are less likely to misbehave. The focus in this unit is on:

- Activities that develop an understanding of the processes and styles of humour
- Activities that highlight how humour can be used to assist with coping in hard times as well as with supporting others
- Activities to help students to differentiate between humour that helps and humour that harms or trivialises or denies
- Five-minute humorous activities that can be used as a stress break in class.

Unit 9—Bullying

No study in any school anywhere in the world has shown an absence of bullying (Rigby 2001). Students have the right to feel safe and protected at school from psychological and physical attack. In schools where there is a culture of bullying this basic right is not being met. A recent Australian study of 9000 young people found that a third reported being recently bullied (Bond et al. 2000). Current research on the outcomes of school bullying illustrates the devastating long-term effects of bullying for all involved: the students participating in the bullying, the students who are being bullied, and the many students and teachers who feel distressed and unable to stop the mistreatment and injustice that is occurring. Bullying is such a serious problem that we have devoted a whole separate chapter in this book (Chapter 8) to the topic of managing bullying at a whole-school level.

In the unit of work on bullying in the Teacher's Resource Books the focus is on:

- Making bullying uncool through activities that demonstrate the similarities between bullying, child abuse, terrorism and historical incidents of oppression and persecution. Examples are drawn from the Holocaust, racial hatred and persecution, sledging in sport and the social mobbing processes such as those used by the Ku Klux Klan and seen in soccer riots.
- Investigating the legal and workplace issues related to bullying.
- Activities that portray bullying as an act of cowardice and weakness and those who bully others as 'social predators'.
- Strategies for understanding and managing peer pressure to take part in harassment or to stand by and do nothing about it.
- Teaching the skills and attitudes that enable bystanders to support those who are being mistreated with minimal risk to themselves. Also teaching bystanders to act responsibly by letting a teacher know what is happening, if necessary.
- Activities that teach students the escalating skills needed to respond to 'social predators' at various points in a bullying situation. Initially these skills relate to methods of staying safe by not attracting attention and identifying and avoiding situations that contain danger. If the mistreatment

continues, they need the skills of outsmarting and escaping from the predators and being assertive by giving the bully warnings to desist. At the very least the student needs skills at this point of 'maintaining face' in order to sustain a sense of self-respect, dignity and empowerment. Lastly, if the situation continues for a long time without resolution, they need the skills of acting responsibly and asking for help in dealing with the situation from a teacher.

Unit 10—Success

The skills of setting and achieving goals, problem solving and being resourceful have been shown to contribute to resilience. Similarly, having a healthy self-esteem based on a realistic self-knowledge and developing the skills of self-discipline and self-management are factors that contribute strongly to resilience. The activities in this unit help students to develop an understanding that the most effective path to a positive and healthy sense of self is one based on mastery and competence and the successful achievement of what is important to them. This unit is based around these acronyms at the three different levels:

- STAR! in the Lower Primary (Level 1) book;
- CHAMP! in the Middle Primary (Level 2) book;
- WINNERS! in the Upper Primary/Junior Secondary (Level 3) book.
  Each acronym helps to teach students key messages for success at age-appropriate levels.
  The focus in the Success unit is on activities that:
- Teach students how to identify their own relative strengths and weaknesses, and to use this self-knowledge to help them be successful across many areas of their life. There is a particular stress on collecting evidence for these conclusions about oneself, not just hoping or making unwarranted, unrealistic and deflated or inflated assumptions.
- Develop skills of self-discipline and self-management (e.g. willpower, time management, and organisational skills).
- Teach the skills and processes of achieving goals (e.g. setting goals, making a plan, taking sensible risks, persisting in the face of obstacles, problem solving and being resourceful when things are challenging or when something goes wrong).
- Challenge students to use their initiative and hence understand the real-life 'rocky up-and-down' process of goal achievement.
- Help them to understand the concept of 'psychological flow' (Csikszentmihalyi 1990), a positive outcome that occurs when they are immersed in an activity that offers them a challenge and fully absorbs their attention in a positive way.

The underlying principles of the BOUNCE BACK! Resiliency Program

This section provides a brief description of the principles that underpin the program and the answers to common questions asked in regard to the implementation of the program.

Earlier is better

The teaching of resilience and the creating of resilient environments should start as soon as a student enters school. It is appropriate to teach resilience at all ages but the earlier the better. It is less effective to focus on resilience only as students enter early adolescence.

Student welfare is integrated with curriculum

Academic learning is integrated with personal and social development. At the same time as students are engaged in activities which address curriculum outcomes across all key learning areas, they can learn the life skills of resilience that meet the expectations of a student welfare program.

There are 'key points' to communicate to students in each unit

The key points at the beginning of each unit in the three Teacher's Resource Books provide a succinct summary of the most important unit concepts for students to understand. Many different activities in each unit offer students opportunities to demonstrate their understanding of these key concepts.

All three levels of Teacher's Resource Books can be adapted for older or younger classes

If you require more ideas on how to teach a particular key point or concept, different activities can be found in the other Teacher's Resource Books. Many of the activities in the three books can be readily adapted to make them age appropriate for younger or older children.

There is a strong focus on literature

Stories are powerful ways to reinforce important resilience principles. They also serve as a stimulus for a range of engaging teaching activities. Each unit of work incorporates picture books, novels and poetry that communicate and reinforce the key messages of the unit or encourage discussion in related areas. An age-appropriate critical literacy approach is adopted through discussion questions and activities. There are further suggestions in Chapter 11 of this book for literature prompts that help students to understand and think critically about the texts. Several of the picture books offer deep psychological insights and social criticisms. These books provide different layers of meaning through their visual and verbal images that appeal to young and old. The books have been chosen to counter the negativity and nihilistic themes that have occurred in a lot of literature for young people over the last few decades (Bokey, Walter & Rey 2000). Also many of the Black Line Masters (BLMs) in the units can be used as literacy activities.

Literacy outcomes are met

All units of work actively engage students in talking, listening, reading and writing. The diverse range of teaching strategies employed in all units ensures that students are actively engaged in interacting with their classmates to facilitate their understanding of key concepts. This dynamic interaction with peers and teacher ensures that the contemporary definition of literacy as social practice (Luke 1993) is met.

There are opportunities for older students to work with younger students

There are many activities that involve older students working directly or indirectly with students in the first four years of their schooling. These activities are usually based on games, literacy activities, or a specific children's picture book. Older children are also encouraged to write and illustrate the text for picture storybooks on resilience themes. As they prepare to work with the younger children, the older students gain a deeper understanding of the resilience concepts so they can effectively teach and work with the younger children. Students who need a boost in self-esteem particularly benefit from opportunities to work with younger children. They are able to feel more knowledgeable. This helps them to regain confidence in their skills and abilities as well as to learn skills in relating positively to others. This cross-year contact can be based around:
- Direct classroom visits to teach to the class, run a game or work with a buddy
- Preparation of lessons, materials or products for younger students to use
- Video conferencing or videorecording.

There is a strong emphasis on cooperative learning in all units

Working cooperatively creates a sense of belonging in the classroom. Cooperative learning has been shown to be effective in engaging students and developing a sense of 'psychological flow' as well as superior academic outcomes across all key learning areas (Johnson, Johnson & Stane 2000). Students learn more about social skills when cooperative learning is used well. For these reasons, the use of cooperative learning is frequently incorporated in units of work. Chapter 10 of this book details a large number of basic cooperative learning structures, with guidelines on how to adapt them to make them age appropriate.

There are multiple entry points into the program, based on Gardner's model of multiple intelligences

Activities engaging each of the eight intelligences, identified in Howard Gardner's model of multiple intelligences, are incorporated in the program. What attracts one student's interest and allows them to demonstrate what they are good at may not do the same for another student. Diversity in teaching and learning strategies creates a greater likelihood that all students will become engaged and succeed in learning than does a 'one size fits all' approach. Multiple entry points to the same topic provide opportunities for all students to learn in ways that are comfortable for them, to experience success and to develop an understanding of their relative strengths and weaknesses across the multiple intelligences.

There are opportunities to develop higher level thinking skills

Giving students a challenging task designed to foster higher order thinking skills doesn't mean they will use these skills. Persisting at a task that is intellectually challenging and stretches you is more likely if you find the task intrinsically interesting. The nature of the BOUNCE BACK! Program ensures that the tasks are relevant to the real world of young people today. Many of the activities are open-ended and encourage students to develop skills in solving problems, making decisions and thinking critically and creatively. These higher order thinking skills are crucial to coping with the complexity of life in the 21st century.

There is a strong focus on 'hands-on' experiential learning

Each unit incorporates many practical activities so students can actively learn key resilience concepts through making, doing, acting out, manipulating, constructing and experimenting. Concrete activities help young children make sense of what they are learning and to remember and act on what they have learned. 'Hands-on' concrete experiences for older students, especially boys, more effectively engages them in the material they are learning and creates more opportunities for them to demonstrate what they have learned and understood.

Songs and music are used to consolidate some of the main understandings of the program

Throughout history music has been used to help maintain people's spirits during difficult times. For example, Australian convicts sang songs such as 'Botany Bay' to raise their spirits. Similarly, gospel singing in America emanated from the times of slavery. Singing together builds a sense of community and the lyrics of songs can convey important messages of hope and strength. Many of the key resilience concepts and messages in the Junior Primary and Middle Primary programs have been incorporated into newly composed songs that are usually based on well-known tunes. Each unit also refers to well-known tunes with resilience themes and incorporates websites where the songs' lyrics and music can be accessed. See Chapter 11 (Music resources) of this book for more information on different sites. Regularly singing the songs creates opportunities for students to revisit the key resilience messages many times. This repetition makes it more likely that students will then transfer this learning to their real-life experiences and problems. In the Upper Primary/ Junior Secondary book, students are encouraged to go 'song hunting' and look for and bring to school songs that they believe are consistent with a particular message about resilience.

Visual and performing arts are a core part of most units

Most units of work in the program include opportunities for students to demonstrate their understandings of resilience concepts through drawing, painting, constructing, modelling, singing or drama. The activities are developmentally appropriate and meet various outcomes for the visual and performing arts syllabus at different levels.

Students are continually encouraged to self-reflect during the activities

Throughout the program, students are asked to reflect on their own strengths and weaknesses, and the effect of their behaviour on themselves and others. They are also asked to reflect on what they can do to improve their learning, their behaviour and their own emotional wellbeing. These skills of self-reflection (linked to their self-knowledge and self-management) have been identified by Howard Gardner (Noble & Grant 1997) as probably the most important skills for surviving in the 21st century.

Technology is incorporated wherever possible

There are many suggestions in each unit as to how students might use the internet and email, develop powerpoint displays, use digital cameras, carry out topic-related internet research, hunt for songs on different internet sites, access internet sites with support materials and use software packages such as Microsoft Publisher or KidPix.

Consolidation activities follow after each unit

All units incorporate consolidation activities such as games, group tasks and word puzzles, and activities that are designed to consolidate core concepts and skills.

Frequently asked questions

Where can the BOUNCE BACK! Resiliency Program be taught?

Ideally, the program is taught separately for one hour a week (usually as Personal Development, Pastoral Care or Life Skills) and also consistently integrated with current curriculum in Social Studies, Health, English, Religious Education, Physical Education, Science, Maths and Creative Arts. Library staff can also integrate BOUNCE BACK! with their activities.

How often is the BOUNCE BACK! Resiliency Program Taught to students?

The key messages and concepts in BOUNCE BACK! are best taught many times across a student's schooling if these coping skills are to have a significant effect on student thinking and behaviour. The preferred model of presentation of the BOUNCE BACK! program is to teach some aspects of each of the ten units at every year level. However, different schools have different needs and constraints and it may be more convenient for some schools to alternate the topics so that some topics are taught one year and then the others the following year.

In what order should the units be taught?

We believe that the best order is as follows.
1. Core values
2. Elasticity
3. People bouncing back
4. Courage
5. Looking on the bright side
6. Emotions
7. Relationships
8. Humour
9. Bullying
10. Success

The first six logically and developmentally follow each other. However, the last four could really be taught in any order, depending on the needs of the school.

Who should teach the BOUNCE BACK! Resiliency Program?

The best person to teach the program is the teacher who has the closest relationship with a particular class of students. In primary systems that is usually the classroom teacher. In secondary systems the Health or English teacher can deliver the program, as can any teacher responsible for Personal Development, Pastoral Care or similar. Many aspects of the program can also be 'picked up' by teachers in other subject areas.

How else can BOUNCE BACK! Resiliency Program be used?

The coping skills in the program are also suitable to train students as Supportive Friends, who act as emotional peer supports. There should also be training for these students in listening skills (see 'Relationships' units) and empathic responding (see 'Emotions' units). Relevant parts of the program can be taught on camps and retreats. For some students extra small-group sessions incorporating aspects of the program may be beneficial at certain times.

How much does it cost to use BOUNCE BACK!?

Very little. The Teacher's Handbook and the three Teacher's Resource Books are an essential resource. Most school libraries already have at least half of the books used in the units. Purchasing some of the other recommended books can be achieved as part of the ongoing library budget.

REFERENCES

Australian Unity Wellbeing Index, 2002, www.australianunity.com.au/info/wellbeingindex.asp.

Bokey, K.M. Walter, G. & Rey, J.M., 2000, 'From Karrawingi the emu to Care factor zero. Mental health issues in contemporary Australian adolescent literature'. *Medical Journal of Australia*, EMJA www.mja.com.au/public/issues/173_11_041200/bokey/bokey.html.

Bond, L., Thomas, L., Toumbourou, J., Patton, G. & Catalano, R., 2000, *Improving the Lives of Young Victorians in Our Community—A Survey of Risk and Protective Factors*. Centre for Adolescent Health, Melbourne. (available from www.dhs.vic.gov.au/commcare)

Buss, D.M., 2000, 'The evolution of happiness'. *American Psychologist*, 55, No. 1, 15–23.

Csikszentmihalyi, M., 1990, *Flow. The Psychology of Optimal Experience*, Harper & Row, New York.

Gardner, H., 1999, *Intelligence Reframed: Multiple Intelligences into the 21st Century*. Basic Books, New York.

Gottman, J., 1994, '*Why marriages succeed or fail.*' Simon & Schuster, New York.

Jacobsen, G. & Wainwright, R., 2001, 'Onward Christian Scholars'. *Sydney Morning Herald* 26/12/01, p. 13.

Johnson, D.W., Johnson, R.T. & Stane, M.B., 2000, *Cooperative Learning Methods: A Meta-Analysis*. www.clcrc.com/pages/cl-methods.html.

Luke, A., 1993, 'The social construction of literacy in the primary school'. In L. Unsworth (ed.) *Literacy, Learning and Teaching. Language as Social Practice in the Primary School*. Macmillan, Sydney, pp. 1–53.

McGrath, H., 1997, *Dirty Tricks. Classroom Games Which Teach Students Social Skills*. Melbourne: Addison Wesley Longman.

McGrath, H. & Anders, E., 2000, *The BOUNCE BACK Program. A Pilot Study*. The Department of Education, Victoria. Turning the Tide in Schools Drug Education Project.

McGrath, H. & Francey, S., 1991, *Friendly Kids, Friendly Classrooms*. Longman, Melbourne.

McGrath, H. & Noble, T., 1993, *Different Kids Same Classrooms: Making Mixed Ability Classrooms Really Work*. Longman Australia, Melbourne.

Myers, D.G., 2000, 'The funds, friends and faith of happy people'. *American Psychologist*, 55, No. 1, 56–67.

Noble, T. & Grant, M., 1997, 'An interview with Howard Gardner', *EQ Australia* 5 (1), 24–26, Curriculum Corporation.

Peterson, C., 2000, 'The future of optimism'. *American Psychologist*, 55, No. 1, 44–55.

Rigby, K., 2001, *Stop the bullying. A Handbook for Schools*. ACER Press, Melbourne.

THE CONCEPT OF RESILIENCE

What is resilience?

There are many different definitions of resilience but all refer to the capacity of the individual to 'overcome odds' and demonstrate the personal strengths needed to cope with some kind of hardship or adversity. Norman Garmezy, one of the first researchers in the study of resilience, defines resilience as manifest competence despite exposure to significant stressors. He sees competence as a variety of adaptive behaviours (Rolf 1999). Benard (1991) suggests resilience is a set of qualities or protective mechanisms that give rise to successful adaptation despite high risk factors during the course of development. We have defined resilience as:

> The ability to bounce back after encountering difficulties, negative events, hard times or adversity and to return to almost the same level of emotional wellbeing; that is, the capacity to maintain a healthy and fulfilling life despite adversity.

The emergence of resilience

The construct of resilience emerged, almost by accident, from longitudinal developmental studies of 'at risk' children. This research showed that, despite encountering many life stressors as they grew up, some children survived and even thrived (Silva & Stanton 1996; Werner & Smith 1993). The resilience research has shifted the focus from those children who are casualties of these risk factors to those children who manage to bounce back from stress, trauma and risk in their lives. The resiliency construct is a dramatic shift in perspective from a deficit model of young people at risk to a model that focuses on the personal and environmental strengths that help young people withstand high levels of 'risk'. Martin Seligman (1995), the author of *The Optimistic Child*, has summarised this shift as follows:

> Modern psychology has been co-opted by the disease model. We've become too preoccupied with repairing damage when our focus should be on building strengths and resilience. Psychology is not just the study of weakness and damage but it is also the study of strength and virtue. Treatment is not just fixing what is broken, it is nurturing what is best within ourselves. (Martin Seligman is a past President of the American Psychological Association.)

This paradigm shift is emerging in the helping professions of teaching, counselling and clinical psychology and social welfare. All these professions are using the term 'resilience' and reviewing ways to adopt a strengths approach to prevention and intervention. A growing number of research studies in these fields have challenged the notion that stress and risk (including abuse, loss and neglect or simply the everyday stresses of life) inevitably lead people to psychopathologies, depression and suicidal thoughts and actions, substance abuse, violent actions, antisocial behaviour patterns or educational failure. The new notion of resilience emphasises that we can help students to identify, develop and access protective resources to minimise the potential damage of such stressors and help them to bounce back.

In the context of education today there is a sense of urgency about adopting a positive model of resilience. Although most young people are happy, well adjusted and optimistic, there is a significant number of children and youth who are not. Recent evidence (e.g. Hibbert, Caust, Patton 1996) suggests that 27% of Australian young people aged 18–24 experience a mental disorder (e.g. anxiety, depression, mood disorders, drug-related illnesses). Seligman (1995) refers to depression as the current common cold of mental illness. Depression frequently combines with or is an outcome of substance-abuse, conduct disorders, anxiety disorders, eating disorders and other behaviour disorders.

Too many of our teachers are starting to lose hope. We are in serious danger of undermining a fundamental truth of educational effectiveness—that the learning and emotional lives of students are profoundly dependent on the learning and emotional lives of teachers. (Hargreaves & Fullan 1998 p. 87)

Teachers today also face a challenge in maintaining their own emotional wellbeing and professional enthusiasm. A recent 18-month-long enquiry around Australia found that teachers face a serious crisis of low morale and low morale works against quality teaching (Crowley 1998, p. 2). According to Fullan (1997), if we are to develop effective schools we have to access our last virtue: hope.

Fullan explains that hope is not just a naive, sunny view of life. Sustaining hope and being resilient gives teachers the capacity to find ways and resources to address difficult problems.

The protective processes and resources that promote resilience

Protective processes and resources are the environmental conditions and personal skills that can alter or even reverse predictions of negative outcomes for young people who encounter hard times or ongoing difficult circumstances. The resilience research identifies protective processes and resources that make some young people more stress-resistant and help them to develop strength, courage and positive mental health.

Young people spend 5 to 6 hours per day at school. Apart from families, schools are the most important socialising agent for providing access to an environment that promotes resilience. Schools can play a critical role in providing resilient class and school environments. They can provide key people who show they care, hold positive expectations and provide opportunities for meaningful participation for all students. School connectedness is particularly important for those children who are not connected to highly resilient families. Schools can also teach students the protective personal skills that will help them bounce back when they experience hardships, frustrations and difficult times.

So what are the key components of environments that foster resilience and how can we recognise resilient children and those who are not resilient? The chart on the next page provides a summary of research outcomes related to the protective environments as well as the protective personal skills that lead to resilience in young people.

Environments that promote resilience	Personal skills and attitudes that empower young people to act resiliently
School connectedness A sense of belonging to a good school Meaningful participation and contribution Opportunities to affirm student strengths Opportunities for taking initiative Prosocial, collaborative school culture Physical and psychological safety at school Strong school rules about bullying and violence Engagement with learning tasks High expectations, academic support and differentiated curriculum	**Helpful and positive thinking skills and attitudes** Optimistic thinking Having a sense of purpose and future Normalising instead of personalising Evidence-based rational thinking Using humour appropriately
Peer connectedness Classroom cohesion and sense of belonging Cooperative learning activities Peer support structures Prosocial peer groups	**Skills and beliefs related to resourcefulness and adaptivity** Having an orientation towards success Skills for setting, planning and achieving realistic goals Decision-making skills Problem-solving skills Creativity, flexibility and adaptivity Holding a belief that effort will pay off Organisational skills Skills to enable adaptive distancing from distressing and unalterable situations
Teacher connectedness Limited number of teachers Teacher knowledge of students Teacher warmth and availability Cooperative and prosocial classroom culture Classrooms that celebrate differences Clear consistent boundaries	**Social skills** Having a belief that relationships matter Group social skills Friendship skills Conflict management skills Help-seeking skills and preparedness to self-disclose
Positive family–school links Family involvement with school programs Strong teacher–family relationships	**Emotional literacy** Skills for recognising and managing own emotions Skills for reading, predicting and responding empathically to others' emotions
Family connectedness Expression of warmth and affection Good communication Positive approach to solving family problems Family loyalty, affirmation and support Shared activities Individual responsibilities and meaningful contribution Prosocial and shared family values Warm relationship with at least one parent	**Healthy self-esteem: a sense of personal competence and self-knowledge** Realistic and positive self-knowledge Skills of self-reflection A prosocial personal value system Feeling confident in several areas of one's life Courage Age-appropriate level of independence Self-discipline—skills for delaying gratification and managing impulses
One caring adult outside the family Availability and interest in student Expresses unconditional positive regard	
Community connectedness Awareness of and access to support services Voluntary community service Involvement in prosocial clubs and teams Community norms against antisocial behaviour Strong cultural identity and pride	
Religious involvement Participation in spiritual communities with shared values	

The BOUNCE BACK! Resiliency Program incorporates practical strategies to assist schools to set up the environmental protective processes and teach the personal coping skills that foster young people's resilience. The following section shows how the program addresses the protective processes and resources.

Environments that promote resilience

School connectedness

School connectedness has become one of those educational buzz words. It simply means the extent to which students feel they belong to a school that accepts, protects and cares about them, affirms them as people with positive qualities, and provides them with meaningful and satisfying learning experiences. School, above all other social institutions, provides unique opportunities for young people to form relationships and meet and work with peers and caring professional adults on a daily basis. School can offer young people hope and pathways for their future. Research over the past decade has clearly demonstrated that the most powerful factor leading to students completing Year 12 is their school connectedness. In order to enhance school connectedness for every student, there needs to be a clearly stated vision shared by the whole school community that can be translated into structures and everyday practices. Such a vision needs to incorporate features such as:

- Strategies for identifying and developing every student's strengths. Howard Gardner's model of multiple intelligences provides a useful framework for this purpose.
- The provision of differentiated and relevant learning activities that actively engage students and give them a sense of satisfying participation and worthwhile outcomes.
- Academic support for students who are struggling with the curriculum.
- Procedures, structures and activities that ensure the students feel valued and supported by both their teachers and their peers.
- A culture of safety and care in which no student feels threatened. There are clear and consistently enforced rules and procedures regarding bullying and violence, and infringements are quickly and firmly dealt with when they occur.
- A diverse range of opportunities which are made easily accessible to all students to help them make a meaningful contribution to the life of the school.
- Student commitment and pride in their school is fostered. This used to be known as 'school spirit' and hasn't featured as strongly in school cultures in recent times.
- Students are given opportunities to take initiative. This means they are given the chance to set their own goals (both academic and enterprise goals), start things up, stay engaged over time, and stick with their plan until completion. Teaching initiative skills also involves helping students learn how to handle the inevitable failures, mistakes and obstacles they will experience along the way (Larson 2000). Typical school experiences do not provide much opportunity for students to learn initiative skills, despite their importance to coping with life in the 21st century.
- The establishment of a prosocial and collaborative school culture that is based on relationships, cooperation, negotiation, and the effective resolution of conflict.

Chapters 5 and 6 of this Teacher's Handbook offer practical class-based and whole-school ideas for implementing many of the above features.

Chapter 8 outlines strategies for the whole-school management of bullying.

Chapters 10 and 11 incorporate teaching and learning strategies for more effective engagement of students. All units of work provide activities designed to meet these criteria.

The classroom units on bullying in the three Teacher's Resource Books contain activities for both preventing and reducing bullying.

Peer connectedness

For most young people, one of the major reasons for coming to school is their desire to socially and emotionally connect with their peers. They look forward to seeing their friends, and enjoy having a sense of belonging to both a friendship group and the larger peer group (Fuller, McGraw & Goodyear 1998). Schools can establish the kind of social structures that enhance the development of such relationships and foster a sense of acceptance, belonging and fitting in. Such structures include cooperative learning groups, classroom meetings and peer support groups.

Many classroom-friendly cooperative learning activities are provided in Chapter 10 of this Teacher's Handbook. The classroom units on 'Core values', 'Success' and 'Relationships' also provide practical activities at each of the three levels for helping students connect with each other in a prosocial way. All of the classroom units incorporate learning activities that facilitate students getting to know each other a little better through the sharing of perceptions and experiences related to the topics covered.

Teacher connectedness

A number of research studies have indicated that students today do not feel closely connected to many of their teachers, especially in secondary schools (Trent 2001; Fuller, McGraw & Goodyear 1998). Often students' perceptions of their low levels of teacher connectedness come as a surprise to their teachers (Van Pelt 2001). Yet the quality of teaching and the teacher–student relationship, above all else, makes the most significant difference to student learning outcomes (Rowe 2001). Feeling connected to their teachers helps students not only to experience more successful learning outcomes but also to become more resilient (Henderson & Milstein 1996) and to stay at school rather than drop out (Christenson & Carroll 1999).

Schools can empower their teachers to establish positive and close relationships with their students in a number of ways. They can limit the number of teachers that students come into contact with; they can make time for teachers to get to know their students well through pastoral care and personal development programs; they can arrange for one teacher (who does not teach the students) to act as a mentor and confidante through a vertical tutoring system; they can make sure teachers have time to meet with those students who need more academic support or personal time with them; they can provide opportunities for teacher professional development in areas such as differentiating the curriculum, personal development, resilience and student counselling and they can 'power up' their student welfare and support services. Teachers can also take up the challenge of becoming more connected to their students and creating a prosocial and resilient classroom culture. They can do this by modelling resilient attitudes and skills, establishing a collaborative classroom climate, communicating warmth and positive expectations, adopting classroom practices which affirm student strengths, having clear and consistent boundaries, respecting and acknowledging the value of individual differences, and by taking the time to get to know their students as people, not just pupils.

Chapter 5 of this Teacher's Handbook offers suggestions as to ways in which teachers can become more connected to their students. It also outlines the kinds of teachers and teacher behaviour that students most prefer and respect. As they teach the BOUNCE BACK! acronym, teachers are very likely to gain a deeper understanding of the core components of resilience and become more resilient themselves (McGrath & Anders 2000). Becoming more resilient enables most teachers to more effectively model resilient skills and attitudes to students and to become more skilled at counselling students by referring to their common understandings from the BOUNCE BACK! acronym.

As well, all classroom units of work at the three levels contain classroom-friendly learning activities that directly and indirectly create greater teacher–student connectedness.

Positive family–school links

Students are more likely to become more resilient, to learn more effectively, and to complete Year 12 when the family and the school work together (Epstein 1995; Christenson & Carroll 1999). Chapter 7 provides guidelines on how schools can develop strong positive links with families. This chapter includes strategies for working with parents and building strong family support for a resiliency program.

Family connectedness

Research clearly indicates that high levels of family connectedness is one of the most important of all the protective environmental resources (Bond et al. 2000; Masten et al. 1999; Werner 1993). Young people who feel they are supported by their families, have parents who set and enforce rules in their homes and feel respected for their individuality while belonging to a cohesive and stable family are likely to be resilient (Werner 1993). All families face challenges at different times. In some families those challenges relate to the typical developmental stages of their children, and of their own couple relationship. In others they relate to death, illness, marital separation, financial hardship, job loss, mental illness, alcohol and substance abuse or other kinds of adversity.

Family connectedness is the extent to which young people feel a sense of involvement and acceptance in their family, and the degree to which they feel close to their parents and siblings. It also relates to the extent to which families communicate effectively with each other, spend time with each other in shared activities, express and enact loyalty and commitment to each other, solve family problems and pull together in the face of adversity. The research into the levels of resilience demonstrated within a family starts from the assumption that all families have strengths that can be accessed in difficult times. The family strengths model does not deny that many families need additional support and care, but it does advocate helping families to understand and develop the strengths they already have as well as helping them to learn resilient skills and attitudes.

Chapter 7 contains activities which can be used at parent information sessions about the BOUNCE BACK! Resiliency Program. This chapter also offers parents suggestions for enhancing family-connectedness and their own family's resilience in small ways.

One caring adult outside the family

Resilience research has shown us that having one adult in their life who is not a parent, but who is accessible and caring towards them and believes in them, is a highly significant protective resource for young people and their resilience (Benard 1999). The adult may be a part of the extended family, such as an older sibling, a grandparent or an aunt, uncle or cousin. They may be a family friend, a youth worker or a teacher. Caring about a young person means seeing the possibilities in them and having a sense of concern and compassion for their wellbeing. It means looking beyond their often negative and challenging words and actions and seeing their underlying feelings of anger, pain, fear, insecurity and confusion (Benard 1999). Caring also means being a sympathetic confidante for their distress and worries by carefully listening to and believing their story, and by showing interest, respect and empathy (Miller 1990).

Community connectedness

Opportunities for positive community involvement such as involvement in sports teams with other young people and membership of youth groups has been identified as one of the most prevalent protective factors in a recent large-scale Australian study of young people (Bond et al. 2000). The other two major protective factors were core values and family connectedness. Community connectedness means positive participation in the life of the wider local community and a willingness to access community resources. Healthy schools, churches, youth clubs, sports clubs and other community institutions can provide an infrastructure for young people's connection with their community.

> Kids can walk around trouble if there is some place to walk to and someone to walk with. (Former gang member, Tito, in McLaughlin, Irby & Langman 1994)

It is salutary to note that informal rather than formal community connections often are more powerful. When asked who helped them to succeed against the odds, resilient young people in the longitudinal study by Werner and Smith (1993) overwhelmingly gave credit to members of their extended family (grandparents, siblings, aunts or uncles), to neighbours and teachers, and to mentors in voluntary community associations such as YMCA or YWCA or church groups. Young people sought support from these informal community networks and valued this kind of support more often than the services of formal community organisations, mental health professionals and social workers.

Being connected to people in one's community has been shown to correlate strongly with having healthy self-esteem, having a feeling of control over one's life, not being involved with antisocial groups, and having higher educational aspirations and achievement (Larson 2000). However, it is not clear as to how much this correlation reflects the fact that young people who are more likely to seek access to the community in the first place are also likely to have high levels of parental support, high ability and high socioeconomic status.

Schools are in an excellent position to provide a focus for their local community and connect different community resources. This focus can be operationalised in different ways. Some schools choose to become full service schools where the school collaborates with community agencies and programs to met students' needs. Full service schools can provide non-fragmented services through the collaboration of professionals in schools with health, family and welfare professionals. Other schools choose to provide community education programs, after school care, or to invite the community to make use of school facilities, such as the gym, after hours. Access to community facilities such as TAFE education can give young people a second chance, and some schools choose to provide early facilitated pathways to these resources for those students who are less likely to want to pursue university qualifications (Werner 1993).

Community connectedness for young people includes their family's connections to their cultural or ethnic group. Different cultures provide different cultural resources to deal with crises. In western culture these might involve legal assistance and counselling and schools can help young people to access these community services. In some ethnic minority cultures dealing with crises might include accessing a strong network of support within the community. Strong identity with one's culture can be a source of pride and positive self-esteem for young people. Schools have long understood the value of acknowledging and celebrating the different ethnic groups that make up the school community. Schools with religious affiliations often have strong connections to the local religious community, providing a sense of continuity and belonging for many of their students.

Involvement in voluntary community service can help young people to develop personal coping skills such as being resourceful, showing initiative and setting goals, and developing prosocial values. The capacity for initiative can also be developed in the context of voluntary community activities such as sports teams, art and drama groups and participation in community organisations. One example of such a project that required initiative was a group of Girl Guides engaged in a campaign to sell biscuits. The girls developed plans for their sales that included rehearsing their sales pitch and developing routes through the neighbourhood. As they gained experience they adjusted their plans and strategies. Their sales pitches became better, their tracking of orders became more systematic and they took over responsibilities initially held by their parents. Their process of learning was collaborative—with parents, peers and customers—and it showed them that the development of initiative is not necessarily an individual process but one that best involves collaboration (Rogoff, Baker-Sennett, Lacasa & Goldsmith 1995).

One major American study of 60 youth community organisations serving 24,000 youths was conducted in low-income neighbourhoods serving multi-ethnic groups of youth in urban and rural settings. All the effective organisations were based on young people displaying initiative. Although the original impetus for the groups came from community youth leaders, the youth participants held responsibilities for setting goals, identifying problems to be solved, raising money, writing grant applications, handling budgets, setting rules and deciding schedules. The organisations depended on the young participants being motivated, if not the projects collapsed (Heath 1997, cited in Larson 2000; McLaughlin et al. 1994). A second feature of these effective organisations was that all engaged the young people in an environment of real-world constraints and the leaders did not hold back on articulating these constraints. These leaders saw the young people's potential, held high expectations for them and focused on their strengths.

The classroom units of work on 'Success' provide opportunities for students to develop initiative and collaboration skills. Schools can consider encouraging the local community to become involved in their use of the BOUNCE BACK! Resiliency Program, especially the policing community, welfare agencies, scouting and guiding communities and sporting groups.

Religious involvement

Engagement in an active religious life makes it likely that an individual will be more resilient and be less likely to be involved in antisocial behaviour, to abuse drugs and alcohol, to divorce and to commit suicide (Myers 2000). People with spiritual faith report higher levels of happiness and life satisfaction (Myers 2000), are more likely to be physically healthier and live longer (Koenig 1997) and are more likely to retain or recover emotional wellbeing after suffering divorce, unemployment, serious illness or bereavement than people without such faith (McIntosh, Silver & Wortman 1993; Ellison 1991).

Many explanations can be offered for the connection between religious involvement and resilience. For example:

- Communities with shared spiritual values usually provide social support and connection for members, as well as a sense of belonging and affirmation. Many religions offer unconditional love and acceptance.
- For many people, a spiritual faith provides a sense of purpose, and satisfies a basic human need of wanting our lives to have some kind of meaning (Myers 2000). Seligman (1992) has argued that loss of meaning and a sense of purpose contributes to today's high levels of depression among young people.
- Many religions offer people a sense of hope, often through prayer, when facing adversity, as well as answers to some of life's deepest questions (Myers 2000).
- The principles and beliefs associated with many religions encourage an acceptance of, and stoicism in the face of, things that can't be changed.
- Some religions encourage the practice of deep self-reflection and the facing of truth and pain with courage.

There is no section in the BOUNCE BACK! Resiliency Program that directly addresses religious faith or involvement. Those schools with religious affiliations will undoubtedly already have such learning experiences and strategies in place. However, the values addressed in the classroom units on 'Core values' have been derived from those that underpin most religions, whether they be Christian, Buddhist, Muslim or Jewish. These values focus on integrity and self-respect, justice, support, care and concern for others, compassion, acceptance of differences, cooperation, friendliness, and respect for the rights of others. Of course, these prosocial core values are not held only by people with religious beliefs. Many people who are not currently affiliated with any religion, and would consider themselves to be agnostic or atheist, also hold and live by these values.

Personal coping skills that empower young people to act more resiliently

Helpful and positive thinking skills and beliefs

The skills in this category have been strongly linked to being resilient. They are:

- Optimistic thinking
- Having a sense of purpose and future
- Normalising instead of personalising
- Evidence-based rational thinking
- Using humour appropriately.

Optimistic thinking

Optimistic thinking involves looking on the bright side of situations. Seligman (1995) has identified three components to optimism:

- Positivity, which involves finding the positives in negative situations, however small
- Mastery, which involves feeling some sense of competence and control over one's life

- Explanatory style, which involves believing that bad situations are temporary, acknowledging that bad situations are usually not all your fault, and believing that bad situations are specific and do not necessarily flow over into all aspects of your life.

Having a sense of purpose and future

Having a sense of purpose and future is also an aspect of optimism. It means believing that things are more likely to turn out well than not, and having goals to aim for.

Normalising

Normalising, instead of personalising, is another indirect aspect of optimism. Normalising means recognising that things that are happening in your life happen to lots of other people too. In contrast, personalising is when you think something that is relatively normal only happens to you, not others. Over time, personalising results in a negative self-perception, that is, a belief that you are jinxed, doomed or inadequate.

Evidence-based rational thinking

Many people become unnecessarily distressed and despairing because they are distorting the picture and not seeing a situation as it really is. Others have irrational and unhelpful beliefs such as:
- I must be perfect and never make any mistakes.
- You can't help the feelings you have. There is nothing you can do about them. They just happen.
- If something CAN go wrong, then it definitely WILL go wrong.
- It is the end of the world if something negative happens in your life.
- If something bad has happened to me once it will happen again.

    These beliefs are not helpful in regards to feeling emotionally in charge of yourself and achieving the outcomes you desire. On the other hand, helpful thinking has these features:
- It is evidence-based and based on cross-checking with others to get a second opinion.
- It acknowledges that how you think affects how you feel and that emotions, though powerful, can be managed.
- It doesn't involve irrational generalising from 'once' to 'all the time'.
- It doesn't involve trying to mind-read.
- It involves considering alternative explanations rather than jumping to conclusions.
- It results in self-soothing and a stronger sense of self-confidence in dealing with problems.

Using humour

Using humour appropriately has been linked to resilience as well as to social success. Humour is a form of optimism that helps to keep things in perspective. When we find a small thing to laugh about in a dark situation, we realise that it probably isn't the total disaster it seemed to be at first, and there is a glimmer of hope.

    The classroom units on 'The bright side', 'Success', 'Humour' and 'People bouncing back' provide activities to teach all the skills and beliefs outlined above which are helpful and optimistic.

Skills and beliefs related to resourcefulness and adaptivity

The skills and beliefs that underpin resourcefulness and adaptivity and link to being more resilient are:
- Having an orientation towards success, which means that you are focused on what you believe you can achieve by your own efforts if you work hard and persist in the face of obstacles.
- Being able to set, plan and achieve realistic goals and being able to organise yourself. Such skills result in a sense of optimism as well as higher levels of self-esteem and self-efficacy (the belief that you can do it).
- Being able to make decisions and solve problems in a creative way and to find resources that will help with problem solving.
- Holding the belief that it is important and helpful to be flexible when the need arises, rather than be restricted to a narrow set of options for dealing with problems.

Being able to 'adaptively distance' oneself from distressing and unalterable situations. This can mean:

> Do not tell people how to do things. Tell them what you want to achieve and they will surprise you with their ingenuity. (George S. Patton)

—Not blaming oneself for things that you aren't responsible for, such as not thinking that you must be the cause of your parents' marital difficulties

—Accepting that there are some things that can't be easily changed, such as having a sibling with a chronic illness or an alcoholic parent

—Finding a therapeutic 'place' where you can go when things are at their worst, such as a quiet and beautiful scenic spot where you feel more able to think clearly

—Engaging in a challenging mental distraction such as working on a non-emotional task or project or making plans or lists

—Thought stopping, where you 'blink' to get rid of distressing thoughts and then move into an exploration of a memory of a special and happy time

—Moving temporarily away from the people who are part of the difficult situation. One example would be going to another room when your siblings are arguing, or going to the park at the end of the street when your parent is drunk on Sunday morning. Adaptive distancing is NOT the same as using substances such as drugs and alcohol, which merely offer the illusion that there is no situation to be dealt with or accommodated.

The classroom units on 'Success', 'Core values' and 'People bouncing back' provide learning activities to teach these skills and beliefs.

Social skills

Many studies have demonstrated that young people who have well-developed social skills are more likely to be resilient (e.g. Benard 1999; Garmezy 1991; Resnick, Harris & Blum 1993; Resnick et al. 1997; Rutter 1987; Weissberg, Barton & Shriver 1997; Werner 1996). Having a belief that relationships really matter is the starting point for the development of group social skills, friendship skills, conflict management skills, and help-seeking skills. Having supportive relationships with others creates a sense of belonging, companionship and healthy self-esteem. Being prepared to seek help and self-disclose are also social skills that allow young people to experience intimacy and closeness as they talk to caring others about their thoughts, feelings, worries, past experiences and future plans. When we self-disclose, we are more likely to feel less helpless and anxious, to gain support, and to clarify our own feelings

Emotional literacy

Many recent researchers have identified the ability to be 'emotionally literate' as a protective factor for resilience (e.g. Beardslee 1990; Goleman 1995). Emotional literacy incorporates having the skills to recognise, accurately name and manage one's own emotions as well as skills for correctly reading, naming, responding empathically to, and predicting the feelings of others.

The classroom units on 'Emotions' contain many activities for teaching these skills.

Healthy self-esteem: a sense of personal competence and self-knowledge

Having healthy self-esteem has been closely linked to resilience (e.g. Garmezy 1991; Resnick, Harris & Blum 1993; Resnick et al. 1997; Werner & Smith 1992). A sense of personal competence is one aspect of healthy self-esteem. Personal competence usually involves:

• Believing that you are a decent person because you have a set of prosocial values which you try to live by

• Having enough self-confidence about your ability to achieve and perform in a number of different areas to enable you to take risks such as the risk of failing

• Being able to act courageously when the need arises

• Having a sense of age-appropriate independence, and

• Being able to manage your own impulses and be reasonably self-disciplined.

A second aspect of healthy self-esteem is having a realistic and positive self-knowledge about your strengths and limitations, which is based on evidence rather than wishful thinking. Achieving this requires self-reflection and reality testing.

The classroom units on 'Success', 'People bouncing back', 'Core values' and 'Courage' feature activities for teaching many of these skills and beliefs.

Myths and realities about resilience

The construct of resilience is gaining in popularity. When a construct is popularised there is a risk that the construct is over-simplified. The following section outlines some of the myths and realities related to the term 'resilience'. The realities draw on the resilience research literature. The complexity of the construct highlights the complexity of the task in helping young people to become more resilient.

Myth 1

The best way to prevent problems for young people today is to focus on what 'causes' the problems (the risk factors) and on the group of young people who seem to have the most risk characteristics.

Reality

The majority of 'high risk' children and adolescents do not develop the anticipated problem behaviours such as abuse of illicit drugs. There is not a simple direct correlation between the risk factors in young people's lives and their problems. Also it is not easy to prevent or change risk factors. A more effective approach is a holistic one that maximises as many protective factors as possible to help young people more successfully cope with the risk factors in their lives. This does not, however, deny the need to continue to create environments in which children and adolescents do not have to suffer abuse, neglect, bullying, violence and poverty.

Myth 2

Young people will never be able to escape the cycles of violence, poverty or failure that have characterised the lives of their parents, family members or community members.

Reality

Fundamental to the concept of resilience is the capacity to bounce back when you experience adversity. This capacity may be linked to a positive change in a person's environment and/or the learning of new coping skills. All people have the capacity for positive change and for the development of some characteristics of resilience throughout their lives. For some young people from difficult home environments, school and peer connectedness and finding a teacher who cares can play a crucial role in helping them develop some resilience to cope with the complexities of their lives. For others learning the personal skills such as how to set and work towards goals can give them a sense of purpose and future. This can help them to distance themselves from the events in their lives that are distressing and can not be changed. A combination of many processes provides more protection than one or two.

Myth 3

Resilience is an inborn characteristic. You either have it or you don't.

Reality

It is evident from research that some children are genetically predisposed to be less resilient and some to be more resilient. The Australian temperament study (Prior 1999) has demonstrated that some characteristics that are present at birth are still present when the child is in his or her teen years. Some of these characteristics are:
• Being bored easily

- Not adapting easily to new situations
- Having intense emotional reactions to situations
- Being hard to calm down and comfort
- Being shy.

Some young people inherit a genetic predisposition towards anxiety, depression or forms of mental illness, even though these may not always be apparent in early life. Others are born with cognitive and/or behavioural disabilities (such as dyslexia, attention deficit disorder and learning difficulties) which make it harder for them to cope and access protective resources. Recent research (Teichner 2000) has suggested that some young children suffer from long-term damage to their developing brain and are more at risk of anxiety and depression as adults as a result of early abuse and neglect. Each risk factor creates an extra challenge for parents, teachers and welfare workers as they try to support and care for such young people.

So the evidence suggests that children are born with differing predispositions to becoming resilient. However, a predisposition is not the same as 'inevitable'. Even with predispositions and disabilities, children can still become more resilient if they are in protective environments and if they are taught resilient skills and attitudes. Resilience is best viewed as a developmental process rather than a fixed trait. Young people who may be predisposed towards being less resilient may be even more in need of programs such as Bounce Back than their peers.

Myth 4

A resilient person will demonstrate resilient behaviours in all situations.

Reality

People can readily demonstrate some resilient capabilities in one context and not so readily in another. For example, a child may be uncooperative and unfriendly at school but different when he is playing with his cousins. A teacher may demonstrate high self-confidence when teaching their students but less self-confidence in speaking to a group of parents. In both these examples the different social contexts provide different levels of threat for the individual. Public speaking to a group of parents can be more threatening to teachers than talking to a group of children because they have had less opportunity to practise these skills. When the social context changes or our environmental circumstances change, then our resilience can alter. Skills learned in one context do not always generalise to other contexts because the new context may contain more threat or new/different circumstances. Resilience is a dynamic process that is highly influenced by not only the individual's personal coping skills but also their current social context.

Myth 5

Resilience can easily be observed in the behaviour of young people.

Reality

The multifaceted nature of resilience, with its affective and cognitive components, makes it sometimes difficult to 'see'. Some children can appear resilient, confident and 'cocky' but then under stress or threat they go to pieces and do 'dumb' things. Others can seem fragile and nonadaptive but surprise you in how well they cope when they are placed in very stressful circumstances.

Myth 6

All professionals working with young people agree on what resilience is and how it is best developed.

Reality

The concept of resilience has multiple meanings within and across different professional groups. For professionals working in the context of welfare, the main focus in the development of resilience will most likely be enhancing protective environmental factors such as an individual or a family's access to community support agencies and building family strengths.

For professionals in psychology and counselling, the main focus will most likely be using counselling research to teach the kinds of personal coping skills that can create resilience.

For teachers, the main focus will most likely be on enhancing both school-related protective factors and teaching their students the personal coping skills of resilience at a whole-class level.

Teachers on the same staff can also hold different views on whether a particular student is resilient or not. One teacher may see acting out, defiant behaviour as not coping, whereas another teacher may see the same behaviour as indicative of this student demonstrating resilient behaviour given their tough life. The concept of a resilient person is socially constructed. Planning and implementing a resilience program requires an understanding of both the environmental protective factors and the personal coping skills and beliefs that are valued in a particular cultural and ethnic community.

Myth 7

You need to identify all the risk factors in a young person's life before you can help them to be more resilient.

Reality

A focus on only the risk factors in a child's life runs the risk of negatively labelling young people and focusing on their problems rather than possible solutions. As one young survivor said: 'Abuse is what happened to me, not who I am' (Rubin, in Davis 1999, p. 3). This person demonstrates survivor's pride, a term coined by Wolin and Wolin (2001) to refer to the well-deserved feelings of accomplishment that result from withstanding the pressures of hardship. Survivors want their struggle to be recognised and honoured, not pitied, and they want to be seen as someone with strength, not as a victim.

A focus on problems can set up a cycle of failure. A cycle of failure leads to a sense of helplessness and a propensity to feel overwhelmed and to give up. Instead it is more productive to engage in a talent search of a young person's strengths and reframe their ability to overcome some of their difficulties as proof of their adaptivity, strength, intelligence, insight, creativity and tenacity. A focus on solutions can set up a cycle of positive actions. A positive cycle can engender a sense of empowerment and hope.

Myth 8

Resilience can easily be developed through simple social and educational interventions. A focus on one protective factor, such as improving social skills, will make a student resilient.

Reality

Resilience is multidimensional and reflects the social context of a child's life as well as their personal coping skills. Teaching only one set of skills, such as increasing students' social competence, will have limited long-term effects if some of the other factors in a child's environment don't change. Any program that incorporates a multifactored approach that includes environmental protective processes as well as personal skills is more likely to help young people develop resilience than a one-dimensional program. Also the earlier a program teaches the personal skills, the more likely the program will help students learn life skills that foster resilience (Seligman 1995).

Myth 9

Resilience solves all problems; if a young person is resilient, then they can survive anything.

Reality

No one is invulnerable. No one escapes completely from life's lessons and challenges. All of us have scars and every one of us has their breaking point. If the risk factors in a young person's life increase and their protective resources reduce, they can find themselves unable to cope either temporarily or for a longer period of time. Resilience is sometimes difficult to foster because of the multiple and complex interacting protective mechanisms and risk factors in children's lives.

Myth 10

Resilient children will demonstrate the same kinds of personal coping skills at all ages.

Reality

Resilience is a developmental process and therefore children will experience different everyday stressors and demonstrate different coping skills at different ages. Everyday stressors are the typical kinds of stressors that young people face as they proceed through the developmental stages. A typical everyday stressor for a preschooler may be separation from their parents when starting preschool or school; for a primary school aged child it may be disappointments relating to sport or school-work or peer teasing; and for adolescents it may be maintaining part-time work as well as achieving at school. Any program designed to help young people successfully manage everyday stressors needs to be made age-appropriate and tailored to the students' cognitive, social-emotional and physical developmental stage.

Myth 11

There are no gender differences in risk factors.

Reality

In general boys are more vulnerable in the first 10 years of life and girls become more vulnerable after 10 years old (Werner & Johnson 1999). In early and middle childhood boys are more likely than girls to have disabilities, learning difficulties, behaviour problems, difficulties in developing friendships and be more adversely affected by the absence of a father and a change in schools than girls. After 10 years, as girls move through adolescence, dependency is rewarded and it is not considered feminine to be assertive and confident (Gilligan 1990). Some girls may then in adolescence become more subdued and unsure of themselves as they attempt to deal with hard times and challenges.

Myth 12

Putting funds and energies into making schools more environmentally protective is enough to help all students develop resilience.

Reality

A focus on the environmental protective factors that schools can put into place can significantly help students feel more connected to their school, teachers and peers. Feeling connected in this way can improve the likelihood that students will complete school and have a sense of future. However, a multifaceted approach that incorporates both the school environmental protective factors and the personal skills of resilience provides a much better chance for young people to manage any difficult events and situations in their lives both in the short term and the long term.

In summary

All definitions of resilience incorporate some reference to an individual's ability to 'overcome odds' and to demonstrate personal strengths to cope with hardship or adversity. The construct of resilience emerged accidentally from longitudinal studies of children at risk. This research has prompted a paradigm shift from studying risk factors to looking at protective factors. The section on the myths and realities of resilience demonstrates the research-based multi-factored nature of the construct of resilience and illustrates the complexity of the task in helping young people to become more resilient. A multidimensional approach that incorporates ways to build environments that foster resilience as well as teaches the personal coping skills of resilience has a much greater chance of success than a program that addresses only one set of factors.

The environmental protective factors that foster resilience in young people include feeling connected to your school, positive family–school links being in place, feeling connected to peers, feeling cared for and supported by your teachers in a prosocial classroom climate, having a sense of belonging and worth in your family, having one caring adult outside the family for support, being involved in community life, and being part of a religious community.

A second category of protective resources are the personal skills and beliefs that enable young people to cope more effectively. These personal skills include knowing how to think helpfully and optimistically, having skills for resourcefulness and adaptivity, demonstrating competence in social skills that help with relationship building and self-disclosure, being emotionally literate, and having elements of a healthy self-esteem.

A successful resilience program endeavours to increase the number of both environmental and personal protective resources for all students. Such a program goes beyond simply describing 'what' the protective factors are and moves to a focus on 'how'. A focus on 'how' provides practical steps that professionals and families can take to foster resilience in young people today. A focus on 'how' acknowledges the dynamic nature of resilience instead of the static position taken by simply describing protective factors. The BOUNCE BACK! Resiliency Program provides practical guidelines on the actions educators can take to build resilient classrooms and schools and teach the personal coping skills that help students develop resilience.

REFERENCES

Beardslee, W.R., 1990, 'The role of self understanding in resilient individuals: The development of a perspective'. *Annual Progress in Child Psychiatry and Child Development*, 52–69.

Benard, B., 1991, 'Fostering resiliency in kids: Protective factors in the family, school and community'. *Far West Laboratory for Educational Research and Development*.

Benard, B., 1999, 'Applications of resilience: Possibilities and promise'. In M.D. Glantz & J.L. Johnson (eds) *Resilience and Development: Positive Life Adaptations*. Kluwer Academic/Plenum Publishers, New York, 269–80.

Bond, L., Thomas, L., Toumbourou, J., Patton, G. & Catalano, R., 2000, *Improving the Lives of Young Victorians in Our Community—A Survey of Risk and Protective Factors*. Centre for Adolescent Health, Melbourne. (available from www.dhs.vic.gov.au/commcare)

Christenson, S.L. & Carroll, E.B., 1999, 'Strengthening the family–school partnership through "Check and Connect"'. In E. Frydenberg, *Learning to Cope: Developing as a Person in Complex Societies*. Oxford University Press, Oxford.

Crowley, R. (Chair), 1998, 'A class act: Inquiry into the status of the teaching profession'. *Senate Committee for Employment, Education and Training References Committee*. Senate Printing Unit, Parliament House, Canberra.

Davis, N.J., 1999, 'School Violence Prevention. Status of Research and Research Based Programs on Resilience'. mentalhealth.org/schoolviolence.

Ellison, C.G., 1991, 'Religious involvement and subjective wellbeing'. *Journal of Health and Social Behaviour*, 32, 80–99.

Epstein, J., 1995, *School/family/community partnerships*. Phi Delta Kappan, 76, 701–12.

Fullan, M., 1997, 'Emotion and hope: Constructive concepts for complex times'. In A. Hargreaves (ed.), *Rethinking Educational Change with Heart and Mind*. ASCD Yearbook (216–33). ASCD, Alexandria, Virginia.

Fuller, A., McGraw, K. & Goodyear, M., 1998, 'The Mind of Youth. Resilience: A Connect Project'. Victorian Department of Education.

Garmezy, N., 1991, 'Resiliency and vulnerability to adverse developmental outcomes associated with poverty'. *American Behavioral Scientist*, 34, 4, 416–30.

Gilligan, C., 1990, *Making Connections: The Relational World of Adolescent Girls at Emma Willard School*. Harvard University Press, Cambridge.

Goleman, D., 1995, *Emotional Intelligence*, Bantam Books, New York.

Hargreaves, A. & Fullan, M., 1998, *What's Worth Fighting for Out There*. Teachers College Press, New York.

Heath 1997, cited in Larson, R.W., 2000, 'Toward a psychology of positive youth development'. *American Psychologist*, 55, No. 1, 170–83.

Henderson, N. & Milstein, M.M., 1996, *Resiliency in Schools: Making It Happen for Students and Educators.* Thousand Oaks, Corwin Press, California.

Hibbert, M., Caust, J. & Patton, G., 1996, *The Health of Young People in Victoria.* Centre for Adolescent Health, Melbourne.

Koenig, H.G., 1997, *Is Religion Good for Your Health? The Effects of Religion on Physical and Mental Health.* Haworth Press, Binghampton, New York.

Larson, R.W., 2000, 'Toward a psychology of positive youth development', *American Psychologist*, 55, (1), 170–83.

Masten, A.S., Hubbard, J.J., Gest, S.D., Tellegen, A., Garmezy, N. & Ramirez, M., 1999, 'Competence in the context of adversity: Pathways to resilience and maladaptation from childhood to late adolescence'. *Development & Psychopathology*, 11, (1), Winter, 143–69.

McGrath, H. & Anders, E., 2000, *The BOUNCE BACK Program. A Pilot Study.* The Department of Education, Victoria. Turning the Tide in Schools Drug Education Project.

McIntosh, D.N., Silver, R.C. & Wortman, C.B., 1993, 'Religion's role in adjustment to a negative life event: Coping with the loss of a child'. *Journal of Personality and Social Psychology*, 65, 812–21.

McLaughlin, M.W., Irby, M.A. & Langman, J., 1994, *Urban Sanctuaries: Neighbourhood Organisations in the Lives and Futures of Inner-city Youth.* Jossey-Bass, San Francisco.

Miller, A., 1990, *The Untouched Key: Tracing Childhood Trauma in Creativity and Destructiveness.* Anchor/Doubleday, New York.

Myers, D.G., 2000, 'The funds, friends and faith of happy people'. *American Psychologist*, 55, (1), 56–67.

Prior, M., 1999, 'Resilience and coping: The role of individual temperament'. In E. Frydenberg, *Learning to Cope: Developing as a Person in Complex Societies.* Oxford University Press, Oxford, 33–52.

Resnick, M.D., Bearman, P.S., Blum, R.W., Bauman, K.E., et al. 1997, 'Protecting adolescents from harm—Findings from the national longitudinal study on adolescent health'. *Journal of the American Medical Association*, 278, 10, 823–32.

Resnick, M.D., Harris, K.M. & Blum, R.W., 1993, 'The impact of caring and connectedness on adolescent health and wellbeing'. *Journal of Paediatrics and Child Health*, 29(1), s3–s9.

Rogoff, B., Baker-Sennett, J., Lacasa, P. & Goldsmith, D., 1995, 'Development through participation in sociocultural activity'. *New Directions for Child Development*, 67, Spring, 45–65.

Rolf, J.E., 1999, 'Resilience. An interview with Norman Garmezy'. In M.D. Glantz & J.L. Johnson (eds), *Resilience and Development: Positive Life Adaptations.* Kluwer Academic/Plenum Publishers, New York, 5–14.

Rowe, K., 2001, *Keynote Address at the Symposium titled Educating Boys in the Middle Years of Schooling.* St Ignatius School, Riverview.

Rutter, M., 1987, 'Psychosocial resilience and protective mechanisms'. *American Journal of Orthopsychiatry*, 57, 3, 316–31.

Seligman, M., 1992, *Learned Optimism.* Random House, Massachusetts.

Seligman, M., 1995, *The Optimistic Child*, Random House, New York.

Silva, P. & Stanton, W. (eds), 1996, *From Child to Adult: The Dunedin Multidisciplinary Health and Development Study.* Oxford University Press, Auckland, NZ.

Teichner, M.H., 2000, 'Wounds that time won't heal: Neurobiology of child abuse'. *Cerebrum*, 2, no. 4.

Trent, F., 2001, *Aliens in the classroom or: The Classroom as an alien place?* Paper presented at the Association of Independent Schools, NSW Sex, Drugs & Rock N Roll Conference, August.

Van Pelt, J., 2001, Assistant Principal, Hampton Primary School, Victoria. Personal communication.

Weissberg, R.P., Barton H.A. & Shriver, T.P., 1997, 'The social competence program for young adolescents'. In G.W. Aalbee & T.P. Gullotta (eds), *Primary Prevention Works.* Thousand Oaks, California, Sage Publication.

Werner, E. & Smith, R., 1992, *Overcoming the Odds: High Risk Children from Birth to Adulthood.* Cornell University Press, New York.

Werner, E.E., 1993, 'Risk, resilience and recovery: Perspectives from the Kauai longitudinal study'. *Development and Psychopathology*, 5, 503–15.

Werner, E.E., 1996, 'Observations on resiliency'. *Resiliency in Action*, 1, 2, 18–29.

Werner, E.E. & Johnson, J.J., 1999, 'Can we apply resilience?' In M.D. Glantz & J.L. Johnson (eds), *Resilience and Development: Positive Life Adaptations.* Kluwer Academic/Plenum Publishers, New York, 5–14.

Werner, E.E. & Smith, R.S., 1993, *Overcoming the Odds: High Risk Children from Birth to Adulthood.* Cornell University Press, Ithaca, New York.

Wolin, S. & Wolin, S.J., 2001, 'Shaping a Brighter Future by Uncovering "Survivor's Pride"'. www.projectresilience.com/article19.htm

THE BIG PICTURE OF RESILIENCE

Most young people live healthy, happy lives and make the transition into adulthood smoothly. Yet a recent Australian study reports that 25–40% of young people aged 11–18 experienced, in the previous six months, feelings of depression, worries about their weight, worries about their self-confidence, not having enough energy, and trouble sleeping (Waters et al. 1999). What makes these young people low on resilience and what are the implications for those of us working with young people today? This section looks at the 'big picture' of how the teaching of resilience fits in with the social, psychological and educational contexts of young people at the beginning of the 21st century. Empowering young people to become resilient enough to cope with the complexities of the world today requires a significant paradigm shift from a deficit model of what's wrong to a positive model for prevention. With a positive model for prevention we focus on resiliency rather than risk. This shift is now reflected in current social welfare, psychological and educational theories and policies.

The world of young people today

At the beginning of the 21st century the key issues of childhood and adolescence are in some ways the same as they have been for generations, but in some significant ways they are very different. Children and adolescents still move through the same developmental stages as their parents and grandparents. Most of their everyday milestones and concerns are the same as those experienced by previous generations. Young people still need support from at least one caring adult to help them move through the normal developmental hurdles and develop resilience to cope with life's stressors, as did their parents.

Although developmental milestones haven't changed much over many decades (with the exception of earlier puberty), the social and cultural factors that influence all children's lives today have changed a great deal. These social and cultural factors make growing up in our society more challenging than ever before. Helping students to develop resilience to effectively cope with these challenges becomes imperative.

What are some of the social and cultural changes young people face today?

Childhood and youth depression

In the past childhood and adolescent depression was rare. Now depression is almost an epidemic and has been described as the common cold of mental illness (Seligman 1995). In a recent large Australian study of 9000 young people approximately 20% reported being depressed and having emotional problems, with girls twice as likely as boys to report these problems (Bond et al. 2000). Another Australian study found over 40% of the young people surveyed felt that they did not have anyone who knew them very well—that is, who understood how they thought or felt. Almost a quarter said they had no one to talk to if they were upset, no one they could trust and no one to depend on (Glover et al. 1998). These findings of the declining social connectedness of young people today, coupled with their concern about environmental threats (such as violent crime, terrorism,

AIDs and nuclear war), are also supported by a large-scale analysis of different studies from the 1950s to the 1990s (Twenge 2000). Such studies indicate that, until young people feel both safe and connected to others, anxiety and depression are likely to remain high. Depression and anxiety are also associated with substance abuse, eating disorders, antisocial behaviour and suicide.

Youth suicide

Depression is implicated in most youth suicides. The rise in suicides among young males has been a striking feature of the trends in youth problems, with Australia showing a tripling of suicide rates among males aged 15–24 over the last 30 years (Cantor et al. 1999). For every completed suicide it has been estimated there are from 50 to 100 unsuccessful suicide attempts (Australia's Young People: Their Health and Wellbeing 1999).

Media exposure to 'awful facts of life'

The greater media exposure today means earlier and more widespread exposure to the 'awful facts of life'. The extraordinary visual images of the terrorist attacks on the World Trade Centre Towers in New York shown around the world as the attack was happening vividly demonstrate this factor. By the time today's children become adolescents they are more aware of the harsher aspects of society such as racial conflict, acts of terrorism, wars, child abuse, murder and violence (including violence in schools) than earlier generations. Many young people experience the direct impact of this increase in violence and abuse.

Media images of physical, emotional, economic and social success

Young people are constantly being bombarded with global media images, especially in television and movies, of women who are physically attractive and thin, of men who are highly dominant and influential, and of young people who have large circles of friends. Rather than comparing themselves to other young people in their community, young people now compare themselves and their own lives to these unattainable media images. They risk perceiving themselves as failures due to their faulty comparisons of their own lives with the lives depicted so glamorously in the media (Buss 2000). Advertising that communicates messages about consumerism and sexuality is specifically aimed at the child and adolescent market. These messages can be very persuasive and very threatening.

High social and cultural diversity

Now Australian families reflect much greater social, cultural and racial diversity than ever before in our history. A quarter of the children in Australian classrooms are from non-English-speaking backgrounds and in many schools the proportion is much higher. Many children experience being members of minority groups, feel different to their peers and live in two cultures. Many families who have migrated from other countries no longer have the family or community support networks that helped them feel connected and to deal with adversity in their country of origin.

Changing family structures

Many children live in families where both parents work, or in single-parent or blended families. Family life is less stable than in previous generations due to the increasing divorce rate (43%), the increasing number of de facto relationships, the increasing number of children born outside marriage (23%), and the high rates of family geographical relocation. One of the most consistent findings in studies of wellbeing is the link to marriage (Diener 1999). Married women and men are significantly happier than single women and men even when other variables such as income and age are controlled.

Many children face challenges of changing family structures and contexts and greater demands on their competence to cope with these changes. It is not uncommon for children to face these challenges more than once. For example, as more second marriages break-down than first marriages, many children twice experience changes in family structure and may lose step-siblings and a loved step-parent. Changes in family life, including increased conflict, abuse and neglect, are likely factors in the social and psychological problems associated with young people today (Eckersley 2002).

Changes in parenting

According to Martin Seligman (1995), one of the major reasons why young people are less resilient today than earlier generations is the change in parenting styles. He argues that parents in the last 25 or so years have over-protected their children, and have focused too much on trying to make their children 'happy'. He believes that, out of misguided love, parents have mistakenly given their children the message that they should be happy, that it is terrible and abnormal to feel unhappy, even for a short time, and that something must be done quickly to 'feel good' again. He gives as an example the way in which many parents offer their children a 'quick fix' such as a trip to a fast-food outlet or a special video if their child is feeling upset. Feedback from schools also suggests that parents today are more likely than in previous times to take action to solve their child's problems rather than helping their child to solve their own problems. For example, many parents ask teachers to place their child in the class they want to be in, or to intervene in minor friendship spats.

Hugh McKay (1997), an Australian psychologist and social commentator, has identified generational differences that support this changed trend in parenting. According to McKay, the earlier generation of Australians who dealt with wartime adversity and restrictions expected that life would not be easy. They were proud of their ability to cope with hardship and retained an optimistic spirit, even in the face of great deprivation and challenge. During this era, most people lived and worked in a relatively small neighbourhood area, and their extended family was usually not far away. So young people had good community support and extended family availability if they needed it. They raised their own children to be responsible members of the community who could look after themselves and survive. Trying to make their children happy was not a direct part of their parenting goals. As Eleanor Roosevelt once said, 'Happiness is not a goal, but a byproduct'.

According to McKay, the children and grandchildren of these earlier generations of Australian parents have had an easier life in many ways, so they perceive that adversity is a terrible and unusual thing, not a reasonably common and predictable occurrence. Their easy access to air travel has meant that family members are more likely to be geographically scattered than in previous times, so there has been less extended family support or small neighbourhood community support. The end result is that the values of post-war parents have focused on the overriding priority of investing time, money and energy in the welfare and happiness of their children. Their main fear is that their children will either become involved with drugs or become depressed and commit suicide. Their answer to this is a tendency to over-protect their children, try to make them 'happy' and prevent them from feeling bad about anything. Ironically, in doing so, they have probably produced less resilient young people.

Fast pace of change

The young people of today are a web-surfing, text-messaging, emailing, interactive, DVD literate, dot.com generation. Engaging and holding their attention in a learning context is more demanding than ever before. Many 'futures' experts predict that one result of the information, communication and technological changes is that, on average, our current students will have three different careers before they are 40 and many will work in jobs that have not yet been created. Conservatively speaking, technological changes are taking place four times faster than last century. By 2025 we will see changes as vast as the ones that took place over the whole of the last century. This creates less clear-cut career paths and more demands for young people to develop resilience and a greater capacity to be flexible and to cope with change than ever before.

High levels of boredom

Recent American and Australian studies suggest that large numbers of young people are feeling bored, alienated or disconnected from any meaningfully challenging activities (Larsen 2000; Trent 2001). For many teenagers Western life does *not* offer abundant daily opportunities to experience and develop initiative. The great majority of adolescent time is spent at school or in leisure activities. School structures and the incentives are generally under teacher control, not student control and the result is often a lack of intrinsic motivation for schoolwork. In most leisure time, including watching TV and interacting with friends, students experience intrinsic motivation but low challenge. Neither endeavour provides opportunities for learning initiative. Yet in the 21st century, where job demands and lifestyle decisions are not clearly predetermined, young people without initiative will be ill prepared.

High youth unemployment in some areas

Economies are less stable and secure than in the past. There are high rates of unemployment and greater competition for jobs. Demands on workers are very high in terms of hours and commitment, with greater needs for multiskilling and more complexity of tasks. High rates of unemployment, especially in the rural sector, correlate with high rates of youth depression and suicide.

The complementary fields of teaching, counselling and social welfare recognise the complexity of the current social and cultural context. The resilience research literature encourages a paradigm shift from a focus on risk factors to a focus on student strengths and the protective mechanisms that help some young people to cope with adversity. This paradigm shift holds promise for professionals working with young people to initiate and sustain prevention and intervention programs to facilitate the development of young people's resilience.

Resilience is a very complex concept and therefore any prevention or intervention programs must be multidimensional and developmental. Resilience programs that address multiple protective factors are more likely to be successful. Multiple protective factors include fostering peer and school connectedness, building strong parent–school links, as well as helping individual students develop internal protective and coping strategies. The following sections look at key messages on resilience emerging in counselling, psychology and education.

Counselling and psychology today

A focus on pathology (or what's gone wrong when people are experiencing mental illness such as depression) dominated psychology in the twentieth century. Psychologists have learned that the study of pathology, weakness and damage does not always move psychology closer to the prevention of serious problems such as depression, substance abuse and school violence. Now psychologists have become more concerned with looking at 'what goes right' in the lives of individuals who are resilient and with preventing problems. A new term, 'positive psychology', has been coined (Seligman & Csikszentmihalyi 2000).

Positive psychology focuses on what works to prevent difficulties or problems. Prevention researchers have discovered that there are human strengths that act as buffers against mental illness and antisocial behaviour and foster resilience. These strengths include courage, future mindedness, optimism, interpersonal skills, faith, work ethic, hope, honesty, perseverance and insight. Many key psychological theories are now changing direction and focusing on this new science of strength and resilience. Positive psychology—based on research evidence about what works to help people cope with adversity, difficulties and hard times—holds promise for everyone. We can all benefit from examples and advice on how to lead richer and more fulfilling lives.

Social welfare today

Strength-based approaches in social welfare are now seen as radical alternatives to the deficits-based mental health paradigm that has previously dominated work with clients in this field. A focus on clients' problems runs the risk of categorising people in terms of their pathology and assigns them disempowering labels that engender feelings of powerlessness (Gray 2001). The strengths-based service delivery is basically a positive, optimistic orientation that does not ignore problems, but relegates problems to their proper place in life: as vehicles for testing the capacities of families and reaffirming their connections. It works on the assumption that all families have strengths, that strengths develop over time and that strengths are tested through normative developmental transitions. The approach acknowledges that crises can tear families apart but can also make family relationships stronger. Families' strengths are seen as the foundation for their positive growth and change in the future (Defrain 2001).

Psychologists, social workers and educators, all of whom work in some way with families, schools and organisations, are now encouraged to focus on strengths, on prevention and on the development of individual resilience. A more positive focus on what works and how to develop resilience to cope with life's difficulties relates well to new policies and directions in education.

Resilience and today's educational context

New policies in school reform, in inclusive schooling, in gifted education and in reshaping the middle years of schooling are all congruent with focusing on student strengths and capabilities. The new school reform agenda has outlined the most important school factors for developing effective schools for students in the 21st century. Many of these school factors are the same protective factors that facilitate student and teacher resilience in schools. The school reform literature also includes the call for schools to develop better skills in diversifying their teaching and learning strategies to cater for the wide range of student differences in our classrooms today. This call is based on the positive paradigm of acknowledging and celebrating student differences rather than focusing on student problems. This shift in perspective from a deficit to a positive view of student differences engenders more hope and more energy for change in teacher practice.

The school reform agenda also highlights the importance of building prosocial collaborative structures and a culture that connects students with their peers and their teachers, teachers with their colleagues and schools with their families and community. The inclusive schooling movement advocates inclusion of all students as active, fully participating members in the school community. The movement is based on the positive principle that all children can learn, views diversity as the norm and requires a paradigm shift in teachers' perceptions from a deficit model of students' problems to a positive model of student strengths.

There has also been a paradigm shift in how we define and address giftedness in education. We now understand that the traditional view of intelligence, which is based on having a high IQ score, denies opportunities for some students, who may be gifted in non-academic domains, to be acknowledged and challenged in their area of intellectual strength. We recognise that all students, including academically gifted students, have jagged intellectual profiles. We also know that academic giftedness and school success do not necessarily equate with job success or life success (Winner 1996). The social and emotional toll on 'at promise' students who underachieve has been seen as one of the contributing factors to high rates of youth depression and low self-esteem (Gross 1993). A differentiated curriculum with negotiated learning tasks and assessment can provide appropriately challenging learning tasks for all. Skills of persevering, setting realistic goals, taking intellectual risks and bouncing back when they experience difficulties or challenges are important life skills to teach to all students, including students who are 'at promise' of becoming gifted adult performers (Winner 1996).

The practices advocated in the middle school literature (Beane 1995; Cumming 1996) are highly compatible with the development of protective factors designed to promote resilience. Both the middle schooling literature and the resilience literature take a positive view of adolescence as a time of hope and promise rather than a negative perception of adolescence as a time of turmoil and trouble. Rather than adopting a deficit perspective on youth issues, both the middle school curriculum and the resilience-focused research seek to identify the positive aspects of adolescents' lives that help them develop life-long skills. The key message underpinning both movements is the need to build stronger school and peer connectedness for students. The transition from primary to secondary school is often a vulnerable time for many students, especially for low-achieving students. Programs that restructure the middle years of schooling help to promote peer and teacher connectedness and a sense of mastery and achievement in students.

These new educational paradigms are moving schools from risk to resiliency.

Resilience and issues of bullying, school violence and behaviour management

The importance of promoting school connectedness for students in the middle years of schooling is also highlighted by the research on school bullying and violence. The most severe forms of bullying occur during the middle years of schooling (Rigby 1996). Yet young people in early adolescence are less willing to discuss bullying than younger students in primary schools or older adolescents (over 15 years of age). School cultures that promote resilience lower the risk of bullying and other forms of school violence and abuse. In Australia racism has been identified as a major cause of violence in school communities (Petrie, Christie & Christie 1999).

Students with low resilience are far more likely than resilient students to talk about being involved in violent interpersonal conflict, particularly at school (Howard & Johnson 2000). In a large American survey of over 36,000 adolescents from Years 7 to 12 school connectedness was shown to be the most salient protective factor for both boys and girls who act out and display antisocial behaviour (Resnick, Harris & Blum 1993). These students identified schools as their primary source for connecting with adults. Both primary (Howard & Johnson 1999) and secondary students (Howard & Johnson 2000; Fuller 1998; Resnick et al. 1993) identified help with their schoolwork as critical to reducing the risk of their acting out and being violent.

Bullying is reduced whenever schools promote a sense of belonging and ensure high levels of involvement between staff and students (Rigby 1996). There is a great deal of evidence demonstrating the effectiveness of school-based programs specifically designed to reduce violence, such as conflict resolution, peer counselling and peer mediation. However, the research indicates that these programs may only be effective when they are linked to more comprehensive prevention approaches. These multistrategic approaches focus on family strengths, family–school connections (Blum 1998), school protective factors and personal coping skills (Kellerman et al. 1998).

Resilience and drug education

Teaching students about the dangers of substance abuse has not been very successful in reducing the rate of students' experimentation with and dependence on drugs or alcohol. A more multistrategic approach that builds the protective factors of connectedness that lead to resilience has been shown to be more likely to reduce the level of problematic substance abuse in young people (Resnick et al. 1997; Hawkins, Catalano & Miller 1992). Many students use drugs and alcohol as a maladaptive coping strategy. When they are bored or stressed, the 'quick fix' of drugs and alcohol are often readily available and likely to be used in the absence of alternative coping strategies. Teaching personal coping skills is one of the new directions for drug education.

Resilience and suicide prevention

Young people who have strong connections to family, peers and school are more likely to have developed personal coping skills and therefore are less likely to develop suicidal thoughts or behaviours (Fuller 1999; Resnick, Harris & Blum 1993). Currently Australia has the highest rate of young male suicide per capita in the world and among boys there is a high level of disillusionment and despair (Trent 2001). The higher incidence of suicide and substance abuse by boys than by girls has been a contributing factor in focusing our attention on boys' education.

Resilience and boys' education

Are boys in trouble in our schools? Over recent years media reports consistently reveal that girls are now 'doing better' than boys in end-of-school results, retention to Year 12 and competence in literacy. Since 1992 more and more boys across the socioeconomic spectrum have not completed Year 12, with a higher rate of non-completion in rural areas (Trent 2001). These results relate to the broader picture of concerns in boys' low engagement and participation in school. Teachers report that a broad range of boys, including an increasing number of 'very bright' boys and not just the stereotypical boy 'at risk', don't care about the consequences of their behaviour or their lack of interest in schoolwork or achievement (Trent 2001).

In schools boys are far more likely to demonstrate behaviour problems and learning difficulties. Schools are forced to spend considerable time, energy and resources on managing small groups of 'bad boys', on developing programs and strategies to handle disruptive behaviour and on repairing damage done by some groups of boys to school property (Gilbert & Gilbert 1998).

These findings have been linked to boys' views on masculinity. To be a 'real man' you must be physically tough, take foolish risks, suppress emotions and be successful in competition, especially in competitive power over others. One study suggests that boys learn to mask emotions by the age of four to six years (West 1996). Although adolescent girls will seek social support, especially peer support, when in need, boys rarely seek support from anyone (Fischmann & Cotterell 2000). Boys' inability to readily express emotions and seek support has being linked to the shocking statistics that suicide is the leading cause of death among young Australian males in the 15–24 age range (Hawkes 2001).

Boys' self-esteem often relies on the traditional views of masculinity such as sporting or fighting skills and superiority over females, which can mean defying female teachers or harassing girls (Fletcher 1998). However, a recent study of 1800 Year 7 to 12 Australian boys found that boys are more likely to attribute boys' problems with schooling to school environmental factors than a masculinity crisis (Trent 2001). Boys listed a broad range of interconnected school factors involving bad teachers, an out-of-date school culture that narrowly defines achievement and success, and a boring, repetitive and irrelevant curriculum. Rather than a deficit approach to 'fixing up the boys', the boys in this study asked for recognition of their successes outside school. Some of the older boys in the study who worked part time also were actively involved in competitive sport and maintained a social life with both male and female friends. In these out-of-school pursuits they demonstrated many positive resilient skills, such as accepting authority, working well in a team, and remaining adaptive and motivated, but they gained little recognition for these strengths and successes at school. Not all boys have these extra-curricular opportunities.

Boys' views on masculinity affect their subject choice, their achievement and the way they participate in school and their behaviour in and out of the classroom—as well as their health and safety in a range of cultural contexts (Gilbert & Gilbert 1998). Boys' membership of antisocial groups or gangs is often motivated by their desire for peer group acceptance. Gaining peer group acceptance through membership of prosocial groups and belonging to a resilient school are protective factors that mitigate delinquent risk-taking behaviours.

Resilience and the teaching of social skills

Peer group acceptance at school is a powerful protective factor for young people. Over 96% of young Australian adolescents feel that being connected to peers is an important protective factor in their own lives and that friendships and socialising are the most important factors in liking school (Fuller et al. 1998). These findings suggest that for young people who may be alienated from their families peer connectedness may be their most important protective factor. Consistent findings from the social skills research demonstrate that students learn the social skills leading to peer group acceptance and resilience better in the naturalistic context of school than in withdrawal programs (McGrath 1998; Johnson & Johnson 1989; Gresham 1988).

In summary

This chapter began by reviewing the world of young people today. The current social context highlights the urgent need to foster resilience in young people. The resilience research literature asserts the need to encourage a paradigm shift from a focus on risk factors and problems to a focus on the personal strengths and skills and protective resources that can help young people to cope with adversity. This paradigm shift holds promise for professionals working with young people in the complementary fields of education, counselling and social welfare. This new paradigm is starting to influence the school reform agenda and policies and practices in different areas of education such as special education, gifted education, middle years of schooling, dealing with bullying and behaviour management, boys' education, youth substance abuse education and suicide prevention and social skills training. A consistent theme in the study of resilience is the importance of prevention as well as a comprehensive, multidimensional approach. The more protective factors and processes in any program, the more likely it will be successful in fostering resilience.

REFERENCES

Australian Institute of Health and Welfare 1999, *Australia's Young People: Their Health and Wellbeing*. www.aihw.gov.au/inet/publications.

Australian Institute of Family Studies, www.aifs.org.au.

Beane, J.A., 1995, *The Middle Years Kit: An exploration of pedagogy, curriculum and work organisation for the middle years of schooling*. National Schools Network, Ryde.

Bond, L., Thomas, L., Toumbourou, J., Patton, G. & Catalano, R., 2000, *Improving the Lives of Young Victorians in Our Community—A Survey of Risk and Protective Factors*. Centre for Adolescent Health, Melbourne.

Buss, D.M., 2000, 'The evolution of happiness'. *American Psychologist* 55(1), 15–23.

Cantor, C.H., Neulinger, K. & DeLeo, D., 1999, 'Australian suicide trends 1964–1997 youth and beyond'. *Medical Journal of Australia*, 171, 137–41.

Cumming, J., 1996, *From Alienation to Engagement: Opportunities for Reform in the Middle Years of Schooling*. Australian Curriculum Studies Association, Canberra.

DeFrain, J., 2001, 'The Family Strengths Perspective'. *Building Family Strengths Conference Program*. University of Newcastle, December.

Diener, E., Suh, E.M., Lucas, R.E. & Smith, H.L., 1999, 'Subjective wellbeing: Three decades of progress'. *Psychological Bulletin*, 125, 276–302.

Eckersley, R., 2002, 'Taking the price or paying the price? Young people and progress'. In L. Rowling, G. Martin & L. Walker (eds), *Mental Health Promotion and Young People: Concepts and Practice*. McGraw Hill, Sydney.

Fischmann, S. & Cotterell, J.L., 2000, 'Coping styles and support sources of at-risk students'. *The Australian Educational and Developmental Psychologist*, 17(2), 58–69.

Fletcher, R. cited in Gilbert, R. & Gilbert, P., 1998, *Masculinity Goes to School*. Allen & Unwin, St Leonards.

Foreman, P., 2001, (ed.), *Integration and Inclusion in Action*. Harcourt, Sydney.

Fuller, A., McGraw, K. & Goodyear, M., 1998, *The Mind of Youth. Resilience: A Connect Project*. Victorian Department of Education.

Fuller, A., 1999, *Resilience*. A keynote address at Australian Association of Cooperative Learning Biennial Conference, Perth.

Gilbert, R. & Gilbert, P., 1998, *Masculinity Goes to School*. Allen & Unwin, St Leonards.

Glover, S., Burns, J., Butler, H. & Patton, G., 1998, 'Social environments and the emotional wellbeing of young people'. *Family Matters*, 49 (Autumn), 11–16.

Gray, M., 2001, 'Strengths-based approaches: A radical alternative'. *Building Family Strengths Conference Program*. University of Newcastle, December.

Gresham, F. M., 1988, 'Social skills: Conceptual and applied aspects of assessment training and social validation.' In J.C. Witt, S.N. Elliot and F.M. Gresham (eds) *Handbook of Behaviour Therapy in Education*. Plenum Press, New York, 526–546.

Gross, M., 1993, *Exceptionally Gifted Children*. Routledge, London.

Hawkes, T., 2001, *Boy Oh Boy. How to Raise and Educate Boys*. Pearson Educational, Sydney.

Hawkins, K., Catalano, R. & Miller, J., 1992, 'Risk and protective factors for alcohol and other drug problems in adolescence and early childhood: Implications for substance abuse prevention'. *Psychological Bulletin*, 112, 1, 64–105.

Howard, S. & Johnson, B., 2000, 'Young adolescents displaying resilient and non-resilient behaviour: Insights from a qualitative study—can schools make a difference?' Paper presented at AARE conference, University of Sydney, December.

Howard, S. & Johnson, B., 1999, 'Tracking student resilience'. *Children Australia*, 24(3), 14–23.

Johnson, D.W. and Johnson, R.T., 1989, *Cooperation and Competition: Theory and Researach*, Interaction Book Company, Minnesota.

Kellerman, A.L., Fuqua-Whitley, D.S., Rivara, F.P. & Mervy, J., 1998, 'Preventing youth violence: what works?' *Annual Review of Public Health*, 19, 271–92.

Larson, R.W., 2000, 'Toward a psychology of positive youth development'. *American Psychologist*, 55, No. 1, 170–83.

McGrath, H.L., 1998, 'An overview of prevention and treatment programs for developing positive peer relations'. In K. Rigby and P. Slee (eds), *Children's Peer Relationships.* Routledge, London.

McKay, H., 1997, *Generations: Baby Boomers, Their Parents and Their Children.* Macmillan, Sydney.

Petrie, S., Christie, G. & Christie, C., 1999, *Reducing and preventing violence in schools.* Paper presented at Australian Institute of Criminology Conference, Brisbane.

Resnick, M.D., Harris, L.J. & Blum, R.W., 1993, 'The impact of caring and connectedness on adolescent health and wellbeing'. *Journal of Paediatrics and Child Health*, 29, 1, 3–9.

Resnick, M.D., Bearman, P.S., Blum, R.W., Bauman, K.E., Harris, K.M., Jones, J., Behhring, T., Sieving, R.E., Shew, M., Ireland, M., Bearinger, L.H. & Udry, J.R., 1997, 'Protecting adolescents from harm—Findings from the National longitudinal study on adolescent health'. *Journal of the American Medical Association*, 278, 10, 823–32.

Rigby, K., 1996, *Bullying in Schools: And What To Do About It.* ACER, Melbourne.

Seligman, M.E.P. & Csikszentmihalyi, M., 2000, 'Positive Psychology'. *American Psychologist*, 55(1), 5–14.

Seligman, M.E.P., 1995, *The Optimistic Child.* Random House, New York.

Trent, F., 2001, *Aliens in the classroom or: The Classroom as an alien place?* Paper presented at the Association of Independent Schools, NSW Sex, Drugs & Rock 'N Roll Conference, August.

Twenge, J.M., 2000, 'The age of anxiety? Birth cohort change in anxiety and neuroticism, 1952–1993'. *Journal of Personality and Social Psychology*, 79(6), 1007–21.

Waters, E., Wake, M., Toumbourou, J., Wright, M. & Salmon, L., 1999, 'Prevalence of emotional and physical concerns among young people in Victoria'. *Journal of Paediatrics and Child Health*, 35, 28–33.

West, P., 1996, *Fathers, Sons and Lovers.* Finch Publishing, Sydney.

Winner, E., 1996, *Gifted Children: Myths and Realities.* Basic Books, New York.

THE PERSONAL COPING SKILLS APPROACH

Human resilience is a complex concept. The best strategy for promoting resilience is to take a multi-faceted approach. The greater the number of protective resources and processes in the life of a young person, the more likely they are to develop resilience. The previous chapter explored the social and educational contexts of youth today. This chapter looks at the personal coping skills component of the BOUNCE BACK! Resiliency Program that can help young people to develop the skills of resilience that they need to manage the complexity of their life in the 21st century. We cannot protect young people from the stress of all potential aversive life events, but we can help them to develop the personal skills and assets necessary to cope with these events. The personal coping skills, assets and attitudes that contribute to resilience are helpful and optimistic thinking, resourcefulness and adaptivity, normalising and using balanced causation instead of personalising, social competency, help seeking, using humour, emotional literacy and having a healthy self-esteem.

In the BOUNCE BACK! Resiliency Program the main foundation for teaching the personal skills for resilience is the BOUNCE BACK! acronym. The letters of BOUNCE BACK! stand for ten coping statements. This chapter looks at the theoretical underpinnings of the coping statements and provides guidelines on teaching these personal coping skills. Posters of these acronyms can be found in BLMs 4.1 and 4.2.

Optimistic thinking

People who think optimistically tend to look on the bright side of things and to hope for the best. They believe that setbacks are normal and can be overcome by their own actions. Optimism has been correlated with so many protective factors to foster resilience that it has been called the 'velcro' construct to which everything else sticks (Peterson 2000). Optimistic thinking has been linked to:
• Taking risks in the belief that you have a good chance of getting the outcome you want
• Persisting when things become difficult or after failure
• Effective problem solving
• Feeling confident and presenting in a confident way
• Being successful
• Being popular
• Having good health
• Living longer and being more physically healthy.

People who tend towards pessimism feel down and helpless. Everything seems too hard to fix and too overwhelming. They tend to look on the worst side of things and feel a sense of hope-lessness and despair. Pessimism is linked to:
• A greater risk of being depressed
• A tendency to think problems are impossible and to give up without even trying
• Failing because they haven't persisted nor taken risks

- Not doing as well at school, at work and at sport as their strengths would predict
- Being socially isolated
- Getting sick more often and being more vulnerable to infection.

There are many different components to optimism. Seligman (1995) has identified three of them.

The first component is '**positivity**', or the degree to which we try to find the positive features of situations, however small. Another term for this is 'positive tracking'.

The second component is '**mastery**', which involves feeling some sense of personal competence and control over one's life. Mastery is usually attained through the successful achievement of goals over time and hence the positive expectation that you can repeat the process. Providing students with opportunities to develop an understanding of their strengths and weaknesses and using this understanding as the basis for problem solving, decision making and goal setting is important to developing resilience and maintaining realistic optimism. Such self-understanding is an element of what Howard Gardner (1999) refers to as intrapersonal intelligence. Conveying positive but realistic expectations to students and encouraging them to persevere can also assist them to develop optimistic thinking. Persevering and being successful, especially when a task is challenging, promotes optimism and self-efficacy—'I can do it'.

The third component is '**explanatory style**', which is the way we explain to ourselves why events happen to us. Our way of explaining events to ourselves determines how energised/optimistic or how helpless/pessimistic we become when we encounter everyday setbacks as well as momentous defeats. There are three dimensions to our explanatory style:

1 How permanent we think a situation will be:
   - *Ongoing*: The pessimistic style stresses the ongoing and long-lasting nature of negative situations.
   - *Temporary*: The optimistic explanatory style stresses that a negative event is likely to not last very long. It is a 'one-off'.
2 How much we think a situation has happened because of our own characteristics and behaviour:
   - *Because of me*: The pessimistic style stresses that negative events happen mostly because of our own defects, stupidity, unworthiness or because we are jinxed and attract bad luck.
   - *Because of other reasons too*: The optimistic explanatory style stresses that negative events have many different causes, including circumstances outside one's control, bad luck and the behaviour of other people.
3 How much of our life we think will be affected by one situation:
   - *Everything!*: The pessimistic style stresses that negative events spoil everything.
   - *Just this*: The optimistic explanatory style stresses that negative events are specific and just affect that one relevant part of your life.

Explanatory style for negative events

The pessimistic explanatory style for **negative** events leads to little sense of control and a loss of hope. On the other hand, the optimistic explanatory style leads to a stronger sense of power over one's life and hence a belief that the future can be bright even if the present seems bleak.

The table on the next page compares two students who are both feeling socially isolated a month after starting at a new school. One uses a pessimistic explanatory style for why they are having difficulties making friends, while the other uses an optimistic explanatory style.

Explanatory style for positive events

Explanatory style for explaining *good* events in our lives is just the *opposite*. Again, there are the three dimensions:

1 How permanent we think a situation will be.
   - *Temporary*: The pessimistic explanatory style stresses that a good event is likely to be short-lived and is a 'one-off' fluke.
   - *Ongoing*: The optimistic style stresses the ongoing and long-lasting nature of good situations.

Pessimistic explanatory style for a negative situation (feeling isolated at a new school)	Optimistic explanatory style for a negative situation (feeling isolated at a new school)
Ongoing No-one will ever want to be friends with me. I'll be on my own forever.	Temporary Things will improve for me when things settle down a bit.
Everything! I hate it that we moved. Everything is going wrong in my life.	Just this I wish I had a better social life at school, but I like our new house and I've made friends in the local netball team that I've joined.
Because of me I'm boring and I can't make friends. Nobody likes me because I'm ugly. This sort of thing always happens to me. It never seems to happen to any of the other kids I know.	Because of other reasons too Maybe I need to try a bit harder but the teacher hasn't helped me to get to know people. The other kids seem a bit 'cliquey'. I remember my cousin had the same problem when she changed schools.

2 How much we think a situation has happened because of our own characteristics and behaviour.
- *Because of other reasons too*: The pessimistic explanatory style stresses that good events have many different causes, such as good luck, accidental circumstances and favourable treatment by others.
- *Because of me*: The optimistic style stresses taking credit for a good event, that is, believing that the good event happened mostly because of our abilities, hard work and personal characteristics.

3 How much of our life we think will be affected by one situation.
- *Just this*: The pessimistic explanatory style stresses that a good event is specific and just affects that one relevant part of our life. There is no carry-over effect.
- *Everything!*: The optimistic style stresses that good events have a positive effect on everything in our lives.

Consider this example of two students who both do well in a maths test. One uses pessimistic explanatory style for why they did well and the other uses an optimistic explanatory style.

Pessimistic explanatory style for a good event (doing well on a test)	Optimistic explanatory style for a good event (doing well on a test)
Temporary What a miracle. This is just a one-off. It won't happen again.	Ongoing This is another test on which I got a good result. I think my work and results are improving.
Just this Sure I did well on today's test, but nothing else in my life works out.	Everything! This week is really looking up!
Because of other reasons too I was just lucky today and the questions we got were ones I knew about. This teacher sets easy tests.	Because of me! The studying I did definitely paid off.

Explanatory style is also linked to self-esteem. Young people who habitually blame themselves whenever things go wrong and don't give themselves credit for the good things that happen in their life are more likely to be depressed and have low self-esteem.

Those who use an approach of balanced causation feel less guilt or shame when bad events happen because they also take into account the behaviour of others or adverse circumstances. They like themselves better and therefore are less likely to feel disempowered by the event. When good things happen in their lives, their self-esteem increases. They tend to 'pat themselves on the back' privately whenever anything they do, however small, is successful. They feel empowered because they believe that their own efforts have made the difference.

The BOUNCE BACK! acronym contains statements which focus on changing students' explanatory style for bad events. It focuses specifically on:

• Understanding that bad events are temporary
• Understanding that one bad event doesn't have to spoil your whole life
• Not personalising bad events and normalising instead, i.e. accepting that some things that happen to us happen to nearly everyone—they're pretty normal
• Not over-emphasising your own faults and blaming yourself completely
• Identifying the bit you might be responsible for and what you can learn from your own actions or mistakes so you can avoid doing the same thing again
• Learning from other people's contributions to what happened so you get a better idea of what to be careful about next time
• Accepting that there are some random factors over which we don't have control. These factors usually are described as bad luck or unfortunate circumstances.

There are activities in 'The Bright Side' units that focus on changing explanatory style for good events.

Pessimistic thinking about bad events is a significant risk factor for anxiety and depression. Not surprisingly, young children who develop a pessimistic style at an early age are the ones who are most likely to get depressed and stay depressed (Seligman 1992). Changing students' explanatory style for bad events from pessimistic to optimistic is seen as an innoculation against mental illness and a protective factor in the development of resilience (Peterson 2000; Seligman 1995). Programs designed to change students' explanatory style from pessimistic to optimistic thinking have been more successful with young people from ten years old to early adolescence than with older adolescents. Evaluations of these programs have shown that students were significantly less depressed and their classroom behaviour significantly improved immediately after the program and at a 6-month and 2-year follow-up (Jaycox et al. 1994; Gilham et al. 1995). However, it is never too early or too late to learn more effective ways of coping. We can start teaching very young children to be more optimistic, so that over time optimistic thinking develops and becomes well established. We can also help older students to learn more optimistic thinking, even if the gains are a bit smaller.

There is one cautionary note to be sounded here. Being overly optimistic can be counter-productive if it is too unrealistic. Constant striving for control over events without the human or material resources to achieve a goal, or without seeing real obstacles, can also lead to a sense of helplessness and depression. Research by Harvard psychologist David McClelland (1985) found that people who achieve the most success show both optimism and pessimism when selecting goals. They anticipate difficulties before they occur and then plan to avoid or overcome them. We all face objective limits to what we can achieve no matter how hard we work.

Maintaining hope in difficult situations

Hope is another aspect of optimism. A hopeful person maintains a belief that if one path is blocked there will be alternative pathways to achieving goals. Hope provides people with a will to live and to work towards making life happier for themselves. It is essential to our physical and psycho-social wellbeing. There are two kinds of hope: conceptual hope and operational hope. Conceptual hope relates to big-picture concepts of hope for the world and hope for humanity. Operational

Optimism is the faith that leads to achievement. Nothing can be done without hope and confidence. (Helen Keller)

At a time of crisis one always has choices. (John Kennedy at the time of the Cuban crisis)

A crisis is a dangerous opportunity. (Chinese proverb)

Nothing is more creative than hope, nothing more important when the present is hard to live through, nothing more necessary to give purpose and direction to life. (Moltmann, in Marsh 2000:152)

hope relates more to one's own life and the capacity to take action. The following four components of hope are derived from the disciplines of psychology and psychiatry, philosophy and theology (Marsh 2000; Moltmann 1967).

1. An orientation towards the future

Hope is maintaining an expectation that what you want or desire is obtainable or achievable. Hope always looks for creative changes—changes for the better. Dreaming about the future helps a person to create new ways to improve present situations.

2. Goal setting

Goal setting is closely linked to being future-oriented. Hope creates the capacity to set goals, to make plans, and to maintain a belief that your goals can be achieved. The goals can be short-term tasks or long term plans. 'High-hope' people can clearly talk about their goals, whereas 'low-hope' people are much more uncertain about their goals (Snyder 1999). 'High-hope' people look for alternative pathways if the original pathway to their goal is blocked. They are motivated to initiate and continue finding different pathways to meet goals. They are more willing to take risks and see a way around most problems. They see problems as an opportunity in disguise. This courage to take risks is also linked to a sense of security and a belief in oneself and one's abilities. In contrast, 'low-hope' people not only are unclear about the best pathway to achieve a goal, but they don't know what actions to take when a goal is blocked.

3. Action

A hopeful person approaches situations with a belief that there will be solutions. The action element of hope is reflected in different ways in the different disciplines. Psychologists focus on the capacity of 'high-hope' people to take action to achieve personal goals. Philosophers and theologians are more likely to focus on the actions that 'high-hope' people are prepared to take on behalf of others, such as social and political activities.

4. Trust in interpersonal relationships

Hope initially develops from trusting relationships with others, especially in early childhood. Young people who fail to develop a sense of trust in early childhood may continue to mistrust people. They may also feel too insecure and dependent on other people's approval to develop an independent personality. 'Low-hope' adults report they were not supported, nurtured or given guidance during their early years (Snyder 1999). A trust in others means that a person with high hope is more likely to seek help from others when a goal is blocked than are 'low-hope' people. Trust in oneself, in others and in one's environment is the genesis of hope.

Normalising

Normalising, instead of personalising, is an indirect aspect of optimism. Normalising means recognising that something that happens in your life is also something that happens to lots of other people too, or is typical of a set of circumstances or a stage of development. In contrast, personalising is when you think something that is relatively normal happens only to you, not others, and that it happens BECAUSE you are who you are. If we personalise, we say 'that occurred to me because I am me and therefore there is nothing I can do about it because it will undoubtedly happen again because I will always be me'. When you personalise you automatically think 'what's wrong with me?' or 'why me?' If you normalise you automatically think 'what's wrong here?' and ask yourself 'is this an out-of-the-ordinary event or the kind of thing that happens quite frequently to other people?' In normalising we say 'that happened to me because it is one of those things that happen to many people in their lifetime, not just me. If others can deal with it, so can I'. Over time, young people who personalise everyday difficulties develop a negative self-perception or a belief that they are jinxed, doomed or inadequate.

Young people need to be shown how to normalise many of the changes in their behaviours, roles and relationships that are due to developmental 'everyday' stressors. We can probably remember from our own experience wondering if what we were experiencing as we proceeded through childhood and adolescence was 'normal' or typical. Challenges to our wellbeing can occur at any time due to illness, accidents, loss or trauma, but there are also everyday stressors at different developmental stages when everyone is likely to experience some anxiety and uncertainty. Many of these are listed in the chart on the next page. Young people need to understand that others are also likely to be experiencing the same kinds of feelings and it is normal at these turning points to experience some anxiety. Sharing their concerns with others helps with this 'normative' process.

It is also important that those working with young people clearly understand the developmental stages and characteristics of each stage of childhood development. Without this understanding there is a risk of over-reacting or under-reacting to young people's problematic symptoms. Understanding the characteristics of young people's thinking at each stage of development and in response to everyday stressors helps teachers and others working with young people to normalise their experiences for them. Normalising, if it is done sensitively and not dismissively, does not trivialise or devalue young people's anxiety, but rather helps them to see that other young people are also experiencing similar feelings. This helps them to respond more constructively and optimistically to the situation.

Young people also need to be taught how to normalise and manage emotional states. Without being patronising or trivialising their feelings, those working with young people can encourage them to understand that it is normal and appropriate to temporarily feel sad, anxious, worried or disappointed when they experience hardship, loss, sadness, disappointments, reversals, setbacks and bad times. In fact such feelings are useful in that they can motivate problem solving and empathy for others. An important message is that others survive difficult or bad events in their lives and they can too.

Everyday stressors and major stressors

Everyday stressors are the typical kinds of stressors that children face as they proceed through developmental stages. They include changes in routine, social disappointments, and changes required in starting school or advancing from one grade to another. Whether these everyday events are stressful for the child will depend on the child's personal coping skills and their home and school environment. Major stressors or risk factors are events like divorce or family trauma. At these times young people will typically need extra support to develop and employ resilient attitudes and skills.

Using humour

Humour is a powerful tool for resilience and we need to use it in every helpful way we can when working with young people. Lefcourt (2001) has argued that humour is a characteristic that is useful to our species, aiding us as we attempt to live in what are often unbearable circumstances. Humour may also have evolved as an antidote to anger and aggression, allowing humans to live together without engaging in continuous conflict. When there is a major world crisis or tragedy there is soon a spate of jokes about it. These jokes help people to manage the stress or anxiety provoked by the tragedy. We are less likely to succumb to feelings of depression and helplessness if we are able to find something funny in the situation that is troubling us.

Everyday stressors	Major stressors
Pre-school (1–4 years) Birth of sibling Adjustment to child care Transition to preschool Separation from attachment figures **Primary School age (5–12 years)** Transition to school Competition with peers Peer relationships Peer teasing Peer pressure (e.g. to go with a fad or do something they don't want to do) Sibling reputation pressures Homework Poor academic outcomes Conflict with the teacher Disappointments connected with sport or other extracurricular activities Class presentation Worry about tests Time pressures (balancing schoolwork demands and extracurricular or home demands) Child–parent conflicts Early puberty **Adolescence (13–19 years)** Hormonal changes Growth changes Physical appearance Peer pressure Heightened sexuality Issues of independence and freedom Relationship issues Increased responsibility for self in school Career and university choices Transition to work Part-time work Gender role issues Romantic partnership issues	**Death** Parent Sibling Close relative Close friend Favourite pet **Serious illness or disability** Self Parent Sibling Close relative Close friend **Other extraordinary trauma** War Fire or flood Legal problems Sexual and/or physical abuse Robbery or assault **Parental** Divorce Remarriage Job loss, job start Abuse/violence Mental illness Alcohol and other substance abuse Being jailed **Change in** Standard of living School district Residence Number of people living in home Parental contact (e.g. parent working long hours/ shift work or loss of contact) Being bullied

Adapted from Arnold, L. (1991) *Childhood Stress*. Wiley, New York. This material is used with permission of John Wiley & Sons, Inc.

The degree to which a person uses humour can tell us a lot about their resilience and coping style. For example:
- Those who use humour under stress are more likely to have a strong sense of their own personal control and feel less helpless. Teaching people to use humour as a coping strategy has been shown to increase their sense of having greater control and power over their own life (Wootton 1992, 1996).

- Children who are perceived as having a good sense of humour also tend to be more assertive and have more of an internal locus of control (Lefcourt 2001).
- A poor sense of humour is associated with an avoidance style of coping and a degree of passive acceptance of the negative effects that accompany stressful experiences (Lefcourt 2001).

Professional humourists can show us the link between humour and hardship. Research has demonstrated that humorous performers have greater self-confidence than other kinds of performer, but also tend to have had harsher childhoods, especially the stand-up comics. They tend to have higher ego-strength. It appears that being funny becomes their way of appeasing adults in their life and surviving the adverse aspects of their childhood environments.

Humour has positive benefits for physical health as well as mental health (Berk 1989a, 1989b, 1994; Wootten 1994, 1996; Lefcourt & Martin 1986; Martin & Dobbin 1985). The emotions and moods we experience directly affect our immune system. After ongoing stress to the body or mind, our adrenal secretions become exhausted. Consequently, insulin secretion is also diminished and our appetite is suppressed. Ultimately, over time, we fail to adequately store nutrients. This interferes with the incorporation of calcium into bone which in turn interferes with the function of growth hormones and the digestive processes necessary for growth and repair. On the other hand, laughter releases pleasure and relaxation chemicals, improves the functioning of the immune system, lowers heart rates and blood pressure, and encourages growth and repair. Research also suggests that we can stay feeling relaxed and in a good mood for up to 45 minutes after a hearty laugh. Laughter does indeed positively affect the body, mind and spirit.

> Comedy and music come into their own at times of stress and strain. They're your only reminders of normality. (Billy Connelly)
>
> A person has two legs and one sense of humour, and if you are faced with the choice, it's better to lose a leg. (Charles Lindner)
>
> He who laughs, lasts. (Mary Pettibone Poole)
>
> Humour allows man to create a perspective, to put distance between himself and whatever may confront him. Humour allows man to detach himself from himself and thereby retain the fullest possible control over himself. (Viktor Frankl)
>
> Humour is a magical thing that allows us to endure life's hardships such as death, sickness, hunger, pain, and fear. It is the bond that can bring us together, and if used as a weapon can tear us apart. (Shaeffer & Hopkins 1988)

Research studies have consistently demonstrated that humour can moderate distress and negative emotions (Lefcourt 2001). Humour, more than anything else in the human make-up, gives one an ability to rise above any situation, even if only for a short time. Humour is a healthy way of putting a little 'distance' between one's self and the problem, a way of standing off and looking at one's problem with perspective. Comic actor Robin Williams once described humour as 'optimism in action'. Humour can create hope by encouraging us to reframe and redefine a negative situation as a little bit more positive. Laughter throws a bit of light onto an otherwise dark and bleak situation.

The cartoon book *Sick Humour*, drawn by critically ill young people and published by the Melbourne Royal Children's Hospital, shows the human capacity to maintain a sense of humour. Their work illustrates that when we laugh about a situation we give ourselves the subtle message: 'this is not completely threatening, because sometimes there's a funny side'. Associate Professor Susan Sawyer, head of the clinical program at the Centre for Adolescent Health which is based at the Royal Children's Hospital, has this to say in her foreword to the book:

> We believe that humour is an aspect of resilience that assists young people to 'bounce back' from the tough times associated with illness in adolescence. This diary [of adolescent patients] is testament to their strength and ability to cope with life with illness and disability (Arnott & Inserra 2000:iii).

Humour also assists in accepting life's imperfections, inevitabilities, difficulties, frustrations and disappointments. It helps us to accept what we cannot control, such as death, the behaviour of other people, incompetence, ageing, physical limitations and illness. Jokes and funny throwaway lines can also communicate messages that help us to understand what is normal and typical. In knowing that others share some of the same feelings, perceptions and troubles, we feel more empowered to deal with these troubles.

When we have to rise above challenges to our public self and our self-respect, humour is an alternative to becoming defensive (Lefcourt 2001). When we laugh at ourselves after falling over in an undignified way, the message we are giving to ourselves is, 'this is not as bad or dangerous as it first seemed' and we feel more able to handle the slight embarrassment. Humour allows us to 'maintain face' in front of others. When others gently laugh with us in similar circumstances, their laughter says 'we understand, and we feel your embarrassment, but we are OK with it and you haven't lost any respect in our eyes'.

There are many social benefits from using humour. For example:

- It can create a sense of community and closeness. We all benefit from closeness to others when we encounter difficulties in our lives. Social support moderates the impact of stressful experiences. Sharing a joke and laughing at similar things together not only gives the message that we are enjoying each other's company but also helps us to develop strong bonds with others and creates group allegiance and solidarity.
- People who use humour, especially self-deprecating humour, often draw other people towards them. Being able to laugh at our own foibles and at aspects of our own crises tends to attract support from others. Other people interpret self-directed humour in the face of adversity as a sign of courage.
- Humour can be a way of showing affection. Being able to gently and humorously 'stir' another can be a sign of friendship and the strength of the relationship.
- Children with a good sense of humour are more popular and socially competent. They are also well liked by teachers as long as the humour is not disruptive and 'silly and immature' (Rockhill & Asher 1992; Troop & Asher 1998; Sletta, Sobstad & Valas 1996).

Humour can also decrease tension in social contexts. For example:

- If the social tension is due to unfamiliarity and possible nervousness, laughter and having fun can break down barriers and create a sense of safety.
- If the social tension is due to fear, humour can act as an icebreaker, especially if there is not much time in which to build a relationship. Humour can communicate trust and safety, when we are aware that the humour is being used in a supportive and caring way to reduce fear. This process is often seen in hospitals, where the medical staff often make light-hearted and joking remarks in the face of a serious medical situation. The humour can be easily terminated when more seriousness is needed.
- If the tension is due to anger and conflict, humour can, used wisely, 'short circuit' a hostile exchange and allow people to 'back off' and change to a more positive and conciliatory direction.
- If the social tension relates to discomfort about talking about certain things, humour can make the 'undiscussable' discussable. People feel more able to talk about their feelings and difficult situations if there is an element of humour to lighten the discussion.

There are gender differences in the use of humour. There are two significant differences between males and females in regards to their use and appreciation of humour. The first difference is that girls and women use and appreciate more self-directed humour and boys and men initiate and appreciate more other-directed and hostile humour. Secondly, boys are more likely to use humour to decrease the intimacy of a situation, whereas girls are more likely to use it to increase the intimacy level.

There are also some 'downsides' to humour. Exploitive and attacking humour allows others to be entertained by another's distress. However, while hostile humour may create a sense of cohesion in an in-group that shares its animosity towards other groups or individuals, there is also a negative aspect to it. Group members soon become suspicious of each other, fearing that they will become the next targets of ridicule (Lefcourt 2001). Humour can be used to trivialise a serious situation and deny the reality of associated feelings and hence reduce efforts to deal with it. It can encourage disengagement from problem solving and avoidance of problem confrontations.

Humour is a powerful tool of resilience and we should use it in our interactions with young people and teach them to use it as part of their repertoire of coping skills. There is a classroom unit on 'Humour' in each BOUNCE BACK! Teacher's Resource Book. The units focus on activities that create a classroom environment that is fun to belong to, and they provide messages about using humour in a resilient way.

Helpful and rational thinking

Helpful and rational thinking derives from the Cognitive Behaviour Therapy (CBT) model developed by Albert Ellis (Ellis & Dryden 1986; Burns 1980; Clark & Beck 1999; Ellis 1988, 1997; Ellis & Harper 1976). CBT is based on the assumption that strong feelings such as anxiety, depression and anger are exaggerated and, in some cases, caused by our own thoughts and beliefs. Like Seligman's explanatory style (which also derives from this model), CBT is based on the principle that changing the way we think enables us to change the way we feel. CBT is a practical, action-oriented approach to coping with problems and enhancing personal growth. CBT has become recognised throughout the world as a highly successful form of treatment for depression, anxiety and anger (Tanner & Ball 1991). Distortions in our thinking play a key role in causing and maintaining low coping skills. What we think about a negative event exaggerates our emotional and behavioural reactions.

The CBT model uses tactics to help people to change their thinking, feelings and behaviour. These tactics are all based on the assumption that unhelpful thinking can be identified and helpful thinking can be substituted. The tactics are:

> Nothing is good nor bad but thinking makes it so. (William Shakespeare, Hamlet)
>
> . . . grant me the courage to change the things I can change, the serenity to accept the things I cannot change, and the wisdom to know the difference. (Reinhold Niebuhr)
>
> A man is hurt not so much by what happens to him as by his opinion of what happens. (Montaigne)

- Challenging and changing distortions in their thinking, such as catastrophising ('The worst outcome is inevitable'), mind-reading ('I can guess what they're thinking about me') and over-generalising ('If a bad thing has happened to me once, it's sure to happen again')
- Encouraging 'reality-checking' by talking to other people in order to understand how others see the situation and checking the 'evidence' and facts which supposedly support conclusions
- Accepting those things which cannot be changed because they are not under one's control
- Not having unrealistic expectations of perfection in oneself or others.

Help-seeking and self-disclosure

Seeking help and talking to others encourages young people to disclose their thoughts, feelings, past experiences and future plans. In this way they can gain support, get a reality check, clarify their thoughts and feelings, and learn to be comfortable with intimacy. Self-disclosure in friendships forges close bonds and trust. Of course there are also some risks attached to self-disclosure and/or asking for help. There is a chance that you will feel stigmatised, you may feel rejected or betrayed if the person you talk to doesn't keep your confidences or follow through for you, or you may get negative feedback about yourself which is hard to deal with. It is also possible that after asking for help, it won't be given in the way you expected. Not surprisingly, boys self-disclose less than girls. In one study of Year 5 children, many boys reported that they thought self-disclosure would be a waste of time (Rose, in Rustad 1999). However, accessing social support, learning to cross-check your perceptions with others and developing caring connections with others are critical protective factors for both boys and girls.

Self-concept, self-esteem and self-efficacy

These three terms are similar but different in small ways.

- Self-concept is a global construct that incorporates our many ideas, feelings and attitudes about our self. It is our 'big-picture' belief about who we are and what kind of person we are.
- Self-esteem is our evaluation of who we are, a judgment of our self-worth. If people evaluate themselves positively, they have high self-esteem.
- Self-efficacy is much more specific than self-concept and refers to our judgments of how well we think we would be able to do a particular task or handle a specific situation.

A person's self-efficacy is a strong predictor of their behaviour in specific situations, whereas their self-concept is a weaker predictor because it is more global. It is possible to have low self-efficacy for singing but for this not to affect your self-esteem because singing is not critical to your job or what you deem important. Greater self-efficacy in an aspect of one's life leads to greater effort and persistence in the face of setbacks. A person with high self-efficacy in relation to a task will also set higher goals, be less afraid of failure and look for new strategies when old ones fail. However, if self-efficacy is low for a task or situation, a person may avoid them altogether or give up easily when problems arise. So high self-efficacy is related to optimistic thinking and persevering in spite of obstacles.

In schools self-efficacy is improved when students learn how to set short-term goals so that it is easier for them to judge their progress. They can be taught specific learning strategies that help them focus attention on what is important to learn so that they are more likely to receive recognition and rewards based on their performance, not just on their engagement. Rewarding student performance signals to the student their increasing competence (Graham & Weiner 1996).

The BOUNCE BACK! coping statements are designed to increase young people's sense of self-efficacy by encouraging them to understand the links between how they think in relation to specific events and how they feel and how they act. The classroom units on 'Success' in the three Teacher's Resource Books are designed to increase students' self-knowledge and self-management skills, such as goal setting, planning, organising, monitoring progress and evaluating performance.

Self-esteem is multifaceted

It is possible for a child to feel confident about their skills and competence in one area, such as their academic skills and competence, but not in another area, such as their ability to make and keep friends. However, the more successes that young people experience, the more they build up a global or general belief in themselves as worthwhile people. The aim is to help students attain multiple self-efficacies across a wide range of areas of their life. This creates a more positive self-concept and hence a stronger sense of self-worth.

One classic analogy, used by Canfield and Wells (1976), is that of accumulating poker chips. Successes are like poker chips. If you have a good supply of poker chips you are more prepared to risk losing some, and by risking more, you often gain more. But if you have only a few poker chips, you take fewer risks and bet more cautiously. This often means you gain less. When they experience a difficulty or problem, young people with many self-efficacies are more willing to take a risk and make mistakes because they can afford to lose one or two 'poker chips'. Young people who have had fewer successes and hence have fewer self-efficacies have not stockpiled many chips, so when they experience difficulties or problems they are less willing to take a risk because they could lose the few 'poker chips' they have accumulated. They conduct their life as 'self-protection' rather than 'self-direction'.

There are three categories of self-esteem: healthy, low and inflated.

Healthy self-esteem

Healthy self-esteem is a positive and optimistic view of one's 'value'. It increases resilience and success and enhances relationships. Young people with healthy self-esteem are more able to make and keep friends, communicate effectively and be independent. When they experience problems with relationships or situations they are more prepared to tackle the difficulty and bounce back. Research tells us that a student with healthy self-esteem is more likely than other students to:

- Take reasonable risks
- Have more favourable attitudes to school
- Display positive classroom behaviour
- Have reasonably accurate self-knowledge
- Highlight their strengths, successes and skills
- Downplay and accept failures, mistakes and imperfections
- Be less afraid of making mistakes
- Believe that personal limitations can be worked on
- Be willing to try, and to take initiative
- Approach new tasks with confidence
- Acknowledge their own contributions to their successes
- Compare themselves to similar people, not 'glossy images'
- Have realistic expectations of self.

Low self-esteem

Low self-esteem is a pessimistic and negative view of one's value. Low self-esteem lowers resilience, decreases success and increases isolation. A student with low self-esteem is more likely than other students to:

- Present a 'neutral' image to the rest of the world because it is safer
- Focus on the things they cannot do, rather than the things they can do
- Highlight and think too often and negatively about mistakes, failures and limitations
- Give up easily, show little confidence in areas that are new and take fewer risks
- Compare themselves only to people who are highly successful or to 'glossy images'
- Downplay their own contributions to successes
- Believe that one can be perfect, and tend to think that other people are perfect
- Copy others and be more easily influenced by peer pressure.

Young people with low self-esteem want the same things as others do. They want to be liked and included, to achieve well, to be good at sport and to be admired for their competencies and attractiveness. However, they get stuck on self-protection and spend a lot of their time trying to avoid humiliation, rejection and failure. Because they lack self-confidence they are more vulnerable. They are more likely to react badly when things don't go smoothly by withdrawing altogether or making inappropriate or even aggressive responses.

Inflated self-esteem

An inflated self-esteem is an exaggerated and unrealistic view of one's value that ultimately lowers resilience, decreases success and increases isolation. The Italians use the term 'braggadocio' or 'empty boasting' to describe this. A student with an inflated self-esteem can be arrogant and is more likely than other students to:

- Have poor self-knowledge, especially about their own limitations
- Exaggerate their own successes and skills and generalise from one set of successes to a sense of superiority
- Choose less threatening people with whom to compare themselves
- Assume their own contributions to successes are the only factor, and ignore the role of good luck and advantageous circumstances
- Go to great lengths to make others seem inferior and to make themselves look good
- Initiate bullying and meanness towards their perceived 'inferiors'.

What schools can do to develop healthy self-esteem

The basic building blocks of healthy self-esteem are positive parental and teacher reactions and expectations, positive peer responses, coping skills and successes that demonstrate mastery and competence. In the past we believed the key to enhancing young people's self-esteem was making them feel good about themselves, even if they had not demonstrated mastery or competence. Many activities in classrooms were simply 'feel good' activities such as 'I like Nick because he has nice brown eyes' or 'You are special and unique because there is no one just like you'. Such activities, although enjoyed by children, have been shown to have no significant effect on bolstering self-esteem or changing behaviour (Baumeister 1993). Martin Seligman explains:

> Armies of . . . teachers, along with . . . parents, are straining to bolster children's self-esteem. That sounds innocuous enough, but the way they do it often erodes children's sense of worth. By emphasizing how a child feels, at the expense of what the child does—mastery, persistence, overcoming frustration and boredom and meeting a challenge—parents and teachers are making this generation of children more vulnerable to depression (Seligman 1995:27).

Chapters 5 and 6 outline ways in which schools can help young people develop mastery and a strong, realistic and healthy sense of self. The classroom units on 'Success' in the Teacher's Resource Books offer ideas for developing self-knowledge, initiative and competence and affirming student strengths.

Interpersonal and intrapersonal intelligence and emotional intelligence

Interpersonal (people) intelligence as defined by Gardner (1999) is the capacity to recognise and make distinctions among others' feelings, beliefs and intentions. Young people who show strengths in interpersonal intelligence are able to empathise with the feelings of others, and can successfully negotiate with their peers, influence others' behaviour and make good friends. Intrapersonal (self) intelligence as defined by Gardner (1999) is the capacity to have a sensitivity to oneself, to understand one's strengths and weaknesses, one's fears, wishes, feelings and goals and to use that self-knowledge to effectively plan and pursue one's life.

Daniel Goleman (1998) has popularised the concept of 'Emotional intelligence'. He identifies five domains of emotional intelligence:

- Knowing one's emotions—self-awareness, naming emotions, being able to identify reasons for emotions
- Managing one's emotions—soothing oneself, calming and regaining balance, verbalising emotions appropriately
- Motivating oneself—stifling impulsiveness, delaying gratification, maintaining focus, being able to set goals and plan towards them
- Recognising emotions in others—using empathy, being attuned to non verbal aspects, being able to understand another's point of view, being sensitive to other's feelings
- Handling relationships—interpersonal effectiveness, social competence, appropriate assertiveness, using effective group decision-making strategies.

Daniel Goleman's (1998) concept of emotional intelligence is a combination of interpersonal and intrapersonal intelligence (Gardner 1999), but Goleman goes past describing and actually prescribes certain ways of behaving as being 'better'. Gardner does not make these judgments.

All classroom units in the BOUNCE BACK! Teacher's Resource Books incorporate a strong emphasis on teaching skills related to both people intelligence and self-intelligence. There is a particular emphasis on people skills in the 'Relationships' units and on emotional intelligence in the 'Emotions' and the 'Success' units.

Teaching the BOUNCE BACK! acronym

This section firstly provides some guidelines for teaching the acronym. Then each coping statement of the BOUNCE BACK! acronym is introduced and the key principles that underpin each statement is explained. The BOUNCE BACK! and BOUNCE! posters are presented on BLMs 4.1 and 4.2.

Guidelines for teaching the acronym

The major focus of the BOUNCE BACK! Resiliency Program is on helping students to understand the coping statements so they are able to apply and use them when they experience difficult times. But if students do not easily remember the skills, then they can't use them effectively. The BOUNCE! and BOUNCE BACK! statements should be rehearsed and learned to full mastery in order for the coping statements to be retained over time.

- Repeating and revisiting the acronym over many years helps students to learn to master and easily remember the coping statements, especially at the time of a problem or difficulty.
- Involving parents in the program provides opportunities for the acronym to be reinforced and discussed at home as well as at school. See Chapter 7 for ideas for involving parents in BOUNCE BACK!
- Three levels of delivery are outlined below. More class time can be spent on levels 1 and 2 and less time at level 3.
  —Level 1: Students focus on the statements and what they objectively mean.
  —Level 2: Students focus on the ideas and concepts as applied to others such as family, friends, puppet or cartoon characters, characters in the news, books and films etc. This allows the concepts to be 'one step removed'.
  —Level 3: Students self-disclose and focus on the ideas and concepts as applied to themselves.
- Psychological safety should operate during all discussions and activities (see page 55 of this chapter).
- Encourage students to refer to the coping statements in the acronym when they are trying to support their friends and classmates.
- Making reference to BOUNCE BACK! coping statements when there is a playground or classroom problem or situation is another way of reinforcing the key coping concepts.
- Wherever possible, link the program to other areas of the curriculum, for example Social Studies and the Environment, Science and Technology, English, Health and Personal Development, Protective Behaviours and Religious Education.

More details about the statements in BOUNCE! and BOUNCE BACK!

These are the key principles that underpin each BOUNCE BACK! statement and which will assist with class discussion:

Bad times don't last. Things always get better.

- Bad times and bad or negative feelings are always temporary. Things in your life will get better so don't give up. It is important to stay optimistic and hopeful.
- Sometimes it takes a while for a difficult situation to improve, but it does always improve.
- When things are really bad, just try to get through one day at a time.

Other people can help if you talk to them. Get a reality check.

- Nothing is so awful that you can't talk about it to someone you trust. Things will be easier if you share your worries but it takes courage to do so.
- Everyone needs someone to talk to now and then. Research has shown that talking to someone about what is troubling you is a sign of strength, not weakness.
- Talking about what is worrying you to someone you trust means they can give you support. If you don't talk to them they won't know that you need help with problem solving.
- Talking to other people allows you to 'cross-check' your ideas and perceptions with them. In this way you can see if they see the situation in the same way as you.
- If you talk to someone you trust you can get a 'reality check' because they will tell you if they think you are not being realistic. Maybe you are getting the facts wrong or you don't have all the facts you need. Maybe you are seeing things in a distorted way.

Unhelpful thinking makes you feel more upset.

- Our thoughts strongly influence our feelings and actions. Changing how we think helps us to manage how we feel.
- Unhelpful thinking involves thinking things like:
  —'Everybody must like me' (there is no one who is liked by everybody)
  —'I must never make a mistake' (everyone needs to make mistakes to learn things)
  —'I must never lose' (everyone has to lose sometimes)
  —'Bad things always happens to me' (they don't, but you are collecting evidence to make the argument and missing the evidence which says otherwise).
- Don't mistake your feelings for facts. Just because you *feel* self-conscious doesn't mean people are looking at you. Sometimes you need to do a 'reality check'.
- Use low-key words for your feelings and they will stay more easily under control. For example, say to yourself: 'I am annoyed' rather than 'I am furious', or 'It is unpleasant and I don't like it' rather than 'It is a disaster and I can't stand it'.

Nobody is perfect—not you and not others.

- There is no such thing as a perfect person. We all have flaws. Perfection is not an option but improvement and striving for high standards are options.
- You're not perfect so don't be too hard on yourself when something doesn't turn out as well as you had hoped. Judge yourself by effort and be kind.
- Others (including parents, teachers, brothers, sisters and friends) are not perfect so don't have unreasonable expectations of them.
- Mistakes are part of learning. We all have to make mistakes to get better at things.

Concentrate on the positives (no matter how small) and use laughter.

- Finding something positive in a difficult situation, no matter how small, helps you to hang on and feel a bit more hopeful.
- Finding something funny in a difficult situation, even if it is only a small thing, will make you feel better able to cope. Laugher helps to relieve stress and worry.

Everybody experiences sadness, hurt, failure, rejection and setbacks sometimes, not just you. They are a normal part of life. Try not to personalise them.

- Bad things happen to everyone, even though you may think they happen only to you.
- Courage is needed when you feel sad or disappointed or when you fail at something.
- Personalising is thinking that when something bad happens it only happens to you. People who say 'I'm a jinx' or 'Bad things always happen to me' are personalising.
- Normalising is more helpful and realistic. This means accepting that bad things such as rejection or failure or frustrations happen to everyone now and again, not just you. Sometimes they seem to happen all at once! It's normal!

Blame fairly. How much of what happened was due to you, to others and to bad luck or circumstances?

- Don't just blame yourself when bad things happen—consider how much of what happened was due to your own behaviour, how much was due to what other people did and how much was due to bad luck or circumstances (such as being in the wrong place at the wrong time or random events).
- When something bad happens, always try to do a pie chart of:
  —How much me?
  —How much others?
  —How much luck and circumstances?

Accept what can't be changed (but try to change what you can change first).

- You can try to change the things that you have some control over. For example, if you are worried about schoolwork there are lots of things you can do to improve your skills, such as asking parents

or your teacher for help, making a plan and practising the skills. If you have had a fight with a friend you can try to talk with them about what is troubling you.
- Some things you are worrying about may be other people's worries, like Mum and Dad's worries, not your worries. It is not helpful to worry about things that you have no control over or cannot change.
- Accepting what you can't change also means accepting other people for what they are even if they don't measure up to what you would like. This does not mean you always like what they do, but you accept that they are who they are. You can't change them, but if you accept them they might be more able to change themselves.

Catastrophising exaggerates your worries. Don't believe the worst possible picture.

- Catastrophising means thinking about the worst possible thing that could happen and believing that it will happen. For example:
  —If I don't do well in this test the whole year will be ruined
  —If I go skiing I'll probably break a leg and make a fool of myself.
- Catastrophising makes you feel worried and miserable. You probably won't feel like doing anything because you expect the worst.

Keep things in perspective. It's only part of your life.

- If you don't keep things in perspective you get upset over very little things and make a mountain out of a molehill. You forget about the good bits and see only the bad bits.
- When something happens, some ways to help you to keep things in perspective are to ask yourself:
  —Does this really matter? Am I getting upset over very little?
  —On a scale from 1 to 10, how important is this to me really?
  —How much of my life has this really affected?
  —How many parts of my life are still exactly the same and still as good as they were?
  —Is it really the end of the world?

How the BOUNCE BACK acronym addresses specific emotional and behavioural patterns

Each of the BOUNCE BACK coping statements incorporates thinking/self talk which is an antidote to the development of specific dysfunctional emotional and behavioural patterns such as anxiety, depression, impulsiveness and aggression. The following table illustrates these links.

B	Depression
O	Anxiety, depression and impulsiveness
U	Anxiety, depression, angry aggression and impulsiveness
N	Anxiety, depression and angry aggression
C	Anxiety and depression
E	Anxiety, depression and angry aggression
B	Depression and angry aggression
A	Anxiety, depression and angry aggression
C	Anxiety
K	Depression and angry aggression

Creating psychological safety when using the BOUNCE BACK! Resiliency Program

It's essential to create a classroom climate of psychological safety so students feel that their self-disclosures and any differences in opinions, feelings, ideas or behaviour will be respected by their classmates and not used against them. It is also important to help students learn about the kinds of personal information about themselves and about others that are appropriate to share in class discussions. This climate of trust can only be built up over time and can easily be destroyed by insensitive comments or 'put-downs'. The program does not strongly focus on students sharing deeply personal information about themselves or people they know. The material is delivered at two levels of personal disclosure.

At the first level, students talk about their own ideas and opinions, give examples of concepts and processes and talk about the concepts and ideas as applied to puppet characters, cartoon characters, book characters, people in the news and so on. For example:

- Can you think of an example of the kind of situation in which someone (or someone your age) might feel worried?
- Why was Henry so sad?
- What do you think courage is?
- What are some good ways for the puppet to respond here?

At the second level, students talk about the ideas and concepts as applied to themselves and, perhaps, other people they know such as family or friends. For example:

- Can you think of a time when someone you know achieved a goal they set for themselves? What did they do to achieve it?
- What kind of situations do you find most scary?

Guidelines for creating psychological safety

Here is a summary of the key points for creating a classroom environment that encourages your students to feel psychologically safe and connected to their teacher and their classmates. The rules to follow in classroom discussions are provided in BLM 4.3, to be used as a class handout.

- Paraphrase and clarify what students say when they make unclear comments.
- Avoid giving tasks which require students to expose too much of their personal lives or feelings.
- Remember that some students find it difficult to self-disclose, even at a relatively superficial level. Don't put pressure on them.
- Remember that some students feel anxious about finding a space in the discussion, so you need to find a way to 'let them in'.
- Use 'protective interrupting' when needed, because some students may be tempted to disclose too much about themselves, their family or people they (and their classmates) know.
- Remember to always debrief students after any form of drama or role-play.
- Ask all students to respect each other's confidentiality but let them know that you cannot guarantee that everyone will do this.
- Keep in mind that boys are less practised at self-disclosure than girls.
- Have a strongly enforced 'No put-downs' rule in place at all times.
- Teach the discussion skills of 'listening well' and 'respectful disagreeing' before students start their discussion. (See the 'Relationships' units and the 'Core Values' units in the Middle Primary and Upper Primary/Junior Secondary books.)
- Be aware of cultural differences beforehand and show sensitivity to them.

Paraphrase and clarify what students say when they make unclear comments

Often students say or ask things that are not clear to other students or even perhaps to themselves. Initially, the language of feelings and relationships is not an easy one for many students. If this happens, re-state what they have said in a simpler or clearer way and check it with them. For example:

Harry: Mates give it to you straight.
Teacher: So, Harry, you're saying that you think whenever you talk to mates about a problem you have, you end up getting a more honest picture. Is that right?

Avoid giving tasks that require students to expose too much of their personal lives or feelings

A useful yardstick is to remember not to ask students to do or discuss anything you would not be comfortable doing or discussing yourself. You perhaps need to consider whether you are 'typical' before using yourself as the benchmark in this way. Do you think you are more disclosing or shyer than the norm?

Understand that some students find it difficult to self-disclose, even at a relatively superficial level

The fact that a student finds it difficult to talk personally, even at a relatively superficial level, does not mean they are not interested in the topic, nor that they are upset about it. They are usually still learning a lot even if they are not speaking a lot. Some students are just shyer than others, or they become more anxious when they are the centre of attention. Others fear peer disapproval. Here are some ideas to facilitate the inclusion of all students in the discussion.

- Remind students that having a different opinion is everyone's right. Even if they don't agree with what someone has said, they need to respect that person's right to differ.
- Give students the right to 'pass' on any question, but encourage them to try to contribute to the discussion where they can, and not to take the 'pass' option too often.
- Use strategies that have an anonymous component, for example Postbox and Predictor Cards (see Chapter 10).
- Use puppets, which allow issues and feelings to be presented and discussed 'one step removed'.
- Gently try to include reluctant speakers in the discussion but don't put them on the spot. For example, ask a few students (by using their names) if there is anything else they would like to add. Include in this group some of those students who have already spoken and those who haven't. This way you don't focus directly on the student who hasn't contributed.
- Structure some small group or partner discussion tasks rather than always running whole-class discussions. Some students feel more uncomfortable being the centre of attention in a whole-class discussion and feel threatened by loose or open-ended discussions in a small group. Encourage the group to 'own' everything that is said within the group and report back about what '*We* talked about' rather than focusing on individual opinions or stories. It can be distressing for a student to hear a group member say, while reporting to the class, 'Josh told us about . . .' This obviously depends a lot on the nature of the discussion. Also encourage everyone to sign any group product to enhance team interdependence and ownership.
- Provide students with less threatening alternatives when offering them opportunities to self-disclose. For example, in Throw the Dice (see Chapter 10) give two options, such as: 'tell about a time when you finished a friendship and say why it happened', or 'comment about why you think friendships end'.
- Invite students to describe a situation or likely emotions from the perspective of someone else or a character in a story or video. The gap between describing the emotions felt by someone else and self-disclosing is not large and they will probably feel more comfortable expressing their own emotions with more practice. For example, you can say:
  —Does anyone have any suggestions to offer us about how a new student of your age might feel about being different in this way?
  —What sort of feelings would Chad be likely to have at this point in the story? Why might he feel that way?
- Remind students that they can choose to self-disclose at a relatively superficial level by giving less detail, simplifying a story or leaving out specific information and so on. It is not dishonest to do so under these circumstances.

Remember that some students feel anxious about finding a space in the discussion, so you need to find a way to 'let them in'

Some students feel anxious about finding a space in the discussion where they won't have to compete for their turn to talk and perhaps find themselves interrupted or 'over-talked'. When there is a 'lull' in the discussion, ask a general question such as 'does anybody else have something to add to what has already been said?' Then scan the room, making specific but brief eye contact with those students whom you perceive as having not said much so far but not pressuring them. You can also consider using strategies which have a built-in structure to ensure that interrupting and overtalking doesn't occur, for example Throw the Dice, using a talking prompt (see Chapter 10).

Understand that some students may be tempted to disclose too much

Occasionally, some students are energised by the opportunity to talk about a personal issue and they blurt out more than they should. At the time they may not think through the consequences of revealing too much about themselves, classmates, friends or family. Afterwards they feel uncomfortable. This doesn't happen very often, but it might. Here are some suggestions to minimise this possibility.

- Have a 'no names' rule in place most of the time. Remind students at the start of a discussion to be thoughtfully cautious about giving identifying details about the people they mention. Instead they could say something like:
  —I know/knew someone who . . .
  —I know of a situation where . . .
  —A relative I know . . .
- Before starting a class discussion, remind your students that you will use 'protective interrupting' if you think they are saying something that is either too personal, only indirectly related to the topic or too complicated to be discussed in a whole-class discussion. Before the discussion say something like:
  —Remember that we have talked before about how sometimes what some of us might talk about would be better discussed at a later point with me, rather than pursued in a whole-class discussion. It may be that I feel that what you mention is a little too personal for our whole-class discussion, or it may not be directly related to what we are discussing. I will say something like 'Excuse me for interrupting you, but perhaps we could talk about this later when we can look at it in more detail rather than in this more general discussion'.

  Stress that you do not want anyone to feel that you have interrupted because you are not interested in what they are saying. Make a note about it and be sure to follow up at a later point.

Always debrief students after any form of drama or role-play

Students can easily confuse how someone pretends to be in a role-play with how they really are. Using puppet drama can minimise this effect somewhat. You could also say something like:

'Welcome back to Year 6 Sue and Simon (their real names) and goodbye Jenny and Con (their role-play names). Now, although we all know that this was just drama, sometimes our brains can confuse the actor with the role. Let's remember that Sue and Simon are not like Jenny and Con, they were just acting like them. Simon, how did you feel about playing the role of Con? How are you different from Con? Sue, how did you feel about playing the role of Jenny? How are you different from Jenny?'

Ask all students to respect each other's confidentiality

Students need some expectation of confidentiality in discussions. You might consider asking all students to agree to sign a confidentiality contract. You could also say something like:

'Remember that anything that is said in this room should stay in this room.'

But you also need to point out to students that while you hope and expect that everyone will honour that rule, you cannot *guarantee* them confidentiality. Ask them to think about what might happen with any personal information they disclose and not to discuss anything about themselves or their family and friends they would not like others to talk about in out-of-class time.

Keep in mind that boys are less practised at self-disclosure than girls

Asking boys to talk about their feelings about specific issues runs the risk of making them feel vulnerable and contradicts their socialisation about being tough and not showing their feelings. So it's reasonable to expect that boys will sometimes feel uncomfortable with talking or writing about their feelings or openly declaring their fears, doubts, insecurities or affection to their classmates. They will often show that discomfort by 'being silly', misbehaving or cracking jokes. But don't make the mistake of thinking that they are not taking in what is being discussed, even if they appear to be dismissive and unengaged.

It is reassuring to note that boys, although usually having more reservations about the process, often report greater satisfaction than girls with being given the opportunity to discuss issues to do with feelings and relationships etc. This is probably because they have just the same concerns about these issues and the need for the relevant skills, but fewer opportunities to discuss or develop them in their peer life. You could say something like:

> 'We might talk about some slightly personal issues here, so please respect the importance of what we're talking about.'

It can also be helpful for boys if you make strong links between their ability to express emotions, to gain personal and social understandings and skills and to develop resilience and their success in other areas, such as:

- Sport. Sport is one occasion where boys and men feel free to express their emotions. Capturing on video the emotions of players and spectators at an important sporting event can provide rich opportunities for boys to empathise with the winners and the losers and to encourage them to write and speak with feeling. Sport can also be the focus when discussing teamwork, coping with loss and so on.
- Careers, the workplace and income. The qualities of successful leaders and coaches include self-knowledge, goal-setting, connecting with others through empathising with employees, good communication and interpersonal skills and the ability to develop a great team.
- A successful workplace. Life at all levels also involves working cooperatively with others, handling conflict and dealing with setbacks and failures.
- Romantic relationships. Successful romantic relationships require self-knowledge, optimism, confidence and social skills. The break-up of romantic relationships requires resilience.
- Future parenting. Fathers are now expected to be comfortable in expressing warmth and affection towards their children and to model resilience for their own children.

Have a strongly enforced 'No put-downs' rule in place at all times

Remind students about the rule before any discussion. Remember to enforce it in a non-humiliating way. Don't forget to include nonverbal put-downs in this category. This rule also relates to the core value of accepting differences in people (see the 'Core values' classroom units in the Teacher's Resource Books) and not negatively judging others because they hold different values, ideas etc. There are more details on strategies for reducing put-downs in the Bullying Units.

Teach the skills of 'listening well' and 'respectful disagreeing' before students start their discussion

These skills need to be taught beforehand and then students need to be reminded to use them before each discussion-based activity or debrief. Here are some strategies to use:

- There are many activities in this book which give students the chance to learn and practise the skill of listening, for example Think–Pair–Share, Partner Retell and Throw the Dice (for all these activities, see Chapter 10). There are also listening activities in all 'Relationships' units in the Teacher's Resource Books.
- Use a talking prompt which is held by the person talking and is a signal for others not to interrupt (see Chapter 10 for more detail).
- The skill of 'respectful disagreeing' involves encouraging students to first restate what the other person said that they agree with before they then state their different opinion. For example, 'I can see what Emma means about parachuting being dangerous (*this is the bit I heard her say and which I can agree with*) because the parachute might fail, but I don't think it would be as dangerous as bungey jumping (*this is where I differ*)'.

Be aware of and show sensitivity to cultural differences

Western psychological therapeutic and counselling principles as well as Western educational principles and practices underpin the BOUNCE BACK! program. Many of these principles are in accord with Eastern philosophies, such as some Buddhist principles (see *The Art of Happiness: A Handbook for Living* by the Dalai Lama and Western psychologist Howard Cutler). However, our society is so diverse in its ethnic and cultural make-up that sensitivity in choosing appropriate activities and adapting concepts may be needed for the students in some classes, in order to take account of their cultural differences in regard to language, values, background and experiences.

Indicators for referring a student for professional help

Teachers are the 'first aid workers' in mental health and often feel concerned about the emotional or social wellbeing of an individual student but feel out of their depth in helping them. Under those circumstances it is best to refer them for professional help. Here are some indicators.

- A student has no one in their life they feel they can easily access and talk to (e.g. as reported on the PEPS and/or PRASE, see Chapter 9) and then they lose a significant relationship.
- There is a pattern of ongoing depressed mood, even in very young children.
- There is a pattern of ongoing social and emotional withdrawal, especially if the student had previously been more socially outgoing.
- The student has been bullied or socially rejected over a long period of time.
- The student appears to have a very limited understanding of social interaction and has problems forming close warm bonds with other students. This may be an indicator of Asperger's Syndrome.
- The student has a history of difficulties with angry outbursts or marked problems with controlling impulses.
- Many absences from school with 'indefinite' reasons (e.g. tiredness, felt unwell). These are often indicators of anxiety and/or depression.
- Frequent visits to sick bay, sometimes (but not always) in a dramatic way or in an agitated emotional state. This can be an early indicator of an anxiety predisposition and may lead on to obsessive compulsive disorder (OCD) and/or depression.
- Talking about suicide. There is no discernible pattern as to who will attempt suicide. Some who talk about it don't do it, and others who talk about it will do it. It should always be taken seriously.
- Marked change in a previous pattern without reason (e.g. no longer submitting homework, not going out with friends any more, discontinuing sporting involvement).
- A previous suicide attempt followed by a markedly buoyant mood within a month or two. The strongest predictor of a suicide attempt is a previous suicide attempt, even if there seems to have been a full recovery.

REFERENCES

Arnold, L., 1991, *Childhood Stress*. Wiley, New York.

Arnott, L. & Inserra, R., 2000, *Sick Humour: A Diary from the Adolescent Unit of the Royal Children's Hospital*. Adolescent Unit, Royal Children's Hospital, Melbourne.

Baumeister, R., 1993, *Self-esteem: The Puzzle of Low Self-regard*. Plenum, New York.

Berk, L., 1994, 'Interview with JR Dunn'. *Humor & Health Letter*, 3(6), 1–8.

Berk, L., 1989(a), 'Neuroendocrine and stress hormone changes during mirthful laughter'. *American Journal of Medical Sciences*, 298, 390–96.

Berk, L., 1989(b), 'Eustress of mirthful laughter modifies natural killer cell activity'. *Clinical Research*, 37(ll5).

Burns, D., 1980, *Feeling Good: The New Mood Therapy*. Avon Books, New York.

Canfield, J. & Wells, H.C., 1976, *100 Ways to Enhance Self-concept in the Classroom: A Handbook for Teachers and Parents.* Prentice Hall, New Jersey.

Clark, D. & Beck, A., 1999, *Scientific Foundations of Cognitive Theory of Depression*, John Wiley, New York.

Ellis, A. et al., 1997, *Stress Counselling: A Rational Emotive Behaviour Approach.* Cassell, London.

Ellis, A. & Dryden, W., 1987, *The Practice of Rational Emotive Therapy*, Springer, New York.

Ellis, A. & Harper, R.A., 1976, *A New Guide to Rational Living.* Wiltshire Book Co, California.

Ellis, A., 1988, *How to Stubbornly Refuse to Make Yourself Miserable about Anything Yes, Anything!.* Pan Macmillan, Sydney.

Gardner, H., 1999, *Intelligence Reframed. Multiple Intelligences in the Twenty-First Century.* Basic Books, New York.

Gilham, J.E., Reivich, K.J., Jaycox, I.H. & Seligman, M.E.P., 1995, 'Preventing depressive symptoms in schoolchildren: Two year follow-up'. *Psychological Science*, 6(6), 343–51.

Goleman, D., 1998, *Emotional Intelligence*, Bantam, New York.

Graham, S. & Weiner, B., 1996, 'Theories and principles of motivation'. In D. Berliner & R. Calfee (eds), *Handbook of Educational Psychology*, Macmillan, New York, 63–84.

Jaycox, L.H., Reivich, K.J., Gilham, J. & Seligman, M.E.P., 1994, 'Preventing depressive symptoms in school children'. *Behaviour Research and Therapy*, 32(8), 801–16.

Lefcourt, H. & Martin, R., 1986, *Humor and Life Stress.* Springer-Verlag, New York.

Lefcourt, H.M., 2001, *Humor: The Psychology of Living Buoyantly.* Plenum Publishers, New York.

Martin, R.A. & Dobbin, J.P., 1985, 'Sense of humor, hassles, and immunoglobulin: Evidence for the stress-moderating effect of humor'. *International Journal of Psychiatry in Medicine*, 18(2), 93–105.

Marsh, M.D., 2000, 'Hope and its relationship to self-esteem and spiritual wellbeing in Australian university students'. Unpublished Doctor of Ministry Thesis, Boston University.

McClelland, D.C., 1985, *Human Motivation*, Scott Foresman, Illinois.

Moltmann, J., 1967, *Theology of Hope.* SCM Press, London.

Peterson, C., 2000, 'The future of optimism'. *American Psychologist*, 55(1), 44–55.

Robinson, V., 1991, *Humor and the Health Professions* (2nd edn). CB Slack, New Jersey.

Rockhill, C.M. & Asher, S., 1992, *Peer Assessment of the Behavioural Characteristics of Poorly Accepted Boys and Girls.* Paper presented at the Annual meeting of the American Educational Research Association, San Francisco.

Seligman, M.E.P., 1995, *The Optimistic Child.* Random House, Sydney.

Seligman, M.E.P., 1992, *Learned Optimism.* Random House, Sydney.

Shaeffer, M. & Hopkins, D., 1988, 'Miss Nelson, Knock Knocks and Nonsense: Connecting through humour'. *Childhood Education*, Winter, 88–93.

Sletta, O., Sobstad, F. & Valas, H., 1995, 'Humour, peer acceptance and perceived social competence in preschool and school aged children'. *British Journal of Educational Psychology*, 65, 175–79.

Snyder, C.R., 1999, *Coping: The Psychology of What Works.* Oxford University Press, New York.

Tanner, S. and Ball, J., 1991, *Beating the Blues.* Doubleday, Sydney.

Troop, W.P. & Asher, S., 1998, *Does Everyone Love a Clown? Peer and Teacher Perceptions of Class Clowns.* Paper presented at the Annual meeting of the American Educational Research Association, San Diego.

Wooten, P., 1992, 'Does a humor workshop affect nurse burnout?' *Journal of Nursing Jocularity*, 2(2), 42–43.

Wooten, P., 1996, 'Humor: An antidote for stress'. *Holistic Nursing Practice*, 10(2), 49–55.

CHAPTER 5

THE ROLE OF TEACHERS IN BUILDING RESILIENCE

The environmental building blocks of resilience

There is no single combination of protective factors and processes that can be identified as better than other combinations—resilient students will draw on what is available. The principle that operates here is: 'the more the better.' The more protective factors and skills that students can draw on, the more likely they are to display resilient behaviour. For some students one or two protective factors may be particularly significant, especially if they endure over time, for example a specific set of personal skills or the presence of a significant and caring other person outside the family. With this is mind the BOUNCE BACK! Resiliency Program takes a comprehensive, multifaceted approach that incorporates both an environmental component and a personal skills component to prevention and intervention.

The important role of schools and teachers in building resilience in young people

Next to families, schools are the most likely place where students can experience the environmental conditions and learn the personal coping skills that foster resiliency. For students who are alienated from their families, school takes on even greater importance as a place that offers the conditions and opportunities in which to develop resilience. School, above all other social institutions, provides unique opportunities for students to connect on a daily basis with their peers and caring teachers. A great number of studies over the last decade have confirmed that students' connectedness to school is the most significant factor in determining whether or not they complete Year 12. For a high proportion of young Australian adolescents, being connected to their peers and having a sense of belonging to a friendship group is, at certain times, more relevant to their lives than feeling connected to their family (Fuller, McGraw & Goodyear 1998). Adolescent girls in particular are far more likely to seek peer support than family support when they are experiencing difficulties (Fischmann & Cotterell 2000). For young people who don't feel connected to their family, their school can play a critical role in fostering their resilience.

The chart in Chapter 2 lists the eight most important environmental resources or processes that contribute to student resilience. These are school connectedness, peer connectedness, teacher connectedness, positive family–school links, having access to one caring adult outside the family, family connectedness, community connectedness and spiritual involvement. Not only are schools important resources in themselves, but they can also play a significant role in linking many of these other environmental resources.

Building resilient schools and classrooms

There are many factors in the lives of students that are beyond the school's control or influence and that puts some limits on what can be achieved by teachers. However, teachers still have a crucial role to play in fostering student resilience. Creating positive, safe and effective classrooms is a complex and challenging task but the outcome in terms of student resilience is worth the time and energy. School matters a great deal to students, and the benefits from satisfying school experiences can be surprisingly long lasting. One of the key writers on resilience, Michael Rutter, has explained it thus:

> It is not high school achievement as such that seems to make a difference, rather, it is positive experiences of a kind that are pleasurable and rewarding and which help children develop a sense of their own worth together with the confidence that they can cope with life's challenges and can control what happens to them. (Rutter 1991:8)

There are many strategies and approaches which schools and teachers can adopt to create more resilient schools and classrooms, where students feel valued, are engaged, achieve academic success, feel a sense of belonging and can learn personal and social skills. In summary, these strategies are:

- Teachers staying optimistic and believing in their own ability to make a difference to the lives of their students
- Teachers reflecting on and enhancing their own levels of resilience
- Teachers connecting with students in a personal way
- Limiting the number of teachers that students have contact with
- Going the extra mile for the less resilient students
- Experimenting with changes in curriculum and teaching strategies to maximise student engagement
- Developing student competence through high expectations, academic support and a differentiated curriculum
- Providing opportunities for students to practise the skills of initiative and goal setting
- Connecting students with each other and building relationships
- Using cooperative learning
- Teaching social skills
- Establishing peer support structures
- Using 'circle time'
- Holding classroom meetings
- Setting up class and school committees
- Setting and enforcing clear, consistent boundaries
- Creating a physically and psychologically safe environment.

Teachers staying optimistic and believing in their own ability to make a difference to the lives of their students

The power of teachers to make a positive difference to the lives of their students cannot be overstated. Teachers' optimism about their ability to make a difference in their students' lives in their own classrooms correlates with higher student performance and greater academic success (Woolfolk 2001). Teachers may not feel empowered to make a difference at the system level of whole school change, but working with their students in their own classrooms is working in their circle of influence. Reflecting on the kinds of teaching practices that foster student resilience in classrooms means not only reviewing 'what' is taught but also 'how' it is taught. Teachers' reflection on their practice is one of the critical elements in their professional growth.

Teachers reflecting on their own level of resilience

A teacher's professional resilience determines how well he or she copes with the increasingly complex demands of the job. High levels of personal resilience are essential to a teacher's capacity to take on

> Treat people as if they were what they ought to be and you help them become what they are capable of being. (Goethe)
>
> Change—real change—comes from the inside out . . . It comes from striking at the root—the fabric of our thoughts, the fundamental essential paradigms, which give direction to our character and create the lens through which we see the world. (Covey 1989:317)

board new initiatives, such as resilience interventions and programs for students. This does not mean that resilient teachers feel any less vulnerable than others to the anxieties related to change and challenges. It does mean, however, that when faced with new initiatives, such teachers are more able to:

- Maintain a high level of productivity and quality in their teaching as they manage change
- Remain emotionally and physically healthy during periods of uncertainty
- Rebound from any difficulties arising from change and challenge to be even stronger than before
- Be flexible about how to proceed when blocked
- Become more organised to avoid being overwhelmed with information
- Be proactive in engaging in any new initiatives rather than running away from them.

Teachers who can reflect on their own styles of coping and make improvements are more likely to handle stress effectively.

Teachers connecting with students in a personal way

Students respond best to teachers whose classrooms are filled with warm and positive emotions, who are approachable and 'real', and who do not give up on them. Many different research studies (e.g. Ruddick 1997; Fullan et al. 1998; Dornbusch 1999; Trent 2001) are remarkably consistent in the picture they present of the teachers and teaching styles that students respond to most positively. These teachers are also the ones who are most likely to increase students' commitment to learning and their connections to school, and be responsible for better student outcomes. These teachers:

- Are relaxed, enjoy their day and are able to laugh, especially at their own mistakes
- Use fun and humour as part of their teaching
- Are fair and consistent in their discipline procedures
- Listen to what their students have to say
- Treat each student with respect and as an individual, remembering names and background details and taking time to greet them, not just making contact when there is a problem
- Share parts of themselves with students, to facilitate building relationships with students
- Have high but realistic expectations of all students
- Don't shout/yell or 'go on about things'
- Don't give up on their students, nor tell them they're no good and should leave school
- Explain the work, make the work interesting, find interesting things to do and don't make their students feel small when they don't understand
- Are enthusiastic about what they teach
- Make their curriculum relevant to their students' lives by firstly finding out what happens in the lives of their students
- Have an enthusiastic and experimental approach to trying out new teaching strategies while keeping learning outcomes in mind
- Are easy to talk to and students feel they can go to them when they are in trouble
- Assist each student to become independent
- Encourage high levels of parental involvement with school but don't over-focus on family factors as explanations.

All these characteristics reflect the value that students place on their teachers' support and interpersonal commitment to them. Yet Australian research demonstrates that most students, especially boys, are reluctant to discuss their problems with their teachers. They are more likely to perceive their teachers as sources of discipline rather than sources of support (Fischmann & Cotterell 2000), especially in secondary settings. In a recent study that involved interviews with 1800 Australian boys from Years 7 to 12, the boys felt that less than 10% of their teachers could be described as 'good' teachers (Trent 2001). Nonetheless most of the boys expressed a desire to achieve at school and they believed that a 'good' teacher could make this possible.

Limiting the number of teachers that students have contact with

The more teachers a student has, the more difficult it is for any one teacher to form a close relationship with that student. The move to middle schooling, with a focus on fewer teachers and more inter-subject collaboration and integration, is one significant trend at the secondary level to address this challenge.

Going the extra mile for the less resilient students

There are three basic principles that teachers can follow in their work with those young people who appear to be less resilient. These are:

- Be persistent and communicate to the student that there is someone who is not going to give up on them or allow them to be distracted from the importance of school and their own wellbeing.
- Provide continuity by making sure there is someone who knows the students' needs and is available across time.
- Ensure that there is consistency in the most important messages from all concerned adults in the student's life—do the work, attend classes, be on time, express frustration in a constructive manner, stay in school, consider the rights of others, talk to someone if you're upset.

Other adults can also take on this role of 'going the extra mile', but teachers and schools are well placed to provide these three elements of persistence, continuity and consistency (Christenson & Carroll 1999).

Experimenting with changes in curriculum and teaching strategies to maximise student engagement

There is a considerable body of evidence that students at all levels, but especially in the middle school years, are now less engaged by their classroom learning experiences than in previous times (Cumming 1996; Hill 1997; Trent 2001). Making the curriculum relevant to the lives of students today and actively engaging them in learning through a wide range of teaching strategies ensures better student outcomes and more school-connectedness.

Developing competence through high expectations, academic support and a differentiated curriculum

Educational research over many years has confirmed the powerful effect of teachers' expectations on student achievement and student resilience. Students whose teachers have positive expectations for them demonstrate higher rates of academic success (Rutter 1979), higher self-efficacy, more optimism (Bandura 1997) and

> Start with what they know; build with what they have. (Lao Tau 100 BC)

lower rates of problematic behaviours (Rutter 1979). Having high but achievable expectations for students also lowers their alcohol and drug abuse (Brook, Nomura & Cohen 1989). Many students who are 'at risk' and low on resilience are students who are not performing well academically. Providing academic support and communicating an expectation that they can be successful is critical to helping these students succeed at school.

Classrooms that communicate high expectations are also characterised by curriculum that is differentiated so that all students can be appropriately intellectually challenged and developed. The provision of a differentiated curriculum instead of the 'one size fits all' curriculum means that students can access multiple entry points into the curriculum and use different ways to demonstrate what they know and understand. Differentiating the curriculum is an organised yet flexible way of proactively adjusting teaching and learning to meet students where they are and to help them to achieve maximum growth as learners (Tomlinson 1999).

A relevant and differentiated curriculum can be based around:

- Real-life topics that reflect the interests and lives of students
- A wide range of teaching strategies to actively engage different students in learning
- Using the revised Bloom's taxonomy to plan activities from simple to complex (Anderson & Krathwohl 2000)
- Using Howard Gardner's model of multiple intelligences to plan a greater range of teaching and learning strategies and more choice than a traditional curriculum (Gardner 1999; McGrath & Noble 1995a, 1995b, 1998; Noble 1999).

All students can benefit from a diversified curriculum but such a curriculum is particularly advantageous for students with learning difficulties and those students who are disengaged and more at risk of dropping out. As Gardner says:

> When a student isn't learning something, you don't make the assumption that the student is stupid—you make the assumption that you haven't found the right key. The more resources you have for finding the right key, the more likely you are to succeed (Gardner, in Noble & Grant 1997:25).

Recognising students' strengths is a starting point in adapting teaching strategies to accommodate and develop those strengths. This can most readily be achieved by using the multiple intelligences model as a curriculum planning tool. Research shows that teachers (and classmates) often develop more positive expectations of students' learning abilities once less-academic students are able to demonstrate their understanding in their area of intellectual strength(s), using MI model (Gardner 1999; Noble 1999). Gardner perceives that MI is

> . . . a hopeful and optimistic theory . . . one that says one can build on strengths and there are many ways to achieve self-esteem and to accomplish something meaningful in school and in the world beyond (Gardner 1994:580).

Students are more likely to be actively engaged in learning not only when working in their area of relative strength, but also when working at a task that is moderately challenging—not too hard and not too easy for a specific student. Under these conditions they are more likely to experience 'flow'. Flow has been defined as a state of intense, focused concentration or absorption in an activity (Czikszentmihalyi 1990). When students experience flow they feel competent, in control and alert. Engaging in activities that trigger 'flow' can also help students when things are difficult and when constructive 'detachment' is helpful.

Sometimes giving students choice in what task they do or how they demonstrate what they know and understand encourages them to set their own challenges and therefore be more likely to experience 'flow'. Observing student engagement in different learning activities helps you understand the student's relative strengths and weaknesses across the different types of intelligence. Encouraging students to reflect on their own level of engagement in the different activities helps them to gain a better sense of themselves as learners. Bloom's model, now revised by a panel of international experts in the area of cognition and learning (Anderson & Krathwohl 2000), is a useful tool for matching levels of difficulty with student competence (McGrath & Noble 1993, 1995a). The *Seven Ways at Once* book series (McGrath & Noble 1995(a), 1995(b), 1998) integrates Bloom's taxonomy with multiple intelligences to provide a tool for curriculum planning to cater for all students in the mixed ability classroom.

Enhancing literacy

Students who are low on resilience often have literacy problems (Howard & Johnson 2000). Their history of academic failure means they don't expect to be successful so they quickly give up in the 'one size fits all' classroom. The current educational emphasis on enhancing all students' skills in literacy illustrates the key role of literacy in empowering students to function in Western society.

Traditionally literacy has been described in syllabus and curriculum documents as listening, speaking, reading and writing. Contemporary literature on literacy now focuses on literacy as an active, dynamic and interactive social practice (Luke 1993). Students gain literacy skills through interacting with classmates, teachers, parents and other people in their lives.

Literacy demands on students in school, in the workplace and in society today are different to the demands made on students last century. Now students are required to be literate in different ways, for example linguistic, mathematical, visual, physical, musical, self understanding and so on. Demands for competence in different literacies are illustrated in a student production of a website. It requires traditional print literacies (to record information and ideas), visual literacies (for overall design and to manipulate images), aural and musical literacies (to build a soundscape around the page) and numeracies (to calculate design dimensions and to keep track of usage and interest). A curriculum based on multiple intelligences not only provides a framework for teaching literacies relevant to the 21st century but also creates opportunities to provide multiple entry points into the curriculum and engage students through their area of relative strength.

Initiative

Our society promotes the idea of young people taking responsibility and ownership, but recent studies (Larson 2000) have shown that boredom, disillusionment and loss of motivation to achieve are more characteristic of today's young people that in previous generations. By providing students with opportunities and encouragement to develop and show initiative, students are more likely to:
* Develop a strong sense of their own competence
* Take greater responsibility for their own actions
* Want to become an adult
* Be more able to independently deal with boredom and hence engage in fewer self-harmful or antisocial activities.
There are three categories of initiative that students in schools can be encouraged to become involved in. They are initiatives that involve:
* The pursuit of a personal or group goal
* Some aspect of community service or volunteer work
* A response to a problem that has some personal relevance.
For students to develop initiative, as many of the following features as possible need to be present. Students are:
* Intrinsically motivated to some extent in the project/plan
* Moderately challenged (not too hard or too easy)
* Given a relatively unstructured starting point that means students need to set goals, make plans and justify them to others
* Required to do a lot of decision making
* Working within some rules and regulations
* Likely to encounter obstacles and setbacks and then have to work on solving these problems
* Working within their class, school or local community, not in isolation.
Teachers or other adults may assist but mostly when asked for expert input.

Some examples of student initiative projects are provided in the list of class committees on pages 72 and 73 and in the 'Success' units in the Teacher's Resource Books.

Hardly ever repeating students

Australian schools have traditionally worked on the assumption that if students are not progressing at the same rate as their classmates, then they could benefit from repeating a year. Recommendations that a student repeat have usually been made with the best interests of the student at heart, as teachers genuinely believe in the efficacy of the strategy. Yet research over 50 years provides convincing evidence that there are no academic advantages for students who repeat, even those who repeat for reasons of so-called 'low maturity' (Owings & Magliaro 1998; McGrath 2000). Some students do make some academic progress during the year in which they repeat a grade but not as much progress as similar children who do not repeat, and these early gains tend to slow down very quickly.

In the long term, students who repeat are far more likely to drop out of school early, have behaviour problems and have lowered self-esteem. Retained students feel a sense of failure, shame and a loss of status. These feelings may be compounded if students in the new younger grade perform at a higher level than they do. Students who repeat also have to start again in terms of developing friendships and social relationships with their new classmates. When they are in a younger grade, their original classmates are less likely to perceive them as appropriate friends.

The students who are most likely to repeat are boys who are smaller in size than average, come from a lower socioeconomic background or a non-English-speaking background, and have learning difficulties or Attention Deficit Disorder. Some have a borderline intellectual disability and, without extra support, will struggle with many aspects of a regular curriculum, whatever their educational circumstances. The policy of inclusion affirms their right to be in regular schools and continue moving through the year levels with their same-age peers.

The decision to repeat a student should be made only after careful consideration and deliberation by a panel of teachers and after consideration of more effective alternatives to repeating and a detailed perusal of the most recent research in this area.

Alternatives to repeating are providing support to the student by:

- Providing additional assistance through another specialised teacher
- Differentiating the curriculum
- Adapting learning tasks by using simpler texts, worksheets, vocabulary, shorter sentences, less information
- Employing assistive technology such as using a dictaphone or voice-activated computer programs for some slower readers and students with dyslexia
- Employing games to engage those students with low attention span or a history of non-success
- Implementing a peer tutoring program
- Using cooperative learning strategies
- Setting up learning centres.

Using cooperative learning

Hundreds of studies demonstrate that cooperative learning builds peer and school connectedness, especially for students at risk. The benefits of cooperative learning fall into three broad categories: higher academic achievement and engagement in learning, greater peer connectedness and class cohesion, and better mental health (social skills, self-esteem and adjustment) (Johnson & Johnson 2000, 1989).

The three key elements that characterise cooperative learning groups and make them different from simple group work are:

- Positive group interdependence: this means that the shared group goal cannot be achieved without all group members sharing their work and resources. No one succeeds unless everyone succeeds.
- Individual accountability and responsibility: a group is not truly cooperative if some members are not pulling their weight. In cooperative learning groups there must be both individual and group accountability.
- The teaching and practising of specified social skills within the group task.

The Cooperative Learning Centre, directed by David and Roger Johnson, has a website at <www.clcrc.com>. This website contains useful articles and information about resources for getting started with cooperative learning. *Different Kids, Same Classroom* (McGrath & Noble 1995) also outlines strategies for cooperative learning. Also refer to Chapter 10 of this book.

Teaching social skills

Having positive relationships with peers is one of the most crucial resources contributing to resilience. Research has demonstrated that the 'discuss and hope' method of teaching social skills is almost a waste of time (McGrath 1998). Discussion and hypothetical problem solving alone will not encourage most students to feel confident about practising social skills. Such skills need to be directly taught just like any mathematical, language or sporting skills. Similarly, there have to be opportunities to practise the newly taught skills (McGrath & Francey 1991; McGrath 1997). The steps that have been shown to be most effective in teaching social skills are:

- Discussing the skill: where would it be used and why is it important?
- Identifying the specific steps of the skill and rehearsing them verbally. Make posters as reminders (e.g. Sounds like, Looks like; Do's and Don'ts).
- Setting up an opportunity to practise that skill in drama where positive feedback and suggestions for improvement can be given in an environment of psychological safety.
- Providing opportunities for students to practise the skill in real-life settings such as cooperative learning groups, games, class discussions, class meetings etc.

Establishing peer support structures

Another way for schools to develop peer connectedness and school connectedness is by establishing peer support systems. Creating opportunities where students can help others is not only effective in regards to enhancing the wellbeing of the 'receiver', but also facilitates a sense of self-efficacy for the helper that is a significant component of resilience. Here are some possibilities:

Supportive friends

Self-nominated or invited students receive some training in basic counselling skills and are available to talk through personal or school-related issues with other students. The BOUNCE BACK! acronym is one way of providing students with small 'c' counselling skills. They would also need:
- Good listening skills
- An understanding and commitment to the principles of psychological safety.

This is a structure more commonly found in upper secondary systems, but some schools have also used it successfully at younger levels. A lot depends on the commitment of the students who participate.

Peer mediation

Self-nominated students are taught mediation skills and are available to help other students (usually younger, but not always) sort out low-level disputes. At the primary level, two daily mediators are selected. They wear special armbands or T-shirts to let other students know who they are. Teachers on yard duty back up a request by a student for mediation and make sure all parties attend the session. The session may be conducted informally in the playground where it occurred, or in a more formal setting such as a mediation room. At the secondary level the process nearly always occurs in the more formal setting and students are rostered 'on duty' for a week. A record book is maintained where mediators record the conflict they were asked to mediate in. Students need to be aware of procedures for requesting mediation.

A study by Johnson and Johnson (1995) found that after peer mediation was introduced into schools:
- Students were able to apply the conflict resolution skills and mediation skills not only at school but in other settings such as home.
- Teachers reported a 60% decrease in discipline problems.
- Principals reported an 80% decrease in incidents referred to them.
- Students' overall academic achievement levels were higher.

Another study showed many positive personal outcomes for students trained as peer mediators (Trela & Conley 1997). These outcomes included increased confidence in handling conflict and in using leadership and problem-solving skills, and enhanced self-esteem. These results indicate that all students would benefit from such training in mediation and conflict resolution.

Circle of friends

Students can offer (or be invited) to assist a student in difficulties in the playground. They may help the student with self-control by making 'calming down' statements when anger erupts. Or they may move near a student who is being harassed or bullied and silently stand close by, glaring at the offender(s) to give the message 'we are here to support this student and don't like what you are doing'. It may also involve being prepared to look for and include socially isolated or shy students.

Peer tutoring

In traditional peer tutoring, an older student usually tutors a younger student in reading or maths or other skills. In same-class peer tutoring, students take turns at being tutor and learner. The key to a successful peer tutoring program is training the student in the social and teaching skills needed for the situation (McGrath & Noble 1993).

Peer buddies

There are many ways in which to use this model. Older students can support and befriend or mentor younger students. For example, a Year 5 student can be a buddy to a student in Year 1. A Year 11 student can be a buddy/mentor to a Year 7, 8 or 9 student or to a student in the nearby primary school. Buddies are people who can be turned to when the younger student is having a problem, such as being harassed or feeling guilty about having done something wrong and not knowing how to put it right. Sometimes the relationship is informal, after an initial 'get to know you' period. Other times the buddy helps the younger student with an activity or a project. It may involve helping younger students with craft activities or with cooking or reading a story. Or it may entail producing something for younger students to use, such as a video, or writing and illustrating a picture storybook that incorporates a BOUNCE BACK! theme or message. One Year 6 class, working in pairs, interviewed a Year 3 student to find out personal details about the student. The Year 6 students, in their pairs, then wrote and illustrated a picture storybook that incorporated the younger student as the main character acting resiliently in the story. Photos were also used. A copy was presented to the Year 3 student and each book was kept by the Year 6 students. The task benefited all parties. The younger student felt connected to the older students in a safe and caring situation. All students learned a lot about resilience. The older students also were able to practise being supportive, setting goals, and the skills related to initiative.

Peer buddies can involve students taking turns to assist a classmate who needs extra support. For example, a student with a hearing impairment may need a buddy to repeat teacher instructions or take notes during a class video. A student with a visual impairment may need help in being cued for obstacles in the classroom or playground. A child with a physical disability may need help with their wheelchair.

'First buddies' is a structure where two students befriend a new student for a period of a term, and help facilitate their social entry. It can also be used at the time of transition to high school. Again, the training of the buddies will be an important consideration. Whole classes of Year 11 students can spend a day playing educational games and completing other fun activities with whole classes of Year 6 students from local primary schools to facilitate their transition in the next year.

Using circle time

Circle time has gained great popularity in the UK due to the documented benefits for students in the areas of self-esteem and classroom behaviour (Bliss, Robinson & Maines 1995). These benefits include children becoming better connected with their peers, developing a deeper understanding of self and others, and creating a classroom climate of trust where students become increasingly more prepared to self-disclose. Circle time is a planned time when students sit in a circle in order to maximise eye contact and feelings of safety. Everyone has the opportunity to speak and be listened to. You may need to reorganise the classroom to accommodate everyone sitting in a circle or find access to a different room. Younger students can sit on the floor in a circle, but chairs in a circle work best with older students. Circle time is incorporated in all the units of work in the BOUNCE BACK! Resiliency Program. In the upper primary/junior secondary school level, a classroom discussion version is used, but the format and structure can be similar. The features of circle time are:

- There is a specific focus each time. Sometimes this will be a personal slant on a relatively neutral topic such as 'Pets'. Sometimes it will be a more personal topic such as 'Fears'. Circle time can also be used to celebrate successes on some occasions. A classroom problem can also be discussed and it may end in a decision to pursue a positive goal as a whole class.

- There is a structure in circle time which includes a short opening activity. Reading an appropriate picture storybook can be a good opening activity, even for young adolescents if it is well selected. This is followed by one or more focused activities such as rounds (where everyone, in turn, has a say) or an open forum discussion. Sometimes the Think–Pair–Share or Partner Retell strategy is used (see Chapter 10). It concludes with a closure activity and sometimes follow-up work.

- It usually takes about 20–40 minutes, depending on the age of the students and the length of the opening activity. There is a need for variety and a relatively fast pace. Children can get bored if they spend too long just listening to others without any active participation or change of focus. One tactic that can help here is to mix the students up during the session. For example, the teacher can say, 'If you have a dog, stand up. Now change places with someone standing up'. Alternatively, before the session starts, each student can be given the name of one of four items in a 'set' of things (e.g. four fruits—pear, apple, orange, plum—or four animals—dog, cat, lion, bear). Then the teacher can say, 'All the animals change places'. This adds an element of active movement, changes combinations if some students haven't settled, and provides alternative pairing for activities. Numbered heads can also be used. Every student selects a number from 1 to 4 by drawing a card from a container. Announce that all number threes are changing places. You could also give every student a different number from 1 to 26 and then pull out a card from a container and ask the student with that number to respond to a specific question.

- The teacher acts as a facilitator encouraging everyone to contribute.

- The rules of psychological safety are reviewed before the session begins. (See page 55 in Chapter 4.)

- There is an emphasis on social skills such as listening well, not interrupting, taking turns and respecting others' views. They are reviewed before each session begins. A talking prompt can be used to assist with the development of listening skills (see Chapter 10).

- Circle time can promote empathy for others' views and feelings and allow students to feel more confident about talking about their feelings and giving their own opinions. Students may tend to copy each other a bit at first, but in time they become more confident at expressing their own ideas.

Holding class meetings

Class meetings can be conducted during circle time. However, separate classroom meetings can also be held. These are problem-solving meetings in which everyone discusses difficulties that have arisen in class or in the playground. For example, the teacher may ask the class 'what can we do about students using put-downs or name calling?' or 'what can we do about students coming late to class?' Students may ask 'how can we convince the teachers that we need an extra fifteen minutes for our sports period?' In the primary school, these are easily slotted in as part of the school day. In the secondary school, they are more likely to be used in the context of Home Rooms.

Classroom meetings are excellent sessions to teach how meetings are run and to practise social skills such as respectful disagreeing and listening. They also teach how to request permission through the Chair to speak, wait for one's turn, express one's opinion, use 'I' messages, conflict management and negotiation. Good problem-solving skills are developed and students can increase their sense of competence in this structured environment. There is a rotating Chairperson and a secretary and minutes are kept and circulated. Sometimes there is also a Timekeeper. An agenda is circulated and meeting procedures are followed. Although the teacher does not run the session they may still participate and, if appropriate, subtly facilitate participation by comments and questions. The teacher's role is mostly to accept and listen to different students' ideas and help the class reach solutions that everyone can accept. The rules for psychological safety operate (see Chapter 4). The 'no names' rule can be overturned by agreement for some sessions if it is necessary.

A 10–15 minute meeting works well for younger year levels and up to 30 minutes for older years. Holding the meeting just before recess, lunch or going-home time ensures there is a natural cut-off, even if it's in the middle of a hot discussion. If this happens the teacher can say 'we seem to have run out of time but we will begin our next meeting with this problem'. However, one primary teacher found that classroom meetings held directly after recess or lunchtime were effective in reducing playground bullying. In their classroom meetings children were able to problem solve directly after an 'incident' occurred.

Setting up class and school committees

Student participation in class, year level or school committees can foster a sense of responsibility for self and others. It also gives students a sense of meaningful participation and can increase their commitment and connectedness to the school. Through committee participation, students can also access opportunities to practise leadership skills. They practise social skills (e.g. cooperation, listening, respectful disagreeing, negotiation and conflict resolution) and resilience skills (e.g. showing initiative, goal setting and monitoring and completing a project). On smaller committees, students usually work with only two or three other students but this can vary. All students should be involved in as many committees as possible over time. Ideally, each committee:

- Has the necessary combined skills to perform its tasks
- Has some idea of good goal-setting skills
- Draws up some negotiated decisions about how the members work as a team
- Has a limited life so that membership can be rotated
- Has members who fully understand their responsibility to their committee and to the class
- Does not get too 'bossy'
- Can co-opt another classmate to temporarily assist the committee if other committee members agree
- Writes a final report at the end of its tenure of the committee's work and achievements (a graphic organiser can be provided); keeps records along the way.

Student Representative Councils are one kind of broad committee. Participation on an SRC can teach students leadership skills, as they represent their fellow students in issues and decisions such as how the school is governed, how school reporting is conducted, school rules, uniform matters, how school welfare and school discipline policies are implemented and so on.

Here are some suggestions for small committees:

- *Absenteeism committee:* advises on absenteeism problems.
- *Administrative committee:* checks class attendance and helps keep the statistics on attendance.
- *Assembly committee:* liaises with senior school staff and organises assemblies.
- *Birthday committee:* is responsible for remembering and celebrating birthdays (teacher's too!).
- *Bulletin board committee:* designs and maintains the bulletin boards, displays and classroom door posters.
- *Catering committee:* organises a cooperative class lunch or morning tea once a term. It plans a menu and budget, collects money to cover costs, shops for items, distributes cooking jobs, organises decorations and cutlery, serviettes and so on.
- *Classroom maintenance committee:* is responsible for cleaning and maintenance of the classroom.
- *Classroom meetings committee:* plans, announces, chairs, takes minutes and reports on class meetings.
- *Communications committee:* conveys and collects messages to the office and other classrooms etc. Distributes newsletters and take-home notes.
- *Creative and performing arts committee:* maintains class costume and props and organises class performances such as music performances, play performances and art displays.
- *Curators committee:* puts together classroom collections based around a current class theme and suggests relevant items, invites students to contribute, keep records to ensure a safe acceptance and return of property, designs reasonable rules to make sure that items are well cared for, organises the display and returns items.
- *Event management committee:* is responsible for remembering and celebrating classmates and teachers' birthdays, as well as other important reasons for celebration such as births and recording and reporting on classmates' positive achievements and actions inside and outside the classroom.

- *Excursion committee:* plans excursions.
- *Fund-raising committee:* organises events and projects.
- *Games club committee:* This is an idea from Surrey Hills Primary School in Victoria. A games club can offer a safe, satisfying and non-stigmatising location for some students at lunchtime. It can also be just plain fun for any student. Two lunchtime sessions are held with a maximum of 25 booked places at any one session. Board games are purchased/borrowed, checked, maintained and organised/stored. One teacher must be free to supervise each session.
- *Garden committee:* cares for, purchases and oversees the class plants and any gardens created by the class (e.g. vegetable gardens), a 'smell' garden, a 'touch' garden, a peace garden, an insect repellent garden.
- *Graphics committee:* provides decorations, certificates, magazine illustrations, cards, posters, cartoons etc. as required by the classroom.
- *Gratitude committee:* finds appropriate formal and informal ways of thanking guests who visit and contribute to the class/school.
- *Grouping committee:* plans and organises fun ways to randomly group students for class cooperative group work, using interesting strategies such as drawing cards from a container which match up with three others. This is good for students with sound mathematical abilities and with good cooperative skills (see Chapter 10—Grouping strategies for ideas).
- *Inter-class liaison committee:* plans ways for two classes to mix, cooperate and get to know each other.
- *Library committee:* liaises with the library, keeps records of classroom reading materials, and offers suggestions as to book and resource purchases.
- *Multiple Intelligences Advisory committee:* is based around one specific intelligence (e.g. spatial-visual) and advises the teacher on where tasks reflecting that intelligence could be integrated into the curriculum. There can be a committee for each of the eight intelligences.
- *Newsletter committee:* organises the publication of a weekly, fortnightly, monthly or term class newsletter.
- *Resources committee:* is responsible for keeping track of resources, storing them, offering suggestions for new ones, and making resources for activities.
- *Sports committee:* plans and implements a structured sporting activity such as a round robin or tournament of some kind.
- *Technology roster and maintenance committee:* makes a roster for and keep records of computer use, organises the technology trolley and supervises a roster for the use of tools and equipment in it.
- *Welfare committee:* is responsible for recording and reporting on classmates' positive achievements and actions inside and outside the classroom.
- *'Word of the Day'/'Problem of the Week' Committee:* researches and then selects an interesting word for the day to be used at every opportunity and a fun maths problem to be attempted each day.
- *Zoo keeping committee:* advises on suitable classroom animals and their maintenance and makes sure that they are well cared for.

Some schools have set up school committees, with a representative sample of students from Year 3 on, that meet once a week to discuss issues or problems that have been raised by students or which concern students. The kinds of issues that can be discussed in such a weekly forum can be:

- How could we improve our school playground?
- What can we do to stop bullying in our school?

A teacher should always be at the forum but in a passive role. Rules for psychological safety should operate (see Chapter 4).

Setting and enforcing clear, consistent boundaries

Clear, consistent rules and boundaries help to create a safe, fair and predictable environment for students. At the beginning of the year, the idea of rules can be discussed in terms of the bigger picture, that is, in the world, the nation, the state etc. Then rules and logical consequences for violations are negotiated between students and teacher. Students need to be made aware that some rules can *not* be negotiable. This exercise can model the participatory process by which the classroom will operate for the rest of the year. The students' input is solicited and valued, thus establishing a positive interpersonal relationship between the students and the teacher that is developed more fully as the year progresses. The teacher ensures that he/she is consistent in applying the rules and consequences so the students see discipline as 'fair', a key characteristic of a 'good teacher' as defined by students.

Creating a physically and psychologically safe environment

One of the most devastating things that can happen to a student is to be on the receiving end of bullying. Bullying is a threat in all schools but it only becomes problematic if a school does not acknowledge the reality of it and take firm steps to eradicate as much of it as they can. Bullying can be kept under control with teacher commitment, a preventative approach, curriculum focus on bullying, and continual monitoring and review. Chapter 8 looks at whole-school management strategies for bullying. The Teacher's Resource Books at all three levels contain an extensive collection of anti-bullying curriculum materials. As well as dealing with bullying, a safe school has strong values and rules against all forms of violence and asks the school community to reinforce this message.

REFERENCES

General

Anderson, L. & Krathwohl, D., 2000, (eds), *A Taxonomy for Learning, Teaching and Assessing: A Revision of Bloom's Taxonomy of Educational Objectives*. Longman, New York.

Bandura, A., 1997, *Self-efficacy: The Exercise of Self Control*. Freeman, New York.

Brook, J., Nomura, C. & Whealdon, K., 1994, 'A network of influences on adolescent drug involvement: Neighbourhood, school, peer and family'. *Genetic, Social & General Psychology Monographs*, 115, 303–21.

Czikszentmihalyi, M., 1990, *Flow: The Psychology of Optimal Experience*. Harper Perennial, New York.

Covey, S., 1989, *The Seven Habits of Highly Effective People: Powerful Lessons in Personal Change*. Simon and Schuster, New York.

Christenson, S.L. & Carroll, E.B., 1999, 'Strengthening the family–school partnership through "Check and Connect"'. In E. Frydenberg, *Learning to Cope: Developing as a Person in Complex Societies*. Oxford University Press, Oxford.

Cumming, J., 1996, *From Alienation to Engagement: Opportunities for Reform in the Middle Years of Schooling*. Australian Curriculum Studies Association, Canberra, ACT.

Dornbusch, S.M., Laird, J. & Crosnoe, B., 1999, 'Parental and school resources that assist adolescents in coping with negative peer influences'. In E. Frydenberg, *Learning to Cope: Developing as a Person in Complex Societies*. Oxford University Press, Oxford.

Fischmannm, S. & Cotterell, J.L., 2000, 'Coping styles and support sources of at-risk students'. *The Australian Educational and Developmental Psychologist*, 17(2), 58–69.

Fullan, M. & Rolheiser, C., 1996, *Staff developers: Changing roles for changing times*. National Staff Development Conference, Vancouver, December.

Fuller, A., McGraw, K. & Goodyear, M., 1998, *The Mind of Youth Resilience: A Connect Project*. Victorian Department of Education.

Gardner, H., 1999, *Intelligence Reframed: Multiple Intelligences for the Twenty-First Century*. Basic Books, New York.

Gardner, H., 1994, 'Intelligences in theory and practice: A response to Elliot W. Eisner, Robert J. Sternberg and Henry M. Levin'. *Teachers College Record*, 95(4), 576–83.

Hill, P., 1997, 'Snapshots of the middle years', *EQ Australia*, Issue 1, 10–11.

Howard, S. & Johnson, B., 2000, 'Young adolescents displaying resilient and non-resilient behaviour: Insights from a qualitative study—Can schools make a difference?' Paper presented at AARE conference, University of Sydney, December.

Johnson, D.W. & Johnson, R.T., 1995, *Teaching Students to Be Peace Makers*. Interaction Book Co, Edina, MN.

Johnson, D.W. & Johnson, R.T., 1989, *Cooperation and Competition: Theory and Research*. Interaction Book Company, Minnesota.

Johnson, D.W., Johnson, R.T. & Stane, M.B., 2000, *Cooperative Learning Methods: A Meta-Analysis*. <www.clcrc.com/pages/cl-methods.html>.

Larson, R.W., 2000, 'Toward a psychology of positive youth development', *American Psychologist*, 55(1), 170–83.

Luke, A., 1993, 'The social construction of literacy in the primary school'. In L. Unsworth (ed.), *Literacy, Learning and Teaching. Language as Social Practice in the Primary School*. Macmillan, Sydney, 1–53.

McGrath, H.L., 1998, 'An overview of prevention and treatment programs for developing positive peer relations'. In K. Rigby & P. Slee (eds), *Children's Peer Relationships*. Routledge, London.

Noble, T., 1999, *Integrating Gardner's multiple intelligences with a revised Bloom's Taxonomy: A new model for school reform?*. Unpublished PhD dissertation, University of Sydney.

Noble, T. & Grant, M., 1997, 'An Interview with Howard Gardner'. *EQ Australia*, 5(1), 24–26.

Owings, W. & Magliaro, S., 1998, 'Grade retention: A history of failure'. *Educational Leadership*, September, 86–88.

Ruddick, J., Day, J. & Wallace, G., 1997, 'Students' perspectives on school improvement'. In A. Hargreaves (ed.), *Rethinking Educational Change with Heart and Mind. The ASCD Yearbook*. ASCD, Alexandria, VA, 73–91.

Rutter, M., 1991, 'Pathways from childhood to adult life'. *Pastoral Care in Education*, 63, 384–99.

Rutter, M., Maughan, B., Mortimore, J., Ouston, J. & Smith, A., 1979, *Fifteen Thousand Hours. Secondary Schools and Their Effects on Children*. Harvard University Press, Cambridge.

Tomlinson, C.A., 1999, *The Differentiated Classroom. Responding to the Needs of All Learners*. ASCD, Alexandria, VA.

Trela, P. & Conley, M., 1997, *Understanding student leadership through peer mediation*. Paper presented at the Annual Meeting of the American Educational Research Association, Chicago.

Trent, F., 2001, *Aliens in the classroom or: The Classroom as an alien place?* Paper presented at the Association of Independent Schools, NSW Sex, Drugs & Rock 'N Roll Conference, August.

Woolfolk, A., 2001, *Educational Psychology*, 8th edn, Allyn & Bacon, Boston.

Applying a multiple intelligences model to the classroom

Campbell, L., Campbell, B. & Dickinson, D., 1996, *Teaching and Learning Through Multiple Intelligences*. Simon Shuster Co., Needham Heights, Mass.

Chapman, C., 1993, *If the Shoe Fits . . . How to Develop Multiple Intelligences in the Classroom*. Hawker Brownlow, Melbourne.

Hoerr, T.R., 2000, *Becoming a Multiple Intelligences School*. ASCD, Alexandria, VA.

Kagan, S. & Kagan, M., 1998, *Multiple Intelligences. The Complete MI Book*. Kagan Cooperative Learning, San Clemente, CA.

Lazear, D., 1994, *Seven Ways of Knowing. Teaching for Multiple Intelligences: A Handbook of Techniques for Expanding Intelligences*. Hawker Brownlow, Highett, Victoria.

McGrath, H. & Noble, T., 1995(a), *Seven Ways at Once: Book 1: Classroom Strategies Based on the Seven Intelligences*, Longman, Melbourne.

McGrath, H. & Noble, T., 1995(b), *Seven Ways at Once: Book 2: Units of Work Based on the Seven Intelligences*. Longman, Melbourne.

McGrath, H. & Noble, T., 1998, *Seven Ways at Once: Book 3: More Strategies and Units of Work Based on the Seven Intelligences*. Longman, Melbourne.

Vialle, W. & Perry, J., 1995, *Nurturing Multiple Intelligences in the Australian Classroom*. Hawker Brownlow, Cheltenham, Melbourne.

Bloom's model of thinking

Achieving excellence 1991, *Units of work for P–8*. Ministry of Education and Training, Victoria.

Anderson, L. & Krathwohl, D., 2000 (eds), *A Taxonomy for Learning, Teaching and Assessing: A Revision of Bloom's Taxonomy of Educational Objectives*. Longman, New York.

Baker, A. & Baker, J., 1994, *Developing Thinking Skills Using Children's Literature*. Eleanor Curtain, Melbourne.

Clements, D., Gilliland, C. & Holko, P., 1992, *Thinking in Themes*. Oxford University Press, Melbourne.

McGrath, H. & Noble, T., 1993, *Different Kids, Same Classroom*. Longman, Melbourne.

McGrath, H. & Noble, T., 1995(a), *Seven Ways at Once: Book 1: Classroom Strategies Based on the Seven Intelligences*. Longman, Melbourne.

McGrath, H. & Noble, T., 1995(b), *Seven Ways at Once: Book 2: Units of Work Based on the Seven Intelligences*. Longman, Melbourne.

McGrath, H. & Noble, T., 1998, *Seven Ways at Once: Book 3: More Strategies and Units of Work Based on the Seven Intelligences*. Longman, Melbourne.

Circle time

Bliss, T., Robinson, G. & Maines, B., 1995, *Developing Circle Time*. Lame Duck Publishing, London.

Social skills

McGrath, H. & Francey, S., 1991, *Friendly Kids, Friendly Classrooms*. Longman, Melbourne.

McGrath, H., 2000, *Behaviour Management: 'Ready to Go' Series*. Blake Education, Sydney.

McGrath, H., 1997, *Dirty Tricks. Classroom Games Which Teach Students Social Skills*. Longman, Melbourne.

McGrath, H. & Noble, T., 1993, *Different Kids, Same Classroom*. Longman, Melbourne.

McGrath, H.L. & Edwards, H., 1999, *Friends: A Practical Guide to Understanding Relationships*. Choice Publications, Melbourne (for older students and adults).

Cooperative learning

Bellanca, J., Fogarty, R. & Dalton, J., 1991, *Blueprints for Thinking in the Cooperative Classroom*. Hawker Brownlow, Melbourne.

Kagan, S., 1995, *Cooperative Learning*. Kagan Cooperative Learning, Capistrano, California.

Johnson, D.W., Johnson, R.T. & Holubec, E.J., 1994, *The Nuts and Bolts of Cooperative Learning*. Interaction Book Company, Minnesota.

McGrath, H. & Noble, T., 1993, *Different Kids, Same Classroom*. Longman, Melbourne.

CHAPTER 6

LEADING RESILIENT SCHOOLS

At the beginning of the 21st century there is a sense of urgency about the need to build schools where staff and students can develop greater resilience to cope with the complexity of life today. This chapter draws on the school change literature and research to review the key factors that lead to success in leading a whole-school implementation of a new program such as the BOUNCE BACK! Resiliency Program. In summary, these factors are:
- Understanding that change is a people process
- Developing 'school spirit'
- Sustaining new programs and using a whole-school approach
- Not expecting too much too soon
- Not letting a program implementation 'go cold'
- Creating opportunities for constructive dissent and problem solving
- Developing collaborative partnerships with the local and broader community.

> A small group of thoughtful concerned citizens can change the world. Indeed it is the only thing that ever has.
> (Margaret Mead, anthropologist)

Understanding that change is a people process

Any new school project that improves relationships between colleagues has a chance of succeeding; any strategy that does not is doomed to fail. Strategies that facilitate positive staff relationships lead to higher productivity, improved problem-solving and better learning. They are also more emotionally satisfying (Hargreaves & Fullan 1998). As Fullan has asserted:

> if we dig deeper into the roles of emotion and hope in interpersonal relationships, we will gain a lasting understanding of how to deal with change more constructively (Fullan 1997:226).

Developing communities of teachers who collaboratively work together is the best way to facilitate change. Active participation in collaborative partnerships with other teachers and feeling supported by senior staff are two major protective factors in developing resilience for individual teachers. Collaboration replaces the traditional isolation of teachers and helps them to feel supported and respected. In contrast, teacher burnout is characterised by low levels of collegial and principal support. Collaboration is based on respectful and reciprocal relationships and can mean changing how staff work, not how much they work. It means trusting processes as well as people. Staff collaboration correlates directly with successful school reform and increased student achievement. Professional development and learning is most powerful, long lasting and sustainable when teachers work with a group of colleagues who struggle together to plan for a given group of students or a new program implementation. It is important to create time and opportunity for staff to work with colleagues.

Developing 'school spirit'

One key challenge for a school leader is how to increase the sense of 'school spirit' in both teachers and students. School spirit both reflects and builds school connectedness.

Students demonstrate school spirit when they make positive comments about their school to outsiders and proudly let other people know of their school's achievements and positive features. Their school spirit is also shown in their support for other students in the school in competitive situations such as sporting events and rock eisteddfods, when they honour and maintain the traditions and rules of the school and when they publicly affirm a connection to the school, for example, by wearing the correct school uniform. Their willingness to be involved in school-based projects and social activities, even if they are out of school time, is another way they affirm their school connectedness.

It takes time to develop school spirit and it is harder to create in students if their teachers don't feel a strong commitment and loyalty to the school. Teachers need to genuinely feel and model school spirit.

Strategies to enhance 'school spirit'

- Students and teachers are invited to be part of a problem-solving process to come up with suggestions as to how school spirit can be increased.
- Establish a system of recognition for achievements by students and teachers. For example, publicise staff and student successes by putting the information on a bulletin board in a high traffic area (e.g. courses completed, teams coached, prizes won).
- Identify ways to better communicate the achievements of the school and its teachers and students to the community (e.g. have a student-staffed stall and display in the main shopping centre).
- Professionally establish and maintain the school website. A surprising number of people visit school websites, and they are often part of the data collected for research purposes. Ideally students are involved in its preparation but with professional advice.
- Use activities to promote the positive features of the school students and staff, such as:
  —Brainstorm 'The best things about our school' at a staff meeting, in class or in home-room time (The Pairs Rally strategy in Chapter 10 can be used here).
  —Have a large sign at the front of the school which promotes the school's best features, including the best qualities of the staff.
  —Have a teacher profile and a student profile once a week in the newsletter or on a bulletin board.
  —Have a positive teacher photo board, accompanied by each teacher's photo (about five teachers at a time), their qualifications, professional interests, recent professional development activities, professional goals for the year and so on. Change the photos regularly to maintain people's interest. Photos of the teachers engaged with their students in their classrooms is a great way of hooking students' and parents' interest. Try adding a dialogue box that includes each teacher's favourite 'saying' (you may have to carry out a student survey to find out what this saying is).
  —Encourage students to interview a teacher in the school newsletter. Different teachers can be profiled each week, accompanied by a photo. Some questions students can ask teachers are:
  What do you like best about teaching?
  What's one good thing about teaching at our school?
  Why did you become a teacher?
  Where did you train as a teacher? What is one good memory you have about your training?
  What is one of your professional goals for the future?
  What's one thing you like to do to relax when you are away from school?
  What is your favourite type of music?
- Encourage the use of the whiteboard in the staffroom to communicate messages of appreciation and encouragement between staff (e.g. 'Jan, thanks for doing my yard duty, Anne').

- Set up activities that involves whole-school collaboration, for example a musical performance, fund-raising events, concerts. Allow time for students to make banners and rosettes for a sports carnival, and perhaps develop a school barracking chant.
- Organise a day when every student displays or performs according to their best 'intelligence' and parents can be invited.
- Involve students in the building of areas in the school environment that will enhance the quality of life for all who coexist in the school. This could mean:
  —Improving the appearance of a wall by artwork;
  —Building a barbecue and leisure-seating area (this is a good opportunity for students to demonstrate practical skills and retired experts in the community are often very happy to help out);
  —Re-painting an area.
- Community service can be used in several ways. First, it allows students an opportunity to feel proud of their school. Second, it develops a sense of social justice and responsibility. Third, it can allow some less-academic students to 'strut their stuff'. Fourth, it allows students to be connected to the larger community of which they are a part. You could consider:
  —Gardening for a community project or for elderly people;
  —Visiting, singing and performing, drawing or reading to/for elderly citizens in hostels and nursing homes;
  —Undertaking work for a local pre-school.

Sustaining new programs and using a whole-school approach

Meaningful change occurs only when the impact of change is felt schoolwide (Fullan 1991; Sagor 1997). A useful starting point for schools that want to implement the BOUNCE BACK! Resiliency Program is to begin by:
- Identifying how the program fits with the articulated and shared school vision and goals, especially those relating to student welfare
- Assessing teachers' current willingness to collaboratively plan and adopt the program.

Freda Briggs (1999) has reviewed the research outcomes on the effectiveness of a variety of different programs designed to teach protective behaviours in young children. Her conclusions were almost identical to those of the National Health and Medical Research Council after their evaluation of effective health and welfare programs (NHMRC 1996). Both found that the most effective programs in these welfare areas were those that:
- Gave teachers opportunities for professional development in the program. Teachers need to be confident about articulations and defending new initiatives and be able to provide supportive research evidence as part of that process
- Were integrated with the curriculum as much as possible
- Provided classroom teachers with a wide range of user-friendly program materials.

The implications of these findings are clear. New programs require effective resources and professional development. It is also important for staff to collaborate on finding ways to integrate new programs into the curriculum. Although BOUNCE BACK! already integrates its resources and activities with the key learning areas, teachers can identify and share the many other ways in which this can be done.

Here are some other ideas for sustaining whole-school commitment to the implementation of BOUNCE BACK!
- Share resources. For example, collate new activities or integrated ideas in an open-access resource file kept in the staff room. A list of appropriate websites and CDs can also be part of the resource file.
- Create opportunities for staff to visit each other's classrooms to see how they are using the program.
- Network with other schools using the program.
- Create opportunities to visit similar classes in other schools to see their program in action.

- Negotiate release time for collaborative team planning. Time for innovation is a perennial problem in schools. Translating a new program into classroom-friendly activities and checking that the new ideas mesh with curriculum outcomes takes considerable time. Often it is time that teachers simply don't have. There needs to be shared problem solving on the issue of providing more time for new programming.
- Provide opportunities in staff meetings for teachers to share program progress and successful ideas.
- Access community networks, especially for students who belong to minority ethnic and racial communities, to ensure that the program is context-sensitive and based on the reality of the settings in which your students live.

Not expecting too much too soon

Many school-based health and welfare initiatives have been abandoned as a result of lack of clarity of purpose and a poor understanding of change management processes (Curtis & Stollar 1996). Over the last decade one key lesson from the literature on staff development and school change is that it takes far more time for staff to learn about and collaborate on a new program than one would predict. In the past there was confidence in the 'instant coffee' approach to innovation; all we needed to do was to find a good program and just add water. A better analogy for today is that the pace of innovation or change is more like the drip filter method of coffee making: a drip by drip method takes a bit longer but leads to a much better result.

Schools may end up abandoning good programs because they expected to see major changes too soon. Here are some suggestions for realistic implementation:

- If frustration or doubt occurs, there need to be reminders that it takes time to successfully implement and gain results from a new initiative. The pace of any significant change is always slow and complex. Change is a process not an event and the implementation of BOUNCE BACK! is a continuing journey that will require several refinements to suit the particular demands of your school.
- Be aware of the implementation dip. When anyone first trials new teaching strategies or curriculum content there is a risk they will initially feel less competent than they are comfortable with. If staff are encouraged to persevere they will eventually feel more professionally competent than when they began the innovation (Fullan 1996).
- Prepare for the long haul. A new program like BOUNCE BACK! must be sustained for three to five years before it becomes a full part of the school. Ideally BOUNCE BACK! extends from one school grade to the next in a sequential manner. Such coordination means that the key environmental and personal skills components of the program will need to be modelled, reinforced and practised over years so that students revisit the key principles again and again as they move through year levels. This continuing exposure and 'mastery' means that the key resilience principles are more likely to become part of the students' behavioural repertoire. Teachers also benefit from this repetition. By teaching key concepts to students, they develop a deeper understanding of these concepts as applied to their own lives.
- Involve all stakeholders. Parents must be part of the program. One school formed a Parent Education Resource Committee (PERC). This committee was responsible for gathering data on the success of new school programs and practices and sharing that success with the whole school community. Their names and contact numbers were printed in the school newsletter and other parents were encouraged to call them. Because this parent team documented the progress of the new program, they became the best advocates for the innovation.
- Provide data that document progress and share successes with the whole school community. When schools and/or teachers are in a position to demonstrate some positive outcomes and benefits for students through their engagement with the BOUNCE BACK! program, then even more widespread support can be gained. Because it is so important to gather data on student progress there is a whole section (Chapter 9) on ways to gather such data. Monitoring and

documenting progress is not only critical to justifying the inclusion and continuation of the program but it can also provide a 'positive feedback loop' to sustain the implementation of the program.

Not letting a program implementation 'go cold'

Successful implementation of the BOUNCE BACK! program can lead to personal and professional growth for all involved. But being involved in a successful project can also lead to opportunities for staff promotion and that can mean a higher level of staff turnover than normal. The issue of staff loss needs to be addressed. As committed staff leave, there can be a 'cooling down' of a successful initiative. New teachers do not feel an ownership of the program and often are unsure of its history and how to implement it. Here are some ways to maintain everyone's energy for a successful ongoing program, to involve new staff, and to keep the BOUNCE BACK! program 'hot':

- During the year, make videos and take photos showing teachers using the program at many different age/stage levels. This can be used to introduce new staff to the program.
- Develop an induction manual for new staff that includes the aims of the program, an outline of the program, examples of student work, and a list of other teachers who are happy to assist or answer questions or to have visitors in their classrooms.
- Collate collaboratively-developed and shared resources and planning ideas in an open file in the staffroom so that these resources do not leave when the teachers leave. Of course they can make copies to take with them.
- Set up a mentoring or peer coaching arrangement between new teachers and teachers who are more experienced in the program.
- Provide each new teacher with a set of BOUNCE BACK! resources.
- Provide release time for professional development in the program and for visits to other classes.

Creating opportunities for constructive dissent and problem solving

Leaders who are implementing a new program in the school should always expect that someone will be dissatisfied with their performance at some stage (Hargreaves & Fullan 1998). Leaders particularly need to develop resilience to cope with staff criticisms, disagreements and concerns during any change process. The implementation of any new program can trigger different feelings for different teachers. Several things can happen when teachers find themselves in a situation of change (Blanchard, in Fullan & Rolheiser 1996). They can find themselves:

- Doing something they are not used to doing and therefore feeling awkward, ill-at-ease and self-conscious
- Thinking first about what they have to give up, rather than what they have to gain
- Feeling alone or isolated, even if others are implementing the same program
- Being able to handle only a small amount of change at any one time
- Being at an earlier level of readiness for the change than many of their colleagues
- Being concerned that there are inadequate resources.

Be aware that a common human response is to revert to the old ways of doing things when the pressure is off. People generally do not readily embrace the unfamiliar and change often is associated with strong emotions and fears. Michael Fullan perceives that creating opportunities for teachers to express their anxieties, fears and concerns about the changes in their teaching practice is crucial to releasing energy for change. He states:

> If you are sincere, you have legitimised dissent. You have made it easy for staff to speak up about concerns (which would come out later anyway in more subtle and inaccessible ways). You listen carefully, suspending your own advocacy, because you know that some fundamental problems will be identified and that people's fears, real or imagined, will need to be examined carefully (Fullan 1997:222).

Once identified, concerns and problems can serve as the starting point for further problem solving, leading to more effective change. The structured strategies outlined below can be useful for creating structured and constructive opportunities for identifying and managing staff concerns and facilitating staff problem solving. Most of these strategies have been used in business organisations as well as in schools.

- De Bono's Six Thinking Hats strategy or PMI (De Bono 1992, 1993)
- Cooperative controversy (Chapter 10)

Developing collaborative partnerships with the local and broader community

> Nothing new that is really interesting comes without collaboration. (James Watson, Nobel Prize Winner)

Gaining external support for a new program can play a key role in its successful implementation. External support boosts internal staff confidence and motivation (Hargreaves & Fullan 1998). Here are some examples of possible collaborative partnerships with outside community organisations that would complement the implementation of the BOUNCE BACK! program:

- The development of strong family–school partnerships (see Chapter 7 for more details)
- The establishment of school–university partnerships to facilitate research and action research
- Collaborating with local health, social welfare, youth, arts and leisure services and agencies to deliver and support new welfare initiatives and to become a full service school
- Forming links with local cultural and ethnic groups to make the program directly relevant to the needs of the school community
- Setting up links between the school and the police so that messages given to young people who overstep the line are consistent
- Making connections with local businesses, service organisations (e.g. Rotary) and industry in ways that can support the program.

In summary

The challenge for leaders is to support their staff in implementing new programs such as BOUNCE BACK! while understanding and working within the inevitable processes of change that have been identified. This involves creating opportunities for teachers to collaborate, develop and maintain a strong commitment to the school by both teachers and students, using a whole school approach, and using pre-planned strategies that will sustain and maintain the program over time and after staff losses. It also involves being realistic about the timeline for implementation, providing opportunities for staff to express concerns and solve problems related to the program, and establishing collaborative partnerships with both the local and broader community. Leading change in this way also means recognising the need to manage the emotional and cognitive challenges for all involved in any new initiatives.

REFERENCES

Briggs, F. & Hawkins, R., 1999, 'Keeping ourselves safe', SET special, NZCER, New Zealand.
Curtis, M. & Stollar, S., 1996, 'Applying principles and practices of organisational change to school reform'. *School Psychology Review*, 25(4): 409–17.
De Bono, E., 1993, *Serious Creativity: Using the Power of Lateral Thinking to Create New Ideas*. Harper-Business, New York.
De Bono, E., 1992, *Six Thinking Hats for Schools*. Hawker Brownlow, Melbourne.
Fullan, M., 1991, *The New Meaning of Educational Change*. Teachers College Press, New York.
Fullan, M., 1996, 'Turning systemic thinking on its head'. *Phi Delta Kappan*, 77(6), February, 420–23.

Fullan, M., 1997, 'Emotion and hope: Constructive concepts for complex times'. In A. Hargreaves (ed.), *Rethinking Educational Change with Heart and Mind*. ASCD Yearbook, 216–33, ASCD, Alexandria, Virginia.

Fullan, M. & Rolheiser, C., 1996, 'Staff developers: Changing roles for changing times'. *National Staff Development Conference*, Vancouver, December.

Hargreaves, A. & Fullan, M., 1998, *What's Worth Fighting for Out There*, Teachers College Press, New York.

National Health & Medical Research Council, 1996, *Effective School Health Promotion: Towards Health Promoting Schools*. The National Health and Medical Research Council's Health Advancement Committee, Australian Government Publishing Service.

Sagor, R., 1997, 'Collaborative action research for educational change'. In A. Hargreaves (ed.), *Rethinking Educational Change with Heart and Mind*. ASCD Yearbook, 169–91, ASCD, Alexandria, Virginia.

7

BUILDING FAMILY RESILIENCE

The two most important protective *environmental* factors for developing young people's resilience are family connectedness and school connectedness. This section reviews the protective processes that can foster family resilience and build stronger family–school connectedness.

Families

Being a 'good enough' parent

Almost everyone we know feels they are not as good at parenting as they'd like to be. Parents often ask their child's teachers for advice on parenting. It's important to communicate an understanding that parenting is challenging for everyone and there are no easy formulas for good parenting. We have seen many parents who have worked hard at being good parents experience difficult times with their children. We have also seen parents who haven't always 'been there' for their kids still manage to raise well-adjusted children. Parenting styles interact with the many different personalities and idiosyncrasies of children, many of which have a genetic base.

There are many good reasons why different families have not been able to develop as large a collection as they would like of protective processes that lead to child and family resilience. Firstly, parenting is very difficult, and some children are more difficult to parent than others because of factors that are hard to influence, such as genetics. Family life is less stable than in previous generations due to various factors such as increasing divorce rates, breakdown in relationships and high rates of family geographical relocation. The high incidence of single-parent families means that many families in our community are sometimes struggling emotionally, economically and physically. Many children create greater challenges for families because of genetic predispositions and/or the interaction of their difficulties with the family context. For different reasons many families do not have the support networks that existed for previous generations. There is very little or no preparation in how to be an effective parent.

Regardless of the type of family (nuclear, sole parent or blended) or the strength of the family and individual family members, every family faces challenges. Three major challenges identified in a recent Australian study of families (Geggie, De Frain, Hitchcock & Silberberg 2000) were:
- Dealing with breakdowns in family communication
- Managing children's behaviour problems and concerns about how to parent appropriately
- Relationship dynamics such as sibling rivalry or tension in the couple's relationship.

Recent research on protective factors contributing to resilience has shifted the focus to family strengths, not family problems. All families have strengths. This does not mean that family challenges or problems are minimised or ignored. Instead family problems are relegated to their proper place in life, as ways of challenging and testing the capabilities of families. Difficult times can tear families apart but can also make families stronger. Through the BOUNCE BACK! Resiliency

Program, schools can play a significant role in communicating to families the key personal and environmental processes that help all families cope with the challenges that are part of everyday life.

Resilient families

The Australian Family Strengths Research Project conducted by the Family Action Centre, University of Newcastle (Geggie, DeFrain, Hitchcock & Silberberg 2000) has identified the strengths of those Australian families who cope well with life's challenges. These strengths are communication, togetherness, sharing activities, affection, support, acceptance and commitment. The study confirms that families that share these strengths demonstrate resilience when faced with challenges. These eight strengths are described in more detail in the chart below. Another recent Australian study by Howard and Johnson (2000) found that young people who demonstrated resilience despite challenging situations were able to discuss problems with their family members and were encouraged by their family to face difficulties in constructive ways. Family members were also able to recognise and challenge the student's self-defeating talk and learned helplessness.

Family strengths

Quality	Key expression
Communication	Good communication means that family members talk regularly with each other and interact with each other mostly in an open, positive, honest manner. Secrets are rare. Humour is often used in their communications and the family values the humour.
Togetherness	Togetherness is the invisible 'glue' that bonds or connects family and gives family members a sense of belonging. An important ingredient of togetherness is that family members share many similar values, beliefs, morals, experiences and connections.
Sharing activities	When families share, they participate with each other (and as a unit) in activities such as sports, camping, playing games, reading stories, socialising, hobbies and holidays.
Affection	Family members can show affection for each other on a regular basis by hugging, kissing, caring, showing concern and interest for each other and acts of thoughtfulness.
Support	Family members show support for each other when they assist, encourage, affirm, reassure and look out for each other. Where support is a key strength in a family, family members feel equally comfortable about both offering and asking for it.
Acceptance	Family members can show acceptance by respecting, appreciating and understanding each other's individuality and uniqueness. Acceptance is a particular strength if family members value each other's differences, and allow each other 'space' to be themselves.
Commitment	Commitment means that family members show dedication and loyalty towards the family as a whole. They view the wellbeing and unity of their family as a high priority. Commitment means not giving up when the going gets tough and not giving up on each other.
Resilience	Families cope when they respond positively to family challenges and adapt to changing circumstances. They deal with challenges through talking, supporting each other, seeking outside support when needed, and pulling together to form a united front to solve problems.

Source: Adapted from the Family Strengths Research Report in Geggie, DeFrain, Hitchcock & Silberberg 2000. This page from Bounce Back® may be photocopied for classroom use.

Clearly it is not helpful if people feel guilty or uncomfortable because their family does not share all of these strengths. If you decide to introduce the Family Strengths study to a group of parents it is important to 'keep things in perspective' by communicating that there is no such thing as the perfect family or perfect parents. The study then serves as a stepping stone to helping families develop a better understanding of the family-based protective factors that allow them to more effectively manage the challenges that every family experiences. You will find ideas on how the Family Strengths study can be used in parent information nights on page 87. Talking to parents about the key messages in the BOUNCE BACK! Resiliency Program provides practical ways to help all families learn the skills of parenting for resilience and encourages them to support the program being taught at school.

Building positive family–school connections

Studies clearly show that everyone in the school community benefits if parents help with student learning or assist in many other ways to facilitate effective schooling. Here are some suggestions for encouraging parent participation in the life of the school.
- Send home a list of ways that parents can become involved at school.
- Send home a questionnaire to find out what expertise or skills parents have to offer to the school.
- Ask parents to make a specific short-term commitment to participate in a particular task or project that has a clear beginning and end (e.g. two hours every Wednesday morning for 6 weeks).
- Display photos of parents and volunteers working with students on a notice board in a high traffic area.
- Thank parents and volunteers who have helped both personally and at a school meeting.
- Ask students to write thank-you letters or make certificates of appreciation for the volunteer parents.
- Publish examples of the students' thank-you letters in the school newsletter.
   Other ideas plus solutions for common problems in working with parents and volunteers can be found in *Different Kids, Same Classrooms* (McGrath & Noble 1993).

Making an extra effort to build positive school–family connections with less resilient students and their families has been shown to be very beneficial for these students and their families. Here are some ways in which schools can make that extra effort for these families.
- Assign someone in the school community to act as a mentor to work with the student and their family on a mutually shared goal: for example encouraging the student to complete school. Have a positive focus on family strengths, solutions, non-blaming.
- Establish a routine communication system between home and school such as email or phone calls so parents can get regular updates on school events and homework assignments.
- Call parents or caretakers of less resilient students on a regular basis, for example monthly, not just when problems arise.
- Write notes free of educational jargon to let parents know what is happening at school.
- Invite parents to be collaborative partners with you in developing the student's resilience, especially in solving school-based concerns that require home and school support, such as school attendance and homework.
- Find out whether parents would like or need suggestions, resources or support to help their child learn at home or to use their time more constructively outside school.
- Work with other school staff and community resources to offer parent support groups or workshops on topics identified by families as important (Christenson & Carroll 1999).

Strategies for involving parents in the BOUNCE BACK! Resiliency Program

Successful school resilience programs see children in the context of their families and families as significant stakeholders in the school community. For many parents the school is a significant social environment. Parents connect with other parents through their children and often develop life-long friendships. Parent evenings and other functions can help to facilitate inter-family connections and families' positive connections with the school.

Previous research on the program has found that many children spontaneously discuss the program with their parents and even report back on how the BOUNCE BACK! coping statements are influencing their parents' behaviour. This section provides ideas on facilitating parent support for and involvement in the BOUNCE BACK! Resiliency Program.

- Send a letter home to parents which describes the program.
- Write a summary in the school newsletter including ongoing information about the program. Consider printing one BOUNCE BACK! acronym coping statement for each month plus information about how some classes are learning the coping statement.
- Provide a list of ways in which the program can be reinforced at home (give two ideas at a time).
- Conduct a parents' information night on the BOUNCE BACK! Resiliency Program.
- Prepare a Parents' BOUNCE BACK! Resource Centre which could include students' work from the program, information sheets, relevant book lists and books to borrow.
- Encourage students to make fridge magnets, badges, posters and bookmarks of the BOUNCE BACK! statements and to take them home to show their parents, display on the fridge and use every day to provide opportunities to practise and reinforce the coping skills.
- Form a BOUNCE BACK! parent team to support the program. Involve the team in gathering data on the implementation of the program. Ideas for evaluating the success of the program are found in Chapter 9. Encourage them to share the success of the program with the whole school community. Print the parent team's names and phone numbers in the school newsletter and encourage other parents to call them if they have any queries about the program. This parent team can become the strongest advocate for the program.

Parent information nights on the BOUNCE BACK! Resiliency Program

This section includes different activities designed to help parents understand the protective factors and resources that underpin the program. Choose the activities that you think will best suit your school community or develop your own activities. Many of the activities in the Teacher's Resource Books can be readily adapted to be workshop activities for parents.

Introducing the BOUNCE BACK! Resiliency Program

Provide a brief overview of the social context of young people today (Chapter 3)
- Define resilience (Chapter 2).
- Use the icebreaker BOUNCE BACK! people scavenger hunt (see next heading below).
- Review the environmental and personal skills (protective factors) that foster resilience and underpin the BOUNCE BACK! program (Chapter 2).
- Hand out the chart on environmental and personal factors that contribute to resilience (pages 15 and 16, Chapter 2).
- Then briefly explain the foundations of the 10 coping statements in the BOUNCE BACK acronym:
  —Optimistic thinking
  —Helpful thinking
  —Using humour
  —Normalising
  —Seeking help.
- Give some examples of how the BOUNCE BACK! statements are being taught at school followed by examples of how your school is addressing some of the environmental protective factors.

People scavenger hunt strategy (see chapter 10) Make a one-page version for each parent

Ask parents to find and write down the name of someone who:
- has found a good way to help their child be more organised at home. Ask them what they do to achieve this.

- has accomplished something recently that they have wanted to do for a long time. Ask them what they accomplished and how they felt about it.
- has a specific goal or dream that they would like to achieve in the next three years. What is their goal or dream and what is one thing they are doing to help them achieve their goal?
- has experienced some kind of difficulty or hardship during the last five years. Ask them what they did to help themselves cope with this difficulty.
- can tell you about a time when humour helped them to cope.
- can tell you about a time when they had to be resourceful in dealing with a problem, that is, they used creative thinking to find a solution.

Parent evenings after the BOUNCE BACK! Resiliency Program has been introduced

The following activities can be used in follow-up sessions after the BOUNCE BACK! Resiliency Program has been introduced. The purpose of these follow-up parent evenings is to sustain parent interest over time in the program. The activities are not in any prioritised order.

- One way to introduce the eight family strengths that lead to family resilience is to ask parents to think about a family they know that demonstrates great family strengths. This family may be their own family or another family they know well. Then ask the parents to work in pairs to interview each other about the family that each of them has in mind. You may like to use the cooperative learning strategy of a timed Think–Pair–Share (McTighe & Lyman 1988) (see Chapter 10) to facilitate an equal sharing of information.
- In groups of three, parents work together to brainstorm what families can do to build family strengths. The ideas from each group can later be collated and sent home to participating parents, or published in the school newsletter. The Family Strengths chart can be given to parents on the night.
- Another strategy for introducing protective family processes to foster resilience is Postbox (Chapter 10). Here are some questions to choose from:
  —List the most significant everyday stressful events or situations that your child encounters.
  —Describe one thing you do to help your child when they are upset about something.
  —What is one of your child's qualities that demonstrates their ability to cope with frustration or something that is difficult for them?
  —If you could wave a magic wand, what is one quality you would give to your child to help them to cope better with the frustrations of life?
  —What is one family activity that your child enjoys sharing with other family members?
  —What is one coping statement you use a lot with your kids (e.g. This too will pass!)?
  —What is one piece of useful advice you got from your own parents about coping?
  —What is one piece of advice you would give young people to help them deal with difficult times in their lives?
  —What is one thing your child has accomplished in recent times that has helped your child feel more competent?
- Use the Partner Retell strategy (see Chapter 10) and ask each parent to share with a partner one useful thing that parents can do to help kids when they experience a frustration or setback (2 minutes each). Then parents report back to another pair.
- Use the Predictor Cards strategy (see Chapter 10). Use an OH transparency to show the five 'how to cope' options to choose from: a sense of humour, accepting what can't be changed, being able to talk to other people, knowing that bad times happen to everyone sometimes, and staying optimistic. Ask each parent to choose the one that they believe has helped them the most to cope with life and write their own response on a piece of paper. Collect and collate them while parents work in a group to predict the results.

In summary

No family is immune from challenges. The extent to which different families are resilient and cope with challenges is linked to their family strengths. Together families and schools offer the most important protective processes to foster resilience in young people today. Strong family–school connections, especially for those students who are most vulnerable, offers hope for helping all in our school community to successfully manage life's challenges. Schools can play a key role in communicating to parents the personal and environmental processes that help all families cope with challenges. Using the BOUNCE BACK program as a tool this chapter describes ways to build strong family–school connectedness. The information sessions on BOUNCE BACK also offer ideas for parenting for resilience. Any school initiative is less likely to survive without parenting support—ideas for gaining parental support for the BOUNCE BACK program are incorporated.

REFERENCES

Christenson, S.L. & Carroll, E.B., 1999, 'Strengthening the family–school partnership through "Check and Connect"'. In E. Frydenberg, *Learning to Cope: Developing as a Person in Complex Societies*. Oxford University Press, Oxford.

Geggie, J., DeFrain, J., Hitchcock, S. & Silberberg, S., 2000, *The Family Strengths Research Report*. Family Action Centre, University of Newcastle.

Howard, S. & Johnson, B., 2000, *Young adolescents displaying resilient and non-resilient behaviour: Insights from a qualitative study—can schools make a difference?* Paper presented at AARE conference, University of Sydney, December.

McGrath, H. & Noble, T., 1993, *Different Kids, Same Classroom*, Longman, Melbourne.

McTighe, J. & Lyman, F., 1988, 'Cueing thinking in the classroom: the promise of theory-embedded tools'. *Educational Leadership*, 45, 7, 18–24.

CHAPTER 8

MANAGING SCHOOL BULLYING

The topic of bullying is in the forefront of media news today. Recent incidents of bullying in schools and other organisations such as the Australian armed services have made media headlines. Media reports on workplace bullying and bullying in sport have further highlighted the extent of the problem.

These incidents have exposed the potential long-term negative effects of being bullied on the academic, psychological and physical wellbeing of young people. Negative outcomes for young people who bully and for the society in which they live have been identified. It is now very clear that students who repeatedly engage in bullying are more likely to become antisocial and unpleasant adults and that bullying which continues without resolution creates cultures of tension, fear, guilt and cruelty. New technology such as emails and mobile phones have made bullying easier and more glamorous and hence harder to tackle.

It's salutary to note that no study in any school anywhere in the world has shown an absence of bullying (Rigby 2001). All schools have *some* problem with bullying, as it nearly always erupts in a large-group situation in which young people co-exist. However it is a *social* problem not just a personal predicament for the unfortunate victim. Growing community concern about peer victimisation and violence in schools has led parents for the first time to start questioning schools about their anti-bullying policies and procedures. Schools are increasingly at risk of legal action if they do not have sound policies and defensible prevention and management practices in place. Our society accepts that all students have the right to feel safe and supported at school. In schools where there is a culture of bullying this basic right is not addressed. The indicators of a school's effectiveness in dealing with bullying are not just whether or not bullying occurs. The real indicators are:

- The extent of bullying
- How seriously the school views the problem
- How quickly, firmly and collaboratively any bullying situation is dealt with by teachers
- How much the school is prepared to invest in preventing the problem in the long term, rather than just trying to manage it in the short term.

The protective environmental processes outlined in earlier sections of the book can help schools to promote a prosocial school culture where bullying is not tolerated. This section builds on these strategies to explain what bullying is, why some students bully their classmates, and what schools and teachers can do to reduce and prevent bullying. The personal skills outlined in the 'People bouncing back' units in the three Teacher's Resource Books provide strategies for helping young people to learn the skills of resilience to lessen their vulnerability to the harmful effects of being bullied. Classroom activities that develop skills to deal specifically with preventing bullying are incorporated in the 'Bullying' units in the Teacher's Resource Books.

The next section outlines **whole-school guidelines** to effective action in preventing and reducing bullying.

Begin with a clear definition of what bullying is

The starting point to preventing and reducing bullying is to begin with a clear definition so everyone in the school community (students, teachers, parents, other staff) shares the same understanding of what bullying means. Bullying is a form of harassment and persecution. In the school context, it could more accurately be termed 'peer abuse'. Bullying involves a pattern of behaviour that incorporates five key factors (Farrington 1993; Olweus 1993; Rigby 2001):

- The recipient is distressed by what is happening.
- The harmful behaviour is intentional and designed to humiliate, hurt, intimidate or disempower the recipient.
- The behaviour constitutes a repeated pattern with the same person(s) being hunted down for mistreatment each time.
- The recipient is unable to leave the situation; young people who are being bullied are expected to attend school and are not in a position where they can readily withdraw from the situation.
- A power imbalance exists between the person(s) carrying out the bullying and the recipient. For example, the bully may:
  —Have others to back them up (whereas the recipient is temporarily without support)
  —Be bigger, older or stronger
  —Have a weapon
  —Be more articulate
  —Have demonstrated that they are prepared to go further in their harmful actions than the recipient is in retaliation.

There are similarities between bullying and other forms of harassment and injustice

The dictionary definitions of 'to bully' are:

> to be overbearing and arrogant; to oppress another; to make repeated attacks on another in order to distress them; to terrorise and tyrannise another in a cowardly manner; to persecute another.

Bullying and oppression/persecution

The dictionary defines oppression as treating another with cruelty and injustice. Persecution is defined as hunting another down in order to persistently harass them and subject them to ill treatment.

Bullying is similar to racial, political and religious oppression and persecution in that:

- The victims in both situations are different in some way that the perpetrators find unacceptable.
- There is stereotyping involved in both situations, where the targets are not seen as individual people but as members of a category, all of whom are the same.
- There is mobbing involved in both situations; that is, people can feel safer being aggressive in a group because there is less fear of the consequences. The likelihood of violence and cruelty always increases where people are able to lose their sense of individual identity and responsibility. It allows them to de-humanise their victims.
- The perpetrators feel self-justified and blame the victim.

Social psychologist Gordon Allport (1954) proposed a step-by step model which explains the processes and dynamics in all forms of bullying, oppression or persecution. The model explains the Holocaust and the Ku Klux Klan just as readily as it explains bullying, especially the kind of bullying that takes place in a 'mob'.

Step One: *Antilocution:* speaking badly about and damaging the reputation of the target in the eyes of others

Step Two: *Stereotyping:* seeing the target as a member of a category rather than an individual, and assuming that all people in that category are the same in a negative way, then using that category name in an insulting way (e.g. Jews, Aboriginals, 'geeks', over-weight people)

Step Three: *Avoidance:* refusing to associate with the target and encouraging others to do the same

Step Four: *Discrimination:* treating the target in a way which denies them the rights that others have

Step Five: *Dehumanisation:* seeing the target as deserving what has happened and hence 'not human' or 'less than human' and therefore not worthy of empathy or concern

Step Six: *Attack:* directly harming the target.

The curriculum materials in the 'Bullying' units in two of the Teacher's Resource Books make age-appropriate comparisons between bullying and contemporary and historical situations of oppression and persecution, such as the Holocaust, the Ku Klux Klan, and the roles of organisations such as Amnesty International in supporting the victims of such oppression and persecution.

Bullying and child sexual abuse

Bullying is also similar to child sexual abuse in that:

- There is a power imbalance in both situations. The targeted person is less powerful in various ways.
- Both forms of harassment and abuse are covert. Other people are not aware of what is happening and the behaviour happens when others who might act to prevent it are not observing.
- Both forms of harassment are exploitative, in that the perpetrator is using the recipient for their own ends.
- Both behaviours are based on threat and intimidation. The victim feels unable to seek support or help for fear of reprisal.

Bullying and terrorism

There are similarities between bullying and acts of terrorism. Terrorism is a deliberate pattern of repeated harmful actions towards another or others which are designed to create a state of fearfulness and give those orchestrating the terrorism a sense of power and domination.

Recognise the different forms of bullying behaviour

Bullying can take many forms and can be both psychological and physical. It can be direct, such as name calling and hitting, or indirect, such as spreading rumours and excluding. Some of the forms are:

- Physical (hitting, pushing, tripping)
- Damage to personal property or violation of privacy (e.g. cutting clothes, hiding pencil cases, writing in diaries)
- Name-calling, verbal insults
- Nonverbal put-downs such as finger signs, rolling eyes, continual staring, laughing at comments or mistakes
- Practical jokes where the victim is humiliated (e.g. accepting invitations and not turning up)
- Insulting emails or phone calls to or about the targeted student
- Spreading of rumours or stories designed to damage reputation
- Deliberate social exclusion, such as turning away, deliberately ignoring, changing seats
- 'Standover' behaviour (e.g. threats of retaliation if students do not behave in certain ways or hand over food or money)
- Forming a group against someone, or persuading others to exclude someone (also known as 'relational aggression')
- Unwanted touching or sexual remarks or intrusions into one's personal life.

Gender differences

Boys who bully

Boys who repeatedly bully or who initiate bullying are more likely to be motivated by a desire for dominance over another and to 'show off' this toughness and dominance to other boys.

Boys are more likely than girls to bully through physical actions such as tripping or hitting but boys also frequently use name-calling and insults. The insults (which are usually untrue) are most often based around one or more of these five themes:

- Homosexuality
- Being overweight
- Being uncoordinated
- Having no friends
- Being 'uncool'.

Girls who bully

Girls are more likely to participate in social bullying or 'relational aggression' (e.g. exclusion, isolation) as well as name-calling and insults. Girls who repeatedly bully tend to be motivated by the desire to be socially powerful over other girls, and to demonstrate their 'popularity' and, this also may be their way of reducing the power or reputation of girls who they feel jealous of or threatened by.

Cross-gender bullying

Verbal bullying is not uncommon across gender lines but girls are subjected to more hurtful and disparaging remarks from boys than vice versa.

Negative social situations which are NOT bullying

There are some negative social situations which contain similar elements, but which are not bullying. In some such situations it is difficult to assess whether an action constitutes bullying or not. For example, 'stirring' can be hard to separate from bullying. Sometimes there is a fine line between stirring and bullying. Students who bully will occasionally take advantage of this fine line to claim that they were only having a bit of fun, not bullying. A helpful response to this claim is, 'If it was just a bit of fun, both parties would be enjoying it, not just one.'

The chart on the following page compares three of the typical socially negative situations with bullying, namely:

- Conflict
- Social isolation and/or rejection
- Random acts of aggression, intimidation or meanness.

Conflict

Bullying is not the same as conflict. Conflict has a mutuality to it and there is usually an issue at the core of the disagreement. Both parties are distressed (although not always equally) and both want a resolution. Peer conflict should be dealt with differently to bullying. Unfortunately some schools get confused and treat a bullying situation as though it is a conflict situation, for example by using mediation procedures where both parties are asked to negotiate a resolution. This is very unfair to the recipient of the bullying whose right to be treated respectfully and to be safe has been violated.

Social rejection and social isolation

Bullying is not the same as social rejection unless it is intended to distress. Intention to distress is seen in the enjoyment of those doing it and in the intensity and deliberateness with which it is done. Seeing a student left out and not wanted in a game is distressing but it needs to be dealt with by using strategies such as classroom activities about prosocial values, requests for cooperation, and sometimes skills training.

Random acts of aggression and intimidation

Bullying is not the same as aggression or intimidation. In the general culture, some people call anyone who intimidates another a 'bully'. However, a student who uses aggression or intimidation has no preference for one specific victim and hence there is no repeated pattern and we do not, in the school context, refer to it as bullying. Aggression and intimidation are antisocial behaviours and totally unacceptable and must be dealt with strongly. However, the most successful strategies

Identifying types of negative social situations in the playground

Social isolation and/or rejection	Conflict
Key features Social exclusion which is not characterised by an intention to distress but by a preference for not playing with or being with another student. Occurs either because of a negative perception of that student or a strong bonding between students in a group which discourages new members. **Appropriate action** • Reference to core values • Classroom meetings to review core values such as acceptance and friendliness • Teaching of social skills (e.g. including others, joining and approaching) • Counselling of the rejected student about strategies for directing social efforts elsewhere	**Key features** A disagreement between students e.g. a falling out between former friends, a dispute between students over a rule, decision or perception of a situation, or an argument of some kind. Characterised by a relative equality of power and a mutuality of distress (e.g. there are mutual accusations and claims). Both parties are seeking a solution to the problem. **Appropriate action** • Teaching of conflict management skills • Classroom meetings to reinforce these skills • Counselling of all parties • Peer mediation or teacher round-table mediation
Random acts of aggression, intimidation or meanness **Key features** Action taken which is intended to harm or distress another student or force them to do something. The targets of the aggression are usually random. There is no pattern, and no one student is targeted on a regular and predictable basis. The aggressor often claims to have been provoked by the behaviour of the target. **Appropriate action** • Warnings • Negative consequences • Counselling for the aggressor and sometimes behavioural contracts	**Bullying or harassment** **Key features** A regular pattern of aggression which is directed towards one student on a regular and predictable basis. The intention is to harm or distress the targeted student. There is a relative imbalance of power in that the student selected for regular harassment is less powerful in some way at the time (e.g. more isolated, less aggressive, smaller, younger, different in some significant way). Only the targeted student is seeking a solution to the problem. • **Appropriate action** • Reference to school rules and core values • Warning cards followed by graduated negative consequences • Counselling for the targeted student and perpetrators • Restorative justice

for dealing with random acts of aggression and intimidation are often subtly different from the strategies which are most successful with bullying.

Have a clear picture as to why some students bully others

It is useful to understand why some students may bully others. It is also helpful to understand why other students DO NOT bully their peers. There also needs to be some awareness of the process that allows some students to become indifferent when they see others being mistreated.

There are 11 main reasons why students engage in bullying behaviour towards peers. In some schools, several of these reasons operate together.

1 There is a school culture which encourages and supports bullying.
2 They are in an immature stage of moral development.
3 They do not realise what they are really doing because they have framed it differently and lack awareness.
4 They get caught up in peer-group dynamics.
5 It enhances the image of the group they belong to.
6 They bully a member of their own group to maintain the group's norms.
7 They are 'policing' conformity to gender stereotypes.
8 They have been bullied themselves and they are now 'passing it on'.
9 They are protecting themselves from being bullied.
10 It is part of the 'aftershock' when a friendship breaks up.
11 They demonstrate signs of an antisocial personality disorder.

1. There is a school culture which encourages and supports bullying

In some schools where there is a culture of dominance, intimidation and bullying, students who bully are admired for their behaviour and their behaviour is rewarded. This culture endorses 'power over' others as a desirable goal and also endorses 'turning a blind eye' to peer persecution as a way of dealing with it. The students who bully get what they want and they get an ego boost. The culture allows them to feel like they are 'top dog' or 'queen bee'. If schools want to reduce and prevent bullying in schools, they must use strategies that transform the broader culture of the school. Bullying flourishes where students learn that it is safer and more comfortable to do nothing when they witness unjust treatment by others. The culture of a school where bullying is occurring even in a small way needs to be changed. This is a complex and long-term strategy and can take up to two or three years to achieve. There are materials in Chapter 5, the 'Bullying' units and the 'Core values' units that can assist with the creation of a prosocial anti-bullying school and classroom culture.

2. They are in an immature stage of moral development

Most children engage in mild and fleeting forms of bullying and intimidating behaviour at some point in their childhood just as they engage in mild lying and stealing. These behaviours are all aspects of the development of moral thinking. The negative responses and consequences they receive to these brief antisocial behaviours, plus the prosocial moral values which are re-stated by adults when they are reprimanded, help them to further develop their conscience. The majority of students can be expected to *not* engage in the bullying of others after the age of approximately eight. From this age most students have the cognitive capacity to see the perspective of another person and thus respond empathically. Initially, however, children's avoidance of bullying will be based on trying to not get into trouble and they will judge the seriousness of an action by its observable outcomes. Thus they will see that a child who bullies and makes another bleed will be 'naughtier' than a child who hurts someone's feelings. There are classroom activities in the 'Core values' units and the 'Bullying' units that help students to develop their moral thinking in regards to how they treat other people.

3. They do not realise what they are really doing

There are three main ways in which students' lack of understanding about what bullying really is can sustain bullying.

- Many students bully because they don't perceive their behaviour as bullying. They 'frame' their bullying as something else such as 'getting back at someone', 'teaching someone a lesson' or they simply justify their behaviour because they 'don't like that person. They are not nice'.
- Some students think that a student who has been bullied by others must therefore deserve bullying and so it's OK if they also bully this student.

- Many students do not realise that taking part, even in small ways, such as laughing at someone's discomfort, is still bullying. They do not understand that they are an integral part of the bullying process.

There are age-appropriate classroom activities in the 'Bullying' units which can assist with teaching students about what bullying really is and help them to think about their own role in any bullying situation.

4. They get caught up in peer-group dynamics

Bullying can offer some students excitement and arousal and sometimes an escape from boredom. Unstructured, unsupervised time such as at the beginning of lessons before teachers arrive can be a time when bullying occurs. The strategies outlined in this book actively engage students in learning and hence reduce the boredom factor. They also help to create peer connectedness and the safety that comes from belonging. 'Mobbing' is a term which means doing something wrong under the protection of being in a large group all of whom are doing the same wrong thing. The key players in bullying situations where mobbing is involved are:

Prime movers/initiators/ringleaders

The initiators of bullying are usually ringleaders or prime movers who may be serial or career bullies with a pattern of bullying others over years. They are sometimes from family backgrounds that are characterised by a lack of close family bonding between members (Rigby 1997). They frequently have an overinflated and unrealistic sense of their own importance and superiority (Bushman and Baumeister 1998). Many are jealous of certain students and try to reduce their reputations and influence. This group is described further under the category of 'antisocial personality disorder'.

Urgers

Many students collaborate in bullying, even though they don't initiate the harassment. For example, they may urge others on by watching and making encouraging remarks, they may use a disliked nickname when they encounter a certain student, they help to spread hurtful rumours or stories, or they may laugh at the targeted student's discomfort. The urger's motivation is threefold—to enjoy the dominance over another person, to establish themselves as secure members of the group and, sometimes, to avoid becoming a target themselves. The 'Bullying' unit includes self-reflection activities designed to assist students who are 'urging' to look at their own behaviour and understand the concept of a 'lethal chain'. Activities for older students also make links between students who 'mob', and historical issues such as the Nuremberg Defence of war criminals after World War Two, and global issues such as the continuing influence of the Ku Klux Klan.

Bystanders

Many students may take no direct part in bullying. There is very clear evidence that the majority of students are distressed by watching another being repeatedly ill-treated and wish it could be stopped (Rigby 2001). However, they usually do not let teachers know what is happening through fear of retaliation and/or because they believe that telling teachers violates a core value of peer playground behaviour. Many concerned students want to intervene in the process but believe that if they were to say anything to the person bullying it wouldn't make any difference to the outcome. Instead they believe by speaking out it might just rebound and hurt them, so they say nothing. They often do not have the skills to speak up. However, whenever they see or hear of a fellow student being mistreated they feel distressed, unsafe, guilty, disempowered and despairing. The 'Bullying' unit contains activities to teach bystanders attitudes and skills which encourage them to support a student who is being bullied.

5. It enhances the image of the group they belong to

Terwel (2000) and others have described 'the dark side of the group process' which is often masked and not seen by teachers. A group of students can become arrogant and have an over-inflated view of their own 'coolness' and superiority. Their group may choose to attack another student to maintain their over-inflated group image in the eyes of themselves and others. Other students are manipulated into 'realising' the superiority of this group. They exclude a student from their group because their inclusion would reduce their 'superior' group image. They bully the other student so others will understand how inferior this targeted student is in relation to their group. They believe that if they simply ignore the student, others may think they accept or tolerate such characteristics. Such group image maintenance also makes the group feel more cohesive and bonded, but in a very nasty way. By adopting this stance they do not have to accept or tolerate individual differences.

6. They bully a member of their own group in order to maintain the group's norms

Sometimes a complex situation is created where the students who are doing the bullying are supposedly friends of the targeted student. When an individual member of a group is bullied by one or two others (but not the whole group) the stability and future of the group is threatened. Therefore other members are less likely to complain or act on behalf of the target. They are also fearful of becoming the target themselves. The individual chosen for intermittent and (usually) mild bullying is more likely to be one whose characteristics or behaviour are less acceptable to the group. The bullying is usually an attempt to make them 'conform' to the group norms. Sometimes it might be a show of power by a less empathic and more exploitative member (who may be a 'serial' bully).

7. They are 'policing' conformity to gender stereotypes

When a boy or girl behaves in ways that do not conform to the gender stereotyping of the culture or the group, many students may take part in bullying this student. Such bullying behaviour is an attempt to make one student conform to what the students perceive to be gender-appropriate behaviour. At the same time these students affirm their own self-satisfaction at behaving in gender-appropriate ways. One example is where a Year 3 girl was called 'boy' and excluded from conversation because she enjoyed playing cricket. Another situation is where a Year 8 boy was followed by groups of peers and called 'faggot' wherever he went because he did not want to play football and preferred chess.

8. They have been bullied themselves and they are now 'passing it on'

Occasionally a student who has been on the receiving end of bullying will then bully another student. This may occur when the student who has been bullied in the past is in a position of power, such as being older or bigger. Their motivation may be to try to re-establish their reputation, or to feel a sense of power after a period of being powerless. This is a less common pattern.

9. They are protecting themselves from being bullied

Some students find that engaging in bullying in a small way does not make them feel totally responsible for what is happening to another. To some extent they are 'placating' those students whom they perceive as threatening and dangerous.

10. Friendship 'aftershocks'

Sometimes bullying is an after-effect of a broken friendship. Students may have had a 'falling out' over an issue or the former friends may have simply drifted apart. One of the former friends then frequently makes unpleasant comments to the other student while in the company of new friends. This kind of bullying is usually motivated by a desire to impress the new friends and to give an impression that they initiated the break-up of the friendship.

11. They demonstrate signs of an antisocial personality disorder

A small number of 'serial', 'persistent' or 'career' bullies stand out for their relative lack of empathy, and their preparedness to achieve their own goals at the expense of others. These students often initiate attacks on classmates for their own gratification and tend to have more than one victim over time. They like the sense of dominance over another and the 'tough and powerful' or 'socially powerful' image they present to peers. These students are demonstrating some of the typical behaviours of someone with an antisocial personality disorder (or conduct disorder) such as:

- Lack of empathy for the distress of others and hence a relative 'cold bloodedness' in how they treat people, even if that is not immediately apparent
- A belief that they are superior people entitled to break rules
- A belief that using or exploiting people to get what they want is OK because they are cleverer than most.

There appear to be two subtypes of this category. One subtype is more likely to hurt people physically, and they are often cruel or indifferent to animals as well. The other subtype is 'charming' and socially manipulative, and often able to 'hook' other people in. Both subtypes of student have a very high likelihood of developing even more serious antisocial patterns as adults. One study (Olweus 1993) found that:

- 60% were criminally charged before they turned 26 years of age, with their crimes ranging from violence and breaking and entering through to 'white collar fraud'.
- They were more at risk of being violent towards their partners and children.

There has always been a myth in schools that students who repeatedly engage in bullying have low self-esteem and bully other students in order to make themselves seem more adequate. However there is strong evidence to the contrary. There is now a considerable body of research which supports the view that students who bully not only do not suffer from low self-esteem but in fact have a highly inflated or 'puffed up' self-esteem which is ill-founded (Baumeister & Campbell 1999; Baumeister, Smart & Boden 1996; Bushman & Baumeister 1998). They exaggerate to themselves and others their own positive characteristics and hence believe themselves to be superior people. To put this another way, such students are unjustifiably arrogant. The dictionary definitions of arrogance are:

> to make unwarranted claims to superior importance; to claim too much for oneself and be contemptuous of others; to be domineering without respecting the rights of others

Such students often maintain their sense of unjustified superiority by seeking ways to show others how tough, popular, clever or influential they are. They are likely to attack those whose characteristics they see as 'inferior' and hence unacceptable. They may also choose to attack the 'competition,' that is, those students who threaten them by having positive characteristics which others may like or be impressed by. Some students with this antisocial pattern stand out, but others are not always easy to identify. These students can be relatively charming, well presented and seemingly successful. They are often able to influence other students to attack and abuse peers.

Understand why some students *don't* bully others

A review of the factors that discourage some students to engage in bullying illustrates that these students are often the more resilient students or those with more advanced empathy and moral development. Knowing why some don't bully helps to provide us with a focus for preventative practices to assist other students to not engage in bullying. Students who don't bully are more likely to have some of the following characteristics.

They feel that bullying is wrong

These students have strong core values such as support and respect for others, courage and an acceptance of differences. They have high empathy for others and dislike seeing others suffer. They may have families who emphasise that mistreating others is wrong and despicable. In a study by Rigby (1997), nearly half of all students indicated that they would feel ashamed of themselves if they bullied someone because they knew their parents would disapprove of them doing so.

They have higher levels of empathy

Most students who refuse to become involved in the harassment of another have high levels of empathy and they feel very emotionally uncomfortable about the idea of intentionally persecuting and harming another. A study by Rigby (1997) confirmed that most students felt distressed when they became aware that bullying was taking place and had a strong desire for it to be stopped.

They are more socially skilled

They are able to get what they want in socially competent ways, through negotiation and mediation, not through mistreatment of others or manipulation of others. They may also have enough skills to feel confident about intervening or expressing their disgust in bullying situations.

They feel more connected to school

They feel connected to their peers at school in a positive, prosocial way. They like their teachers and feel their teachers care about them and have high positive expectations of them. They do not wish to cause their teachers to disapprove of their behaviour. They feel that the school values, supports and protects them.

Bullying is inconsistent with their self-image

These students have a healthy self-image and gain a positive sense of self through their achievement in one or more domains such as schoolwork, creative arts, sport or friendships. They perceive the role of bully as inconsistent with their other roles such as peer support member, good student, good friend, member of SRC and so on.

They identify with positive role models

They identify with same-age or older students and adults such as parents and teachers who are caring people who accept and value individual differences.

They believe that bullying does not pay off

They understand the possible negative consequences of bullying to others and to themselves and see no value in bullying.

Understand why some students are more likely to be bullied

Although any student can be bullied because of circumstances and school cultures, students who are more likely to be bullied are those who:
- Are shy, emotional and anxious and perhaps lack close friends at that school. This type of student is the most commonly selected target because they tend to provide the students who are doing the bullying with strong emotional reactions
- Are poorly coordinated
- Tend to be inflexible in their thinking and hence excessively rule-oriented
- Lack peer support because they are new at the school or their friends have moved
- Have a 'short fuse' or are overly sensitive and therefore provide more entertainment when upset
- Threaten the image of an individual or group because of their 'difference' (e.g. they might be not trendy, unattractive, too short or tall, effeminate, have a disability, be a member of a minority ethnic or socioeconomic group)
- Are relatively non-aggressive and pacifist in their approach and are less likely to fiercely retaliate if bullied.

The negative effects of being bullied

The psychological damage sustained by the students who are the targets of bullying is usually very severe and can be long-lasting. Many different research studies have identified the following potential negative outcomes for the students who are the targets of bullying behaviour (e.g. Olweus 1994; Rigby 1997, 2001):

Loss of self-esteem

For most students, the desire to be accepted and belong is overriding. The greatest fear of most students is being exposed as inadequate or unacceptable to the rest of the group in which they co-exist. Being bullied does just that to them. Bullying in schools often happens while many people watch. This creates public humiliation, rumours and damage to a student's reputation. Being bullied can also lead to students constructing a 'victim' self-image which makes them feel less powerful in their endeavours. They may believe that the bullying is somehow their fault or that they must deserve some of the unjust and unpleasant things that have happened to them. When they are continually being told that they are inadequate and unacceptable, or they are repeatedly excluded or ill-treated, they start to believe that the messages that they are receiving about themselves must be true. Unlike other students, they have less opportunity to select from a wide range of experiences those which help them to create their own image of themselves. Their view of themselves is imposed upon them by the repeated comments and behaviour of others.

Reduced school achievement

If all of your thoughts are on your intense feelings of anger, fear and humiliation you cannot concentrate on your schoolwork. Students who are bullied always show a reduction in their academic performance.

School absenteeism

Many students will truant or plead sickness in order to stay at home so that they avoid being bullied. They feel they have no other way to protect themselves.

Physical illnesses

Students who are bullied have a higher rate of physical illnesses, especially illnesses which reflect lowered effectiveness of their immune system.

Depression and sometimes attempted or completed suicide

A significant number of students who are being bullied become depressed. Some attempt suicide and some succeed. The ongoing pain, humiliation and isolation create a loss of hope that they can be helped and protected. For others, the depression and suicide attempts occur later in life and are an indirect result of their earlier experiences of humiliation and despair, and their long-term loss of self-esteem. Their earlier experiences of mistreatment that their teachers did not know about or did not stop have led to a loss of hope for a brighter future.

Lack of trust

Once you have been mistreated and abused, you find it more difficult to trust people to be good to you. Students who have been abused by peers, without resolution or support, develop a lack of trust in the school, and in adults and organisations. They also develop a lack of trust in life in general. They learn to perceive others as potential attackers and find it more difficult to form affectionate bonds or take risks in relationships. Sometimes they find that a student who has tormented them as part of a group is also quite pleasant to them on a one-to-one basis and they become quite confused about who can be trusted.

Loss of empathy

Students who have been bullied may become less empathic to others as a result of what they see as a non-empathic approach to them. They start to mistrust and ignore their own feelings of kindness and compassion. As one student put it, 'Why should I care about other people when nobody has shown that they care about what happens to me'. They may begin to see the world as a vicious and unsafe place where you have to get in first to protect yourself.

Parental distress

Parents of students who are bullied also experience psychological distress and more physical illnesses. They feel powerless to protect their child.

The 'Bullying' units in the three Teacher's Resource Books provide activities which teach all students strategies for responding to being bullied. However, it must be emphasised that the bullying is not caused by the behaviour of the student who is on the receiving end. Even if a student is behaving in annoying ways, they still have the right to not be abused and harassed. This is a moral right as well as a right enshrined in our legal system. However, there are skills and attitudes which can assist students to deflect bullying, provide some defence against their attacker's actions, and gain support and protection from those who are empowered and mandated to do so, that is, their teachers.

There are also skills that do not have much impact on the bullying but allow the student on the receiving end to 'maintain face' and feel dignified in the way they respond to it. This is similar to how we feel when we beep our horn at someone who has driven their car in a way that has infringed our rights or endangered us. We have no illusions that our simple gesture will stop that person from behaving like that again, but we feel better because we have done 'something'.

What schools can do about bullying

Changing and preventing a culture of bullying goes hand in hand with building resilient schools and classrooms. This section provides practical guidelines on how to find out what is happening in your school, how to prevent bullying and how to manage bullying when it occurs.

There are four main directions that schools need to take if they are to seriously and effectively address the issue of bullying. These are:

1. Awareness and policy making

Raise the awareness of everyone in the school community about what bullying is and what needs to be done to prevent and reduce bullying. Then the school can start the process of developing a sustainable anti-bullying policy.

2. Identification

All schools have bullying situations. Therefore it makes sense to gain a clearer picture of what you have to deal with by finding out what is happening in your own school, not just once, but on a regular basis. In the next section specific strategies for identification are outlined.

3. Prevention

The prevention of bullying requires increased vigilance, the development of a prosocial school and classroom culture, teacher audit of their own practices, integrated curriculum activities which challenge attitudes and teach skills, a focus on student self-reflection, the creation of safe playgrounds and recess times, the development of supportive peer networks and rigorous teacher supervision. In the next section specific strategies for prevention will be outlined. Classroom materials and activities for prevention are provided in the 'Bullying' units.

4. Management

Many schools will already have in place clearly articulated management steps for bullying. This section provides a review of possible management strategies. The key elements of management are confidential and empathic responding which minimises further harm, the use of warning slips followed by firm and graduated negative consequences for both perpetrators and urgers, mediation only when situations are ambiguous, counselling and support, keeping records, the use of restorative justice, and parental involvement. Details of these aspects of management will be outlined in the following section.

Developing an anti-bullying policy

An anti-bullying policy empowers everyone to deal successfully with bullying. Everyone in the school community should be involved at every stage. This includes students, teachers, parents and at times even those who are more indirectly involved with the school such as the canteen staff, bus drivers and other similar staff. Involving everyone in the process of policy development fosters a whole-school community approach and ensures that the policy is relevant to your particular school's social context. The policy needs to be discussed, drafted, put out for response, revised, implemented and then regularly reviewed. An effective anti-bullying policy should include:

- A statement of the school's stand against bullying
- A definition of bullying with examples of bullying behaviour
- A declaration of the rights of all individuals in the school community (students, teachers, support staff, parents) to be free of bullying
- A statement of the responsibility of members of the school community, that is, to abstain personally from bullying, to actively discourage bullying when it occurs, to report bullying when they become aware of it, and to give support to students who are targets of bullying
- Steps and procedures for teachers to follow when they become aware of a potential bullying situation so that they feel empowered to deal with it; these steps can be based on agreed school management procedures and include the names of staff members who will deal with cases of bullying (Rigby 2001)
- A general description of how the school will prevent and manage incidents of bullying (e.g. counselling, consequences, interviews with parents, restorative justice meetings, suspension and so on)
- An undertaking to evaluate the policy within a specific time frame (Rigby 2001).

Wide dissemination of the policy ensures that everyone in the school community is familiar with it. The policy must be seen to be implemented if students are to have any confidence in it. You can also develop support materials that outline:

- Practical steps for parents to follow if their child becomes involved in a bullying problem at school
- Practical steps for students to follow if they are targets of bullying or if they see someone being bullied.

Identification

Finding out what is happening in your school

Schools can identify the extent of the bullying in the school, where bullying is most likely and who are the main perpetrators and targets by using some of the following strategies.

Observations and teacher data

The starting point is making everyday observations of how students interact with each other in classrooms and playgrounds. Observations can also be made of how staff interact with each other and the quality of their interactions with students and their parents. Teachers may have uncorroborated information which they can write down and have placed in an 'at-risk' file which is only handled by a few senior staff. However, most bullying is covert—teachers do not usually directly observe bullying happening. Therefore to get a true picture of the extent of bullying in your school you will need additional procedures.

Surveys (see BLM 8.1)

Short questionnaires answered anonymously by members of the whole school community can provide reliable estimates of the nature, extent and consequences of bullying for a school community. Schools can devise their own questionnaires to be sent out to parents, staff and students. For example, students can be asked to identify on a class list (or just write names down) anyone whom they have observed bullying someone else or being bullied. The definition of 'bullying' and 'bullied' will need to be explicit, for example:

- A person who deliberately and repeatedly tries to stop others from being included
- A person who repeatedly calls someone names and insults them
- Someone who is regularly insulted or hurt or tormented by others.

Some names will be selected more often and then teachers can keep an eye on those students and collect further observations. If a name is mentioned at least five or six times there is probably something going on. Parents could also be asked to indicate on a questionnaire any information they have about bullying situations and the students involved.

There are also a number of more formal questionnaires developed by Ken Rigby and his colleagues to get information on bullying. There are versions for 5–8 year olds and primary and secondary students. Further details can be obtained at: <www.education.unisa.edu.au/bullying>.

Bully register

Establish a bully register. A sheet can be carried by every teacher on yard duty and they can fill in any information about reported or suspected bullying incidents during recess and lunch times. One teacher should have access to the complete register. In this way patterns can be identified and students who come to the attention of several teachers over time can be warned and, if appropriate, counselled.

A 'hot spot' map

Students can be given a map of the school and asked to place a red dot to show where they have observed bullying to have happened fairly often. This information helps with yard duty supervision.

Balloons

Younger students can be given a sheet of balloons, each one containing the name of a child in the class. They can then be asked to colour in blue the name of any person who has hurt them or their feelings a lot of times. This can be done individually with those children who do not have the reading skills to complete the task. Look for children whose name is mentioned often but also keep a eye on any child whose name is mentioned. Younger children's reports can be less reliable because of the difficulties with conceptualising the concepts of 'hurt' and 'a lot'.

Preventing bullying

The prevention of bullying requires a multifaceted approach that employs preventative environmental processes and also teaches all students the personal skills and values that enable them to respond in bullying situations. Short-term bursts of curriculum activities on bullying have been shown to be ineffective. The preventative efforts and the curriculum activities must be integrated, long term and ongoing across all year levels in the school. Visits to the school by local police or lawyers can highlight to students the severity of bullying. The 'Core values' units in the Teacher's Resource Books contain curriculum activities that contribute to the development of safe, supportive, friendly and respectful classrooms. The 'Bullying' units in the Teacher's Resource Books contain many curriculum activities to provide an anti-bullying curriculum and teach appropriate skills and values. In particular the focus is on:

- Making bullying 'uncool' by:
  —Highlighting the long-term effects of bullying on both the students who take part in bullying and those who are on the receiving end
  —Portraying it as an act of weakness, cowardice and abuse
  —Portraying bullies as predators against whom students need to defend and protect themselves (see BLMs 11.7 and 11.8 for examples) of this link

—Making comparisons between bullying and other forms of global and/or historical abuse, oppression, terrorism and persecution (e.g. the Holocaust, the terrorist attack on the World Trade Centre, the Ku Klux Klan, racial hatred and vilification and sledging in sport)
- Framing the issue of bullying as one of injustice and civil rights
- Pointing out that bullying in the workplace is a serious contemporary and legal issue which has its roots in school bullying
- Challenging the attitude that bullying only happens to those who deserve it
- Analysing the process of 'mobbing' in other contexts such as bar room brawls, soccer riots, lynch mobs and riots
- Encouraging students to reflect on their own contributions to a bullying situation
- Helping students to differentiate between dobbing, acting responsibly and asking for support to solve a problem
- Developing student awareness of the dark side of peer pressure and teaching self-reflective skills to enable them to make good but realistic decisions about what they take part in. The slogans used here are:
  —Don't be a sheep (Lower)
  —Think for yourself (Middle and Upper)
  —A stupid thing is still a stupid thing even if 1000 people say it (Middle and Upper)
- Challenging students' perceptions that if it is not happening to them then it is not their problem and encouraging them to accept that bullying is the responsibility of everyone in the community. The slogans used here are:
  —Bullying spoils things for all of us
  —Everyone is responsible for making sure that the bullying stops
- Developing the courage of bystanders and giving them skills to support a student who is being mistreated
- Looking at the legal issues involved so that students have a strong sense of the law to counterbalance cultural attitudes
- Teaching skills which students can use in bullying situations where they are the potential or actual target. For example:
  —Not attracting the attention of bullies
  —Fooling the bully into stopping
  —Giving assertive warnings
  —Maintaining face so as to appear dignified and not humiliated
  —Accessing adult support in order to redress a situation where their rights have been violated.

A 'five finger' training program for younger students is also outlined. This is based on an idea developed by Gill Brown and Liz Harrop from the Doveton Heights and Wallarano Social Adjustment Centre in Victoria. It involves taking these actions in this order:
- Ignore
- Move away
- Say politely 'leave me alone'
- Call out loudly 'stop annoying me'
- Ask a teacher for support.

There are also many environmental processes which can be implemented which are designed to prevent bullying in a school. These are:
- Building a prosocial school culture
- Increasing school vigilance
- Establishing safe places and stimulating playgrounds
- Facilitating supportive peer networks
- Encouraging students to report incidents of bullying
- Teachers' auditing of their own practices.

Building a prosocial culture

Schools can become training grounds for violence, cruelty and indifference to the distress of others. The answer to this problem lies in the creation of healthy, safe, prosocial and supportive schools and classroom environments. Such a culture starts with the establishment of structures and discussions focused around 'respect and protect'. If older students take a supportive, cooperative and relatively equal role around younger students, they are less likely to attack them. The school and class environmental processes that foster resilience, such as collaborative teacher interaction, positive teacher–student interaction, cooperative learning groups, cross-age peer support and peer mediation, all contribute to an anti-bullying culture as well (see Chapters 5 and 6). If everyone in a school articulates and shares the core values of courage, support, cooperation, acceptance, respect and friendliness, then bullying will be reduced. Students can be taught to identify inappropriate hurtful peer behaviour but they need a conceptual framework and a common vocabulary to do so. The 'Core values' units and the 'Courage' units in the Teacher's Resource Books contain activities which develop these values and concepts.

Eliminating put-downs in the classroom

Put-downs can be defined as critical words or actions whose purpose is to hurt the reputations or self-concept of the recipient. If teachers ignore any put-down that is made towards another student in the classroom they are opening the door to bullying. If there is a pattern of put-downs being made more often towards one or more students you already have a problem with bullying. There has to be a firm 'no put-downs' rule in place. See the 'Bullying' unit in each Teacher's Resource Book for more information about put-downs. The book *Dirty Tricks* (McGrath 1997) contains more details of strategies for reducing put-downs in the classroom.

Increasing school vigilance

Once upon a time teachers were unaware of how much child abuse occurred. Now they know how extensive it can be, and teachers are legally required to look for and report any possible evidence of a child who is being abused or neglected. Similarly, teachers used to be unaware of 75% of the bullying that occurred in schools (Rigby 1996). Now teachers are aware that bullying is a serious and often widespread behaviour in schools, and there is a clear need for greater vigilance and reporting. Bullying occurs in *every* school, so all schools need to be more vigilant in looking for signs of it. Any potential bullying situation which is ignored can be interpreted by students, incorrectly, as acceptance of the behaviour by teachers. Bystanders receive the message that they could be the next to be bullied and that no-one will do anything to prevent it or stop it. Research says that only one-third of students think their teachers are always interested in stopping bullying (Rigby 1996). Yard duty teachers can use a clipboard with pre-printed forms to keep a record of suspected bullying incidents and all students and witnesses involved to identify patterns. These 'at-risk' observations or reports can be either directly dealt with or, if less clear cut, filed with nominated senior staff in the 'at-risk' register. Bullying is most likely to occur:

• Where teachers are not in direct supervision of students (e.g. sports changing rooms, when teachers are late for class or out of the room)
• Where there is overcrowding and hence accidental contact but also protection by numbers (e.g. corridors, canteens, crowded buses)
• Where students are bored.

Establishing safe places and stimulating playground environments

The structure and design of the school playground can increase or reduce the possibility of bullying situations. School playgrounds have not changed much over the last 100 years but students' lives have changed a great deal. Poorly supervised, unstimulating playgrounds and unstructured free time can lead to boredom and unsafe situations in some contexts. Some schools run organised outdoor games at lunchtime with older students acting as referees or organisers. The presence of the older students makes the activities high status. Schools can also designate some rooms or settings as 'safe places', such as:

- A classroom supervised by a teacher for half of lunchtime
- The library, where the librarian reads stories to interested children or runs a book club.

Lunchtime safety without stigma also can be created by the provision of activity groups or clubs. These are run by students for students and being on the committee of these clubs can be an opportunity for a student to have a leadership and/or organising role. Structured activities are available and anyone can join in. For students who are feeling vulnerable or isolated, activity groups and clubs can provide a safe, easy way of feeling protected and becoming involved with other students. Indoor clubs can be based around card games, board games, art, computers, craft activities and puzzles. Outdoor groups can be based around physical activities or treasure hunts. One teacher needs to be in a semi-supervisory role but does not necessarily need to be always present.

Facilitating supportive peer networks

Develop 'supportive friends' structures between older and younger students or between peers. Set up a 'circle of friends' who undertake to go and stand near a student when that student is being bullied. Peer networks can also be used for supportive discussion of how to cope with what is happening in the initial stages, although they should never take the place of teacher action to stop a bullying situation. If there is a peer mediation structure in place, and the students have been well skilled in the techniques of mediation, then mediation can be used as well, but only if:

- The bullying is relatively minor, and
- The bullying has only just started to happen.

Encouraging students to report incidents of bullying

If there is a culture in which reporting of bullying to teachers receives retaliation or condemnation from other students, then students will find it difficult to report bullying situations. This issue of peer pressure is picked up in classroom activities in the 'Bullying' units of the Teacher's Resource Books. Take all reports seriously. It may be difficult for teachers to know who is telling the truth. Just because more than one student in a group provides the same version of a story does not mean that the larger group is telling the truth. There will only occasionally be a neutral witness to verify what actually happened. However, if teachers are known to listen to students who complain of being bullied, they demonstrate to students that it is worth reporting bullying situations. Incident reports on pre-printed forms should be kept on every potential bullying situation. They should include the date, time, place, the people involved, details of what happened, written and signed versions from the people involved in the situation, the names of witnesses, action taken, follow up and the teacher's signature. An anonymous reporting box can work well if it is strategically located for confidentiality, and if it is understood that an anonymous report does not give facts but it does suggest possibilities to be investigated or monitored. Students should also be made aware of the difference between 'dobbing', 'acting responsibly' and 'asking for support'.

- 'Dobbing' occurs when a student is mainly trying to get another student into trouble without trying to firstly solve the problem themselves.
- 'Asking for support' involves seeking a teacher's help in solving the problem when bullying continues and the students cannot stop the situation by themselves. An analogy is when we ask for the support of the police or our supervisor. The slogan is, 'Don't suffer in silence'.
- 'Acting responsibly' means reporting bullying situations to a teacher because someone is at risk of being harmed or is actually being harmed. Harm may be physical or psychological. A student who is being bullied should also be helped to see that if they act responsibly and report what is happening to a teacher, they may also be showing citizenship by making sure that the bullying doesn't happen to other students too.

The difference between dobbing, asking for support and acting responsibility, and the issue of citizenship are picked up in classroom activities in the 'Bullying' units of the Teacher's Resource Books.

Teachers' auditing of their own practices

Teachers are in a position of power with young people. Senior staff are in a position of power over junior staff. Some teachers are insensitive, aggressive or cruel towards their students, but not many. Sometimes teachers under stress unwittingly use sarcasm and intimidation to achieve some sense of control (Rigby 2001). It is therefore worthwhile for teachers to assess their own practices. Are they unwittingly creating a negative culture of dominance and intolerance by the way they interact with some students, and/or by tacit approval for certain types of student behaviour? Verbal responses such as 'not you again!' or nonverbal responses such as raised eyes when acts of bullying are reported can convey negative expectations. Sometimes teachers unwittingly create situations which facilitate bullying, for example by using grouping practices or team selection processes which facilitate peer exclusion. The way in which teachers at a school interact with each other is often reflected in the way that students treat each other. It is helpful for teachers to consider working together as a staff to develop their own code of conduct both towards students and towards their colleagues. The code might contain:

- Not using sarcasm
- Treating each other with respect
- Talking to the person with whom you have a grievance before going to a senior staff member
- Asking for mediation when there is a problem
- Honouring everyone's right to dignity.

Establishing a student anti-bullying committee

Schools can create student committees whose brief is to plan campaigns and projects that will reduce bullying in the school. Committee members may also be asked to take on the role of someone with whom a student can discuss what to do about a bullying situation.

Establishing buddy systems

Buddy systems allow a student to feel that there is another, older, student to whom they can turn if they have a problem with bullying. This system can be in place routinely for all students (e.g. Year 5/6 with Year K–2; Year 11 with Year 7/8/9). It can also be put in place on an individual basis by request or on the advice of a teacher. This can be a first response action without more intrusive teacher intervention. However, even when there is a buddy to help a student deal with a bullying situation, it is still vital that the school continues to monitor the situation and if the student and the buddy cannot change the situation the school needs to step in. The buddies also need to be trained in support skills.

Managing bullying

Every incident of bullying must be dealt with immediately, swiftly and unambiguously. There needs to be a clear message to the school community that bullying behaviour is totally unacceptable and always will be and that it will be immediately dealt with. It is a good idea to monitor the ongoing interactions and relationships between students after dealing with bullying situations and incidents. Sometimes, when students perceive that the 'heat is off', they resume bullying the same student as before.

Confidential, unambiguous, immediate and empathic responding which minimises further harm

Teachers should ensure that when a student reports to them that they are being bullied, the student is not placed at further risk by their actions. For example, they need to make sure that other students do not get the impression that the recipient 'dobbed'. Instead teachers can say to the student(s) involved in the bullying situation, 'Other teachers (teachers on yard duty) and/or some students in this grade/other grades have reported to me that you have been observed bullying other students'.

Alternatively, let the bullies know that their names were mentioned frequently in the 'bully' category in the surveys which have been conducted.

As adults, we would ask a manager in a restaurant to deal with an offensive drunk at another table if they did not respond to our requests to stop their behaviour towards us. The manager has power and authority in that situation which we don't have. We would feel insulted, disempowered and angry if the manager did not take us seriously or did not believe our story. The bullied student needs to feel supported and protected in a climate of trust, confidentiality and hope. The student should also be able to negotiate solutions to the problem with a clear understanding as to what limitations are placed upon them.

The use of warnings followed by firm, graduated consequences

A school's anti-bullying policy should include a list of graduated strong sanctions for bullying. A warning slip can be the first step, followed by community service punishments. More serious consequences can follow, such as exclusion from certain activities and from the social life of the playground. An example of a 'warning slip' is:

> Some of the teachers and students in this school have observed/reported that you have been harassing other students. This is your first and last warning to stop this behaviour. Your behaviour will now be closely monitored by all teachers. If this behaviour continues, your parents will be called in and you face possible suspension.

The issuing of a warning slip automatically places a student 'on watch'; that is, teachers are asked to keep an eye on them in high-risk situations. Teachers can make explicit to the student who is bullying that they understand the motivation behind the harassing behaviour as another way of giving a first warning. They can then re-state the rule. For example:

> 'Jodie, it seems to me that you are trying to make Carly feel small and impress the other girls with your social power. This is not acceptable and is against the rules of our class. Please stop doing it now. There will be a penalty if the harassment is repeated.'

Prosocial consequences are punishments that generate positive outcomes for others in the school or class community. They offer a way for students to compensate for their antisocial behaviour towards a member of the school community. Prosocial consequences should result in improved interactions, relationships and group cohesion or affirm the rights and self-esteem of others. They can't be enjoyable tasks and the student should do the activities alone instead of being with others or doing other enjoyable activities. Some examples can be:
* Tidying up the classroom
* Weeding gardens
* Cleaning up the playground
* Putting stuff away.
* Writing an essay on bullying
* Reviewing a book about bullying
* Preparing written materials for younger students with the message 'don't bully'
* Attending a small-group re-education session on bullying at lunchtime
* Being restricted to a certain area of the playground
* Being moved to another part of the classroom or to another class altogether for a short period of time
* Being required to check in with the yard duty teacher twice every lunchtime.

Schools can make it clear to students that urging or collaborating in bullying even in small ways will also attract punishments, as they are 'accessories to the act'.

Counselling and support

Counselling support should be provided for students who have been bullied as well as for students who bully others. Students who have been bullied can negotiate initially with their teachers on the ways they want to access support. For example, they can ask for teacher intervention, individual

counselling, request a social support group of peers with whom to discuss the problem or receive support in the situation, or ask to work on the problem with an older student. Counselling should focus on:
- Reiterating who really has the problem (the students who are doing the bullying ALWAYS have the problem)
- Strategies for coping emotionally with the perceived loss of face
- How to maintain face when on the receiving end of harassment
- Ways to make themselves invisible to students who bully.

Counselling of students who have been engaging in bullying may be provided in a one-on-one setting or in a 're-learning group' and should focus on:
- Training in empathy and becoming aware of the effects on the student being bullied. People who are very close to the context or who participate in the process of bullying often do not seem to understand the feelings of the victim (Terwel 2000)
- Moral reasoning and a sense of 'fair play'
- Helping them to understand the negative outcomes for this student in the long term if they continue to bully others (e.g. loss of self respect, alienation), loss of reputation, parent involvement.

At the same time schools should be tough-minded about rules and punishments in regard to bullying, especially after Year 4. It is not reasonable or realistic to expect the student who has been bullied to resolve the situation themself.

Interviewing and isolating individual students involved in an incident

It is best to interview each student involved in a suspected or confirmed bullying incident separately in an attempt to break down the peer pressure and group bonding aspects of the bullying behaviour. Give each student a summary of the problem and outline the distress that their bullying has caused and the consequences that can follow. Ask the student to provide a plan for changing their behaviour. They can be given a warning about what will happen if they engage in bullying again. The 'Pikas Method of Shared Concern' (Pikas 1989) developed in Sweden might be used in a situation where there seems to be no history of bullying in the background of the students involved. These are the steps.
- Interview each group member separately and ask each student what they know about the bullying situation.
- Help them to acknowledge and understand the suffering of the student who is being bullied.
- Ask them what they feel they could do to help the situation.
- Then interview the student who has been bullied with a view to discussing what they might be able to change about their own responses. Never imply that their behaviour was the cause of the situation because that is never true. Explain to them that even when it is not their fault, there are still some things they can do to not attract the attention of people who are likely to harm them.

This is not an appropriate strategy when there has been a history of previous bullying or when this bullying situation has been going on for some time or has already been confronted on a previous occasion. It can be useful in situations where the students used to be friends.

Keeping records

All incidents with any suspected or obvious bullying component should be documented. It is time consuming to 'get the story straight' but it is a necessary part of the process of achieving social justice. We would expect the same principles to be followed if we made a complaint to the police or a senior person about the behaviour of another. A form can be used which contains information about date, time and location of the incident, people involved, witnesses, each student's written version of what happened and the teacher's version of what they observed or what was reported and their action. The bullying behaviour can be dealt with at the time of the incident but also the form can be filed in the 'at-risk' register so that patterns can be observed over time. It's advisable that everyone involved signs and dates each document. It is helpful to remind yourself that the document could at some stage become a piece of legal evidence. This process also emphasises the severity of the behaviour.

Mediation when the situation is ambiguous

Sometimes situations can be ambiguous and it is useful to try to identify whether the incident is mostly one of bullying, conflict, or peer rejection, or an isolated incident of aggression/intimidation. This assists in the selection of an approach to deal most effectively with the situation. Mediation procedures between one student and another can be appropriate management strategies if there is some ambiguity about the situation or when the situation appears to be more a conflict situation than bullying. With mediation, there is a round-table meeting and each person explains their point of view and listens to the point of view of the other. Then the teacher, or another student who has been trained as a mediator, helps the students involved to negotiate an agreement for peace. However if one person (or persons) is clearly the attacker, mediation is not a fair or useful strategy to employ. One exception is, as stated earlier, when there is a peer mediation structure in place, and the bullying is relatively minor and has only just started.

Using a restorative justice conference (sometimes called community conferencing)

This is a concept drawn from the world of policing. Police officers encounter many situations where one person could be charged with offences against another person in their family or immediate community. Laying charges and going through the courts is an expensive and time-consuming process. The outcome is usually a caution, a fine or minor community service. The victim is often left without a sense of justice having been served. Where these offences are not major in nature (e.g. a neighbour harassing another, an ex-partner stalking another in annoying but not harmful ways), the police often give the 'victim' an alternative approach to going through the courts. The approach has also been used with graffiti damage. The 'victims' can ask for a restorative justice conference in place of more direct legal action. This involves a round-table conference with the victim, the perpetrator, a police officer and, if required, advocates (not necessarily a lawyer—sometimes a family member or friend) for the victim and the perpetrator. The emphasis is on repairing harm. The victim outlines what they want from the perpetrator as a form of compensatory justice. This may include an apology, a written agreement not to repeat the offence against the victim, the replacement of damaged property or whatever else they deem to be appropriate. If the terms can be negotiated, then court action is averted. There is a record of the process and, if the perpetrator does offend again, then charges are usually laid against them for the new offence and sometimes for the previous one. This concept can also be used in schools for bullying situations. The Principal is always part of the process. Students who have been bullied may ask for:

- An apology
- A written contract to discontinue the harassment
- A voluntary 'intervention order' in which the student(s) doing the bullying agrees to keep out of the other student's specified space
- The perpetrator(s) to agree to stay within a certain part of the playground
- Replacement for damaged property
- The perpetrator to be moved into another class or to another seat.

Parental involvement

Parents are part of the school community and will value the opportunity to be part of the process of identifying, reporting and dealing with bullying. Parental involvement in the development of the school's anti-bullying policy will also ensure greater parental support.

Parents whose child has been bullied can feel as though they are the victim too. They can be more distressed over their child being bullied than for any other school situation, despite understanding how difficult it is for teachers to be aware of what is happening and to stop it. Parents often feel angry because of the unfairness and disempowerment of bullying. They may feel guilty because they chose the school as a safe place for their child and it did not turn out to be as safe as they had hoped. They may feel embarrassed because they fear that others do not like their child or see him or her as 'weak'.

Parents may be tempted to deal with the situation and speak directly to the bullying child or their parents. It's important to reassure them that the school will deal with the problem and ask them not to intervene directly unless it is happening outside the school context. Sensitive procedures for handling the situation are critical to successful management. Parents want:

* To be heard and understood
* To receive empathy and concern
* To be reassured that the problem is being taken seriously and that action will be taken in both the smaller picture and the bigger school picture
* To be reassured of the child's strengths and successes, especially in the social area
* To be kept informed of any further incidents
* To be given updates as to whether or not the action taken by the school has been successful in eliminating the problem.

A combination of several factors tends to propel parents towards the removal of their child from the school or towards litigation, for example:

* An indifferent attitude or response by the school
* Blame being attributed to their child for what has happened
* Failure of the school to take specific action to stop the problem
* The school's keeping further incidents secret
* An attitude to either the child or themselves of 'not you again!' by the school.

There is a high risk that parents who are unhappy about the way the school handled the bullying of their child will tell many other parents. Such talk can seriously damage a school's reputation.

Schools as safe places where all students feel protected

Students have the right to attend schools where they feel safe and protected and where bullying is recognised for what it is, peer abuse. The effects of bullying on targeted students have been shown to be serious and long lasting. There is a growing intolerance in schools and the community for bullying and the associated social injustice. The positive and effective steps being taken in some schools provide a rationale for a sense of optimism about the possibilities of lowering the incidence of bullying in our schools and enhancing the resilience of students involved in bullying, even in minor ways. The preventative and management strategies that schools can take are actions to build resilient schools.

REFERENCES

Allport, G., 1954, *The Nature of Prejudice*. Doubleday, New York.

Baumeister, R.F. & Campbell, W.K., 1999, 'The intrinsic appeal of evil: Sadism, sensational thrills, and threatened egotism'. *Personality and Social Psychology Review*, 3(3), 210–21.

Baumeister, R.F., Smart, L. & Boden, J.M., 1996, 'Relation of threatened egotism to violence and aggression: The dark side of high self-esteem'. *Psychological Review*, 103, 1, 5–33.

Bushman, B.J. & Baumeister, R., 1998, 'Threatened egotism, narcissism, self-esteem, and direct and displaced aggression: Does self-love or self-hate lead to violence?'. *Journal of Personality and Social Psychology*, 75, 219–29.

Farrington, D.P., 1993, 'Understanding and preventing bullying'. In M. Tonney & N. Morris (eds), *Crime and Justice: Volume 17*, University of Chicago Press, Chicago.

McGrath, H., 1997, *Dirty Tricks. Classroom Games Which Teach Students Social Skills*. Longman, Melbourne.

Olweus, D., 1993, *Bullying at School: What We Know and What We Can Do*, Blackwell, Oxford, UK.

Olweus, D., 1994, 'Bullying at school: Long term outcomes for the victims and an effective school-based intervention program'. In R. Huesmann (ed.), *Aggressive behaviour: Current Perspectives*, Plenum Press, New York, 97–130.

Pikas, A., 1989, 'The common concern method for the treatment of mobbing'. In E. Roland & E. Munthe (eds), *Bullying: An International Perspective*. David Fulton, London.

Rigby, K., 1996, *Bullying in Australian Schools and What to Do About It*. ACER, Melbourne.

Rigby, K., 1997, 'What children tell us about bullying in schools'. *Children Australia*, 22, 2, 28–34.

Rigby, K., 2001, *Stop the Bullying: A Handbook for Schools*. ACER, Melbourne.

Terwel, J., 2000, *The group as arena: The dark side of group process*. Paper presented at the American Educational Research Association conference.

MEASURING ASPECTS OF RESILIENCE

This chapter includes assessment instruments for both students and teachers.

For students, there are questionnaires which provide:

• A self-report of the number of environmental protective processes and resources in their lives
• A self-report of how well they think and act resiliently
• A report of their perceptions of the level of class connectedness in their classroom (primary only).

For teachers there are two tools for self-reflection which assess:

• Their perceptions of the level of class connectedness in their classroom (primary only)
• The degree to which their current classroom practices foster student resilience.

All of these measures rely on self-reporting and self-report measures have some limitations. The most telling statement about self-report instruments is 'garbage in means garbage out'. If the young person completing a self-report does not understand the question or gives what they think is the 'correct' answer, or simply does not know very much about themselves, then the results will be less reliable. A student's report of their skills, attitudes or behaviour does not necessarily reflect their actual behaviour. Low scores on the instruments can, however, alert teachers to areas that require further investigation and possible intervention.

The purpose of the measurement instruments

The assessment instruments have two broad purposes. These are:

Identification and needs analysis

All of the instruments can be used to identify less resilient students and their areas of need, and to offer some direction for addressing those needs.

Evaluation of change

All of the instruments can also be used to assess changes after specific interventions or after the implementation of the BOUNCE BACK! Resiliency Program.

The table on the following page provides a list of the different assessment measures, with a summary statement of the specific purpose of each measure.

In summary, these are the assessment options:

At the Lower primary level (Years K-2)

• The teacher can read out to each child the questions (modified if necessary) from the middle version of the PEPS (page 119) and record their answers
• The teacher can complete the TARFIC (primary version page 142) to reflect on and assess the degree to which their current classroom practices foster student resilience.

A SUMMARY OF ASSESSMENT MEASURES IN THIS CHAPTER

Area assessed	Names of instrument	Where	Purpose	Who completes it			
				Teachers	Students: Lower (5–8 yrs)	Students: Middle (9–10 yrs)	Students: Upper (11–15 yrs)
Classroom practices which foster resilience	TARFIC Teacher Assessment of Resilience Factors In their Classroom	Page 140 onwards	Self-reflection by teachers about the degree to which their classroom practices foster student resilience. To identify areas where changes can be made.	Yes One primary and one secondary version			
The number of external protective processes and resources in a student's life	PEPS Protective Environmental Processes Scale	Page 116	To assess the number of external protective resources in a student's life. To identify students who need the school to 'fill in the gaps' with school-based resources where possible.		Middle version can be administered individually to children by the teacher	Yes	Yes
Resilient skills and attitudes	PRASE Protective Resilience Attitudes & Skills Evaluation	Page 122	To assess students' self-reported resilient attitudes & skills. To identify areas where extra teaching of personal coping skills and attitudes would be helpful. To assess the progress of the program.			Yes	Yes
Classroom connectedness	SPOCC Student's Perception Of Class Connectedness	Page 136	To assess a student's perception of the degree of class connectedness in their class.			Yes	Yes—but only primary students or secondary students with one main teacher
	TOCC Teacher's Observations of Class Connectedness	Page 139	To assess a teacher's perception of the degree of class connectedness in their class.	Yes One version for primary teachers only			

At the Middle primary level (Years 3–4)

Students can complete:
- the PEPS (Middle version page 119) to report on the environment protective processes in their lives
- the PRASE (Middle version page 130) to self-report their level of resilient skills and beliefs
- the SPOCC (Primary version page 137) to communicate their perceptions of the degree of connectedness in their classroom.

Teachers can complete:
- the TOCC (Primary version page 140) to report on their perceptions of the level of connectedness in their classroom
- the TARFIC (Primary version page 142) to reflect on and assess the degree to which their current classroom practices foster student resilience.

At the Upper primary level (Years 5–6)

Students can complete:
- the PEPS (Upper version page 116) to report on the environmental protective processes in their lives
- the PRASE (Upper version page 123) to self-report on their level of resilient skills and beliefs
- the SPOCC (Primary version page 137) to communicate their perceptions of the degree of connectedness in their classroom.

Teachers can complete:
- the TOCC (Primary version page 140) to report on their perceptions of the level of connectedness in their classroom
- the TARFIC (Primary version page 142) to reflect on and assess the degree to which their current classroom practices foster student resilience.

At the Lower secondary level (Years 7–8 or above)

Students can complete:
- the PEPS (Upper version page 116) to report on the environmental protective processes in their lives
- the PRASE (Upper version page 123) to self-report on their level of resilient skills and beliefs.

Teachers can complete the TARFIC (secondary version page 147) to reflect on and assess the degree to which their current classroom practices foster student resilience.

The PEPS: Protective Environmental Processes Scale

The PEPS is a student self-report instrument that assesses the number of external processes and resources for developing resilience in an individual student's life. There are two versions of the PEPS:
- PEPS Middle version for students aged approximately 8 to 10 years
- PEPS Upper version for students aged approximately 11 to 15 years.

How the PEPS can be used

The PEPS can be used to:
- Assist teachers to identify students who have a comparatively low number of protective external processes and resources for developing resilience. If a student is identified as having fewer external resources than most, then the school can consider:
    —Setting up a relationship for that student with one caring adult, not necessarily a teacher
    —Helping the student feel more connected to school in a number of ways (see Chapter 5).
- Identify students who do not feel connected to a teacher. This can then be addressed by actions by the teacher(s).
- Assess, after re-administration, whether specific students have more or fewer external protective processes and resources than on the first administration.

PEPS: Protective Environmental Processes Scale—Upper version

| My name is |
| My class is |
| Today's date is |

Please answer these questions. Tick YES if it is TRUE.
Tick NO if it is NOT TRUE.

Item	Yes	No
1. I have at least one parent who I feel close to. I can talk to them when I'm worried.		
2. I often hang around with kids who don't get into trouble and live near me.		
3. I regularly go to church or another place of worship.		
4. I can name one teacher at my school who is interested in me and how I'm going.		
5. My school puts on some good activities that I like doing.		
6. I think the kids in my class would care about me if I was sick or upset about something.		
7. I belong to a sporting team or a club outside school.		
8. I can name someone about my age who I could talk to if I had a problem.		
9. I think this is a safe school to go to because other students don't hurt or pick on others very much.		

Item	Yes	No
10. At least one of my parents is really interested in my schoolwork and what happens to me at school.		
11. There is one other adult besides my parents or teachers who I feel close to. This person cares about me and is interested in what is happening in my life.		
12. I regularly spend some time with people who go to the same church or place of worship as I do.		
13. I know a teacher who I would talk to if I needed help.		
14. When I'm at school I usually have friends to spend time with at recess and lunchtime.		
15. I look forward to school because I like spending time with the kids in my class(es).		
16. If I had a problem or needed help there is one adult besides my parents or teachers that I could turn to.		
17. I hardly ever feel lonely or left out in class activities.		
18. I think my family really care about me and can see my good points. They would stand up for me.		
19. I'm learning things at school that will help me in my future.		
20. There is at least one teacher at my school who knows me pretty well.		
TOTAL		

PEPS: Result chart—Upper version

This result chart provides an opportunity to break down the student's total score into each of seven protective environmental processes/resources that foster resilience.

Score one point for each 'Yes' statement. The highest possible score is 20. The higher the score the more protective environmental processes and resources that are available to the student. In general, a score lower than 12 is of concern.

Name of student:			
Date:			
Aspect of resilience	**Items**	**The highest possible scores are:**	**Student's score**
Participation in a spiritual community • Attending a place of worship • Socialising with church members	3, 12	2	
Family belonging • Parental closeness and support • Parental interest in school life • Family appreciation and loyalty	1, 10, 18	3	
Supportive friends/Peer connectedness • Feeling cared about by peers • Peer support and concern • Peer companionship • Enjoyment of being with classmates • Not feeling lonely or left out	6, 8, 14, 15, 17	5	
Teacher connectedness • Teacher interest • Teacher support • Teacher knowledge of student	4, 13, 20	3	
School/class connectedness • Engagement in school life • Safety • Meaningful purpose to school	5, 9, 19	3	
One caring adult • Interest and care • Appreciation and support	11, 16	2	
Community connectedness • Association with prosocial neighbours • Team or club participation	2, 7	2	
TOTAL		20	

PEPS: Protective Environmental Processes Scale—Middle version

My name is
My class is
Today's date is

Please answer these questions. Tick YES if it is TRUE.
                            Tick NO if it is NOT TRUE.

Item	Yes	No
1. I can talk to my mum or my dad when I feel sad or worried.		
2. I go to church.		
3. My teacher likes me.		
4. I like the work we do in my class.		
5. The other children in my class like me and care about what happens to me.		
6. I have a friend my age whom I can talk to if I feel sad or worried or upset.		
7. I feel safe at this school because other kids don't hurt me or say mean things to me.		
8. My mum or dad talks to me about my schoolwork and what happens to me at school.		
9. There is another grown up (not my parents or teacher) who likes me and helps me.		
10. I usually have other children to play with at school.		

Item	Yes	No
11. My teacher would be happy to talk to me if I had a problem or I was feeling sad or worried.		
12. I belong to a club or team outside school.		
13. The people in my family really care about me and see the good things about me. They stand up for me.		
14. I spend a lot of time doing good things with my family.		
15. I look forward to school because I enjoy being with the other children in my class.		
16. My school has many ways for you to show what you are good at.		
17. I have a brother or sister who cares about me and I can talk to them if I feel worried or upset.		
TOTAL		

PEPS: Result chart—Middle version

This result chart provides an opportunity to break down the student's total score into each of seven protective environmental processes/resources that foster resilience.

Score one point for each Yes statement. The highest possible score is 17. The higher the score, the more protective environmental processes and resources that are available to the student. In general, a score below 11 is of concern.

Name of student:			
Date:			
Aspect of resilience	**Items**	**The highest possible scores are:**	**Student's score**
Participation in a spiritual community • Attending a place of worship	2	1	
Family belonging • Parental closeness and support • Parental interest • Family appreciation and loyalty • Family sharing of activities • Sibling support	1, 8, 13, 14, 17	5	
Supportive friends/Peer connectedness • Peer liking and caring • Peer support and concern • Enjoyment of being with classmates	5, 6, 10, 15	4	
Teacher connectedness • Teacher liking • Teacher support	3, 11	2	
School/class connectedness • Liking for the class activities • Safety • Opportunities for affirmation	4, 7, 16	3	
One caring adult • Interest and support	9	1	
Community connectedness • Team or club participation	12	1	
TOTAL		17	

The PRASE: Protective Resilient Attitudes and Skills Evaluation

The PRASE is a self-report instrument which assesses:
- The resilient attitudes held by students
- Their confidence about coping in certain situations, and
- Their perceptions of their coping skills.

There are two versions of the PRASE. These are:
- PRASE Middle version for students aged approximately 8–10 years
- PRASE Upper version for students aged approximately 11–15 years.

Upper version (for students aged approximately 11–15 years)

The 28 items in the Upper version reflect the ten statements in the BOUNCE BACK! acronym as well as three aspects of future success; recognising the importance of persistence, hard work and effort, and having a sense of control over one's future (through goal setting etc.).
- For nine of the ten BOUNCE BACK! coping statements there is one item in a positive direction and one item in a negative direction.
- For the tenth coping statement ('concentrate on the good bits and use laughter') there are two items in a positive direction and two in a negative direction. The 'good bits' and the 'laughter' are seen as two similar but different aspects of coping and so they are assessed separately.
- For each of the three aspects of future success there is one item in a positive direction and one item in a negative direction.

Middle version (for students aged approximately 9–10 years)

The 20 items in the Middle version reflect the ten statements in the BOUNCE BACK! acronym. For each of the ten core coping statements there is one item in a positive direction and one item in a negative direction.

How the PRASE can be used

The PRASE can identify non-resilient attitudes and skills or low confidence about coping that inhibit the development of resilience in an individual. Having this knowledge about an individual student gives teachers a chance to:
- Focus on developing those identified coping skills and attitudes in interactions and discussions with that student
- Select those coping skills and attitudes for special focus in class activities or small-group work.

The PRASE can also identify whole-class patterns that are helpful in directing extra attention in the program to specific coping skills and attitudes.

The PRASE can be re-administered to ascertain progress in student learning of the skills and attitudes taught through the BOUNCE BACK! acronym.

Protective Resilient Attitudes and Skills Evaluation (PRASE)—Upper version

My name is	
My class is	
Today's date is	

Instructions: Place a tick in the box that shows how you feel about each statement:

TRUE: I think this is TRUE.
UNSURE: I am UNSURE about this.
NOT TRUE: I think this is NOT TRUE.

Item	True	Unsure	Not true
1. If one thing goes wrong for me, then everything else usually goes wrong too.	x	u	a
2. When you're upset about something, the best thing to do is to talk about it with someone who cares about you.	a	u	x
3. When things go wrong for me, it's usually because it's all my fault.	x	u	a
4. When things go wrong, it's a total waste of time looking for anything good in the situation.	x	u	a
5. Everyone makes mistakes sometimes and its normal. Mistakes help you learn things.	a	u	x

Item	True	Unsure	Not true
6. I can often find the funny side of a bad situation after a while.	a	u	x
7. It's OK to have problems or worries sometimes. Everybody does.	a	u	x
8. When something goes wrong in one part of my life, I try to remember that the rest of my life is OK.	a	u	x
9. Even when I know something can't be changed, I still get really upset about it.	x	u	a
10. It doesn't make any sense to worry too much about something bad that could happen but hasn't happened yet.	a	u	x
11. When bad things happen in your life, they're likely to affect your life for a long time.	x	u	a
12. Making mistakes and getting things wrong means that you're dumb or stupid.	x	u	a
13. I have some plans for my future life and I think my future should be pretty good.	a	u	x
14. To make your life better, you have to take some reasonable risks and sometimes move out of your comfort zone.	a	u	x

Item	True	Unsure	Not true
15. I don't see much point in working on something when it gets hard to do.	x	u	a
16. People should sort out their own personal problems and not have to ask for help.	x	u	a
17. You can choose how badly you feel about something that upsets you.	a	u	x
18. When a bad thing happens in my life there's never anything funny about it.	x	u	a
19. Some people can go through life with no problems, setbacks or worries.	x	u	a
20. When something goes wrong for me, there are many different reasons why. It's not always just my fault.	a	u	x
21. Sometimes you have to put up with something you don't like and just learn to live with it.	a	u	x
22. If something bad *could* happen, then I worry about it because it probably *will* happen.	x	u	a
23. Finding the good things in a bad situation, even though they are small, often helps you feel a bit better.	a	u	x

Item	True	Unsure	Not true
24. If I succeed at something it's usually because I've tried hard and didn't give up.	a	u	x
25. I often feel that I have little or no control over what happens to me.	x	u	a
26. If I think there is any risk of failing or embarrassing myself or looking stupid in a situation I try to avoid that situation.	x	u	a
27. When something goes wrong in my life, I might feel unhappy for a while but then things usually get better quickly.	a	u	x
28. Feelings just happen to you and there is nothing you can do to change how you think and feel about a situation.	x	u	a

Coping statements in the PRASE—Upper version

The following table shows the items that relate to each coping statement and whether the item is scored in a positive or negative direction.

		Positive direction	Negative direction
B1	Bad times don't last. Things always get better.	27	11
O	Other people can help if you talk to them. Get a reality check.	2	16
U	Unhelpful thinking makes you feel more upset.	17	28
N	No-one is perfect—not you and not others.	5	12
C1	Concentrate on the good things (no matter how small) and use laughter.	6, 23	4, 18
E	Everybody experiences sadness, hurt, failure, rejection and setbacks sometimes. They are a normal part of life.	7	19
B2	Blame fairly—how much was due to you, others and bad luck?	20	3
A	Accept the things you can't change (but try to change what you can first).	21	9
C2	Catastrophising exaggerates your worries. Don't believe the worst possible picture.	10	22
K	Keep things in perspective. It's only one part of your life.	8	1
	A recognition that hard work and effort and persistence results in goal achievement	24	15
	Having some sense of control over one's future	13	25
	Believing that taking some reasonable risks is necessary to improve one's life	14	26

Scoring details for PRASE—Upper version

For the items scored in a positive direction score 2 for a true answer, 1 for an unsure answer and 0 for a not true answer.

For the items scored in a negative direction score 0 for a true answer, 1 for an unsure answer and 2 for a not true answer.

On the answer sheet, the following symbols are used for ease of scoring

a = 2 points

x = 0 points

u = 1 point

The highest possible score on the PRASE (Upper) is 56. The higher the score the more resilient attitudes and skills that the student has.

Scoring for PRASE—Upper version

Item	True	Unsure	Not true
1.	0	1	2
2.	2	1	0
3.	0	1	2
4.	0	1	2
5.	2	1	0
6.	2	1	0
7.	2	1	0
8.	2	1	0
9.	0	1	2
10.	2	1	0
11.	0	1	2
12.	0	1	2
13.	2	1	0
14.	2	1	0
15.	0	1	2
16.	0	1	2
17.	2	1	0
18.	0	1	2
19.	0	1	2
20.	2	1	0
21.	2	1	0
22.	0	1	2
23.	2	1	0
24.	2	1	0
25.	0	1	2
26.	0	1	2
27.	2	1	0
28.	0	1	2

Result sheet for PRASE—Upper version

			Highest possible score	This student's score
Student's name:				
Student's class				
Date of assessment:				
B1	Bad times don't last. Things always get better.	27 & 11	4	
O	Other people can help if you talk to them. Get a reality check.	2 &16	4	
U	Unhelpful thinking makes you feel more upset.	17 & 28	4	
N	No-one is perfect—not you and not others.	5 & 12	4	
C1	Concentrate on the good things (no matter how small) and use laughter.	6 & 23 4 & 18	8	
E	Everybody experiences sadness, hurt, failure, rejection, and setbacks sometimes. They are a normal part of life.	7 & 19	4	
B2	Blame fairly—how much was due to you, others and bad luck?	20 & 3	4	
A	Accept the things you can't change (but try to change what you can first).	21 & 9	4	
C2	Catastrophising exaggerates your worries. Don't believe the worst possible picture.	10 & 22	4	
K	Keep things in perspective. It's only one part of your life.	8 & 1	4	
	A recognition that hard work and effort and persistence results in goal achievement	24 & 15	4	
	Having some sense of control over one's future	13 & 25	4	
	Believing that taking some reasonable risks is necessary to improve one's life	14 & 26	4	
	TOTAL SCORE		56	

Protective Resilient Attitudes and Skills Evaluation (PRASE)—Middle version

My name is
My class is
Today's date is

Instructions: Place a tick in the box that shows how you feel about each statement:

TRUE: I think this is TRUE.
UNSURE: I am UNSURE about this.
NOT TRUE: I think this is NOT TRUE.

Item	True	Unsure	Not true
1. If one thing goes wrong for me, then everything else always goes wrong too.	x	u	a
2. If you have a problem you should talk to someone about it.	a	u	x
3. When things go wrong for me, it's always my fault.	x	u	a
4. When a bad thing happens to me, it's impossible to find anything funny or good about it.	x	u	a
5. It's OK not to get everything right all the time. Nobody's perfect and mistakes help you learn things.	a	u	x
6. Even when I know something can't be changed, I still get really upset about it.	x	u	a

Item	True	Unsure	Not true
7. It's OK sometimes to have problems or worries. Everybody does.	a	u	x
8. When something goes wrong in one part of my life, I think about the parts of my life that are still good.	a	u	x
9. If you look hard you can find some funny parts and some good bits even in a bad situation.	a	u	x
10. If something bad *could* happen I don't worry too much about it because it probably won't happen.	a	u	x
11. When bad things happen to you they go on forever.	x	u	a
12. Making mistakes and getting things wrong means that you're dumb.	x	u	a
13. People shouldn't have to ask other people to help them solve their problems.	x	u	a
14. If you try, you can change your feelings, even if you're really upset.	a	u	x
15. Some people never have any problems or worries.	x	u	a
16. Sometimes bad things happen to me just because of bad luck.	a	u	x

Item	True	Unsure	Not true
17. Sometimes you have to put up with something you don't like because you can't change it.	a	u	x
18. If something bad *could* happen, then I worry about it a lot because it probably will happen.	x	u	a
19. When something goes wrong in my life, I might feel unhappy for a while but then things get better quickly.	a	u	x
20. Feelings just happen to you and there's nothing you can do about them.	x	u	a

Coping statements in the PRASE—Middle version

The following table shows the items that relate to each coping statement and whether the item is scored in a positive or negative direction.

		Positive direction	Negative direction
B1	Bad times don't last. Things always get better.	19	11
O	Other people can help if you talk to them. Get a reality check.	2	13
U	Unhelpful thinking makes you feel more upset.	14	20
N	No-one is perfect—not you and not others.	5	12
C1	Concentrate on the good things (no matter how small) and use laughter.	9	4
E	Everybody experiences sadness, hurt, failure, rejection and setbacks sometimes. They are a normal part of life.	7	15
B2	Blame fairly—how much was due to you, others and bad luck?	16	3
A	Accept the things you can't change (but try to change what you can first).	17	6
C2	Catastrophising exaggerates your worries. Don't believe the worst possible picture.	10	18
K	Keep things in perspective. It's only one part of your life.	8	1

Scoring details for PRASE—Middle version

The items scored in a positive direction score 2 for a true answer, 1 for an unsure answer and 0 for a not true answer.

The items scored in a negative direction score 0 for a true answer, 1 for an unsure answer and 2 for a not true answer.

On the answer sheet, the following symbols are used for ease of scoring

a = 2points

x = 0 points

u = 1 point

The highest possible score on the PRASE (Middle) is 40. The higher the score the more resilient attitudes and skills that the student has.

Scoring for PRASE—Middle version

Item	True	Unsure	Not true
1.	0	1	2
2.	2	1	0
3.	0	1	2
4.	0	1	2
5.	2	1	0
6.	0	1	2
7.	2	1	0
8.	2	1	0
9.	2	1	0
10.	2	1	0
11.	0	1	2
12.	0	1	2
13.	0	1	2
14.	2	1	0
15.	0	1	2
16.	2	1	0
17.	2	1	0
18.	0	1	2
19.	2	1	0
20.	0	1	2

Result sheet for PRASE—Middle version

				Highest possible score	This student's score
	Student's name:				
	Student's class				
	Date of assessment:				
			Items		
B1	Bad times don't last. Things always get better.		11 & 19	4	
O	Other people can help if you talk to them. Get a reality check.		2 &13	4	
U	Unhelpful thinking makes you feel more upset.		14 & 20	4	
N	No-one is perfect—not you and not others.		5 & 12	4	
C1	Concentrate on the good things (no matter how small) and use laughter.		4 & 9	4	
E	Everybody experiences sadness, hurt, failure, rejection, and setbacks sometimes. They are a normal part of life.		7 & 15	4	
B2	Blame fairly—how much was due to you, others and bad luck?		3 & 16	4	
A	Accept the things you can't change (but try to change what you can first).		6 & 17	4	
C2	Catastrophising exaggerates your worries. Don't believe the worst possible picture.		10 & 18	4	
K	Keep things in perspective. It's only one part of your life.		1 & 8	4	
	TOTAL SCORE			40	

Student's Perceptions of Classroom Connectedness (SPOCC)

The SPOCC assesses students' perceptions of the emotional and social climate of their classroom and their sense of classroom connectedness. There is only a primary version of the SPOCC, as at the secondary level it is likely that students would respond differently for different classes. However, the SPOCC can be used by secondary teachers with a class of students with whom they spend a significant amount of time.

How the SPOCC can be used

The SPOCC can be used to:
- Identify individual students who do not feel connected to their classmates and/or their teacher or who do not feel safe in the classroom
- Assess the perception by the whole class of the emotional and social class climate, by collating the frequency of the responses of all students in the class
- Identify the areas that concern or disappoint many of the students in the class so they can be addressed
- Ascertain, after re-administration, if there have been improvements in the class climate and class connectedness as reflected by more positive perceptions by individual students and the class as a whole.

Scoring the SPOCC

All items are scored in a positive direction.
- Each 'Mostly true' response = 3 points
- Each 'Sometimes true' response = 2 points
- Each 'Not true' response = 1 point.
  The highest possible score is 45. The higher the score, the more the students feel connected with their classmates and the teacher.

SPOCC: Student's Perceptions of Classroom Connectedness—Primary

| My name is |
| My class is . |
| Today's date is |

Instructions: Place a tick in the box that shows how you feel about each statement:

Item	Mostly true	Some-times true	Not true
1. Most of the kids in this class like each other.			
2. I like being in this class.			
3. People in this class hardly ever treat each other in a mean way.			
4. There are very few fights among kids in this class.			
5. Students in this class are kind towards each other.			
6. The kids and the teacher in this class know each other pretty well.			
7. No-one feels left out and lonely in this class.			
8. This is a safe class to be in because no-one tries to hurt you or your feelings.			

Item	Mostly true	Some-times true	Not true
9. I look forward to being with the other kids in this class.			
10. I feel like I belong and am accepted in this class.			
11. 'Put-downs' rarely happen in this class.			
12. Our class gets on well with our teacher.			
13. Most people in this class think more about the good things that happen than the bad.			
14. Most kids in this class work with each other to solve problems that happen in the class.			
15. Most students in this class care about what happens to their classmates.			
SCORES FOR EACH COLUMN			
TOTAL SCORE			

Teacher's Observations of Classroom Connectedness (TOCC)

How the TOCC can be used

This instrument assesses teachers' observations and perceptions of the emotional and social climate in their classroom. It can be used to:
- Identify those areas observed by the teacher to be reflective of a negative social climate and low levels of class connectedness
- Identify discrepancies between the students' perceptions as a class and their teacher's perceptions.

Scoring the TOCC

All items are scored in a positive direction.
- Each 'Mostly true' response = 3 points
- Each 'Sometimes true' response = 2 points
- Each 'Not true' response = 1 point.

The highest possible score is 45. A high score indicates that the teacher believes that there is a strong positive emotional and social climate in their classroom and hence high levels of class connectedness. If there are large discrepancies between the whole class's results on the SPOCC and the teacher's result on the TOCC, then the TOCC is less likely to be an accurate reflection of what is really happening in the classroom.

TOCC: Teacher's Observations of Classroom Connectedness—Primary

Instructions: To what extent are these statements true for your class? Tick the box that best shows to what extent you agree with each statement.

		Mostly true	Sometimes true	Not true
1.	Most students in this class like each other.			
2.	Students like being in this class.			
3.	Students hardly ever treat each other in a mean way.			
4.	There are very few fights between students.			
5.	Students get on reasonably well with each other.			
6.	The students and I know each other pretty well in this class.			
7.	No-one feels left out and lonely in this class.			
8.	Students feel safe. They don't expect to be hurt or have their feelings hurt.			
9.	Students look forward to seeing each other.			
10.	Students feel like they belong and are accepted by their classmates.			
11.	'Put-downs' rarely happen.			
12.	I get along well with the class.			
13.	Most students have a positive attitude and focus more on the good things that happen than the bad.			
14.	There is a strong sense of hope and confidence in this class.			
15.	Students care about what happens to their classmates.			
	SCORES FOR EACH COLUMN			
	TOTAL SCORE			

Teacher Assessment of Resilience Factors In their Classes (TARFIC)

There are two versions of the TARFIC.

Version one is for teachers in a primary school setting. It contains 63 items, with 7 items in each of the following nine categories:

- Creating a safe classroom environment
- Building healthy self-esteem
- Supporting students
- Teaching initiative, goal setting and problem-solving skills
- Developing helpful and optimistic thinking
- Creating a prosocial classroom culture
- Encouraging cooperation
- Building relationships
- Teaching the skills of conflict management.

Version two is for teachers in a secondary school setting. It contains 48 items, with 6 items in each of the following eight categories:

- Creating a safe classroom environment
- Building healthy self-esteem
- Supporting students
- Teaching initiative, goal setting and problem-solving skills
- Developing helpful and optimistic thinking
- Creating a prosocial classroom culture
- Encouraging cooperation
- Building relationships.

How the TARFIC can be used

The TARFIC can be completed by teachers in order to:

- Reflect on their classroom practices, organisation and management in order to identify areas which need development in the interests of fostering resiliency in students
- Assess the level of changes they have made in their class by completing it again at a later stage
- Remind themselves of the classroom protective factors that contribute to student resilience
- Identify areas where the whole school is doing well and areas where the whole school staff can develop their practice. If teachers collate their results and hand in a result sheet anonymously, the whole-staff findings can be helpful in identifying school needs in regards to professional development or program planning.

TARFIC: Teacher Assessment of Resilience Factors In their Classroom—Primary

Tick the box that best shows how you feel about each statement.

SATISFIED: I am satisfied with my efforts and results in relation to this aspect of my teaching and classroom management.

OK: This aspect of my teaching and classroom management is OK but I am continuing to work on it.

UNDERDEVELOPED: This aspect of my teaching and classroom management is underdeveloped and needs more planning and input.

	Satisfied (3)	OK (2)	Under-developed (1)
Creating a safe classroom environment			
I am fully aware of my school's procedures for dealing with bullying.			
I see bullying as a serious issue and I act swiftly to deal with bullying when it occurs.			
I clearly communicate to my students that bullying is not acceptable under any circumstances.			
I make sure that there are no put-downs in my class.			
I follow up on any incidents of nasty behaviour towards a class member.			
I teach my students the skill of disagreeing with each other in a respectful way .			
Each term, I give students the opportunity to anonymously tell me about any bullying.			
TOTAL SCORE			
Building healthy self-esteem			
I let my students know that I aim to build them up, not bring them down.			
I identify and build on students' strengths more than I focus on their limitations.			
I give students positive feedback on their work and behaviour whenever I can.			
I operate from a 'multiple intelligences' framework to identify students' strengths and to diversify my curriculum.			
I plan opportunities for my students to showcase their strengths to others and practise public performance.			
I remember to differentiate between students' actions and who they are as people.			

	Satisfied (3)	OK (2)	Under-developed (1)
I have realistic but high expectations for every student.			
TOTAL SCORE			
Supporting students			
I identify areas where students need extra academic or emotional support and then provide it.			
I persist in trying to support difficult and challenging students even when I feel discouraged and don't seem to be getting anywhere.			
I am approachable and available for students to talk to about their personal concerns.			
I know a lot about each student's background details, interests and learning needs.			
I keep ongoing records and notes on each student, apart from formal records.			
I structure opportunities to talk to students when I know they have a problem.			
I have a written individual behaviour or learning support plan for students who need behavioural support or learning support.			
TOTAL SCORE			
Teaching initiative, goal setting and problem-solving skills			
I provide many opportunities for students to show initiative, that is, take responsibility for thinking of ideas, planning and completing a project.			
I provide many opportunities for students to make decisions and have choices about their work and their school environment.			
I stress the importance of persistence and effort.			
I teach the skills of creative thinking and problem solving using many real-life problems.			
I encourage students to set specific goals and monitor progress.			
I encourage students to work with me to solve any problems that arise in the classroom.			
At the end of each term, I ask students to reflect on their achievements and on goals they have achieved.			
TOTAL SCORE			

	Satisfied (3)	OK (2)	Under-developed (1)
Developing optimistic and helpful thinking			
I convey a sense of optimism when discussing global issues (e.g. the environment, endangered species).			
I make it clear that I see mistakes as necessary learning experiences.			
I model being optimistic about situations that affect both my students and myself.			
When things go wrong, I stress the temporary nature of the problem.			
I model not expecting perfection from myself or others.			
I 'positive track' throughout the day i.e. highlight the positives.			
I use humour as much as I can in my classroom.			
TOTAL SCORE			
Developing a prosocial classroom culture			
I make it clear that I expect students to be kind, friendly, respectful and supportive towards each other and I model this in my interactions with them.			
I directly teach social skills and don't just hope they will happen in group work.			
I provide opportunities for students to practise social skills in planned class activities and games.			
I negotiate classroom rules, expectations and consequences with my students.			
I consistently enforce their consequences if students break the class rules but not in a negative way.			
I give students the opportunity to offer constructive and positive feedback and affirmation in response to the contributions of other students.			
I highlight and model the importance of understanding and accepting differences between people.			
TOTAL SCORE			
Encouraging cooperation			
I use cooperative learning structures on a regular basis.			
I find opportunities to work collaboratively with my colleagues and make students aware of this.			
I have some assignments and long-term projects where students work in a team.			

	Satisfied (3)	OK (2)	Under-developed (1)
I re-teach the skills of cooperation before I set tasks for students that require these skills.			
I use mostly random grouping to mix students up and break down 'cliques' that might exclude others.			
I model the process of negotiation by negotiating whatever I can with students.			
I highlight examples of effective teamwork and cooperation in the media.			
TOTAL SCORE			
Building relationships			
I organise structured opportunities so that my students can get to know each other more.			
I share part of myself with my students so they can get to know me as a person.			
I teach students skills for identifying and managing their anger.			
I make sure that I have many fun group activities and games in my classroom where they can enjoy each other's company.			
I make sure that students who have been away know they have been missed and that I and their classmates are pleased to see them back.			
I make sure that all students get a chance to work with all other students as much as possible.			
I create opportunities for students to be part of buddy systems and peer support programs.			
TOTAL SCORE			
Teaching the skills of conflict management			
I see conflict as a normal part of life and communicate that understanding to my students.			
I directly teach conflict management skills in my classroom.			
I encourage my students to resolve their own conflict issues in a way that everyone wins.			
I have an area in my classroom where students in conflict can go to sort things out.			
If students can't sort out their own conflicts, I offer to mediate.			
I have posters around the room which remind students about how to manage disagreements.			
I hold classroom meetings to help resolve conflict and deal with issues that arise in the classroom.			
TOTAL SCORE			

TARFIC: Scoring my personal profile—Primary

A score can be calculated for each section as well as for the overall checklist.

- Each response of SATISFIED is given a score of 3.
- Each response of OK is given a score of 2.
- Each response of UNDERDEVELOPED is given a score of 1.
  The profile sheet below gives you a quick picture of your results on the TARFIC.

	Total possible score	My score
Creating a safe classroom environment	21	
Building healthy self-esteem	21	
Supporting students	21	
Developing initiative, goal setting and problem-solving skills	21	
Developing helpful and optimistic thinking	21	
Developing a prosocial classroom culture	21	
Encouraging cooperation	21	
Building relationships	21	
Teaching the skills of conflict management	21	
TOTAL SCORE	189	

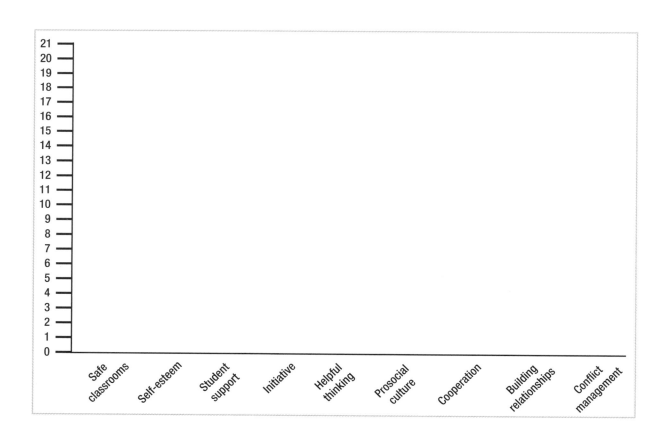

TARFIC: Teacher Assessment of Resilience Factors In their Classroom—Secondary

Tick the box that best shows how you feel about each statement.

SATISFIED: I am satisfied with my efforts and results in relation to this aspect of my teaching and classroom management.

OK: This aspect of my teaching and classroom management is OK but I am continuing to work on it.

UNDERDEVELOPED: This aspect of my teaching and classroom management is underdeveloped and needs more planning and input

	Satisfied (3)	OK (2)	Under-developed (1)
Creating a safe classroom environment			
I am fully aware of my school's procedures for dealing with bullying.			
I see bullying as a serious issue and I act swiftly to deal with bullying when it occurs.			
I clearly communicate to my students that bullying is not acceptable under any circumstances.			
I make sure that there are no put-downs in my classes.			
I follow up on any incidents of nasty behaviour towards a class member.			
I teach my students the skill of disagreeing with each other in a respectful way.			
TOTAL SCORE			
Building healthy self-esteem			
I identify and build on students' strengths more than I focus on their limitations.			
I give students genuine positive feedback on their work and behaviour whenever I can.			
I operate from a multiple intelligences framework to identify students' strengths and to diversify my curriculum.			
I remember to differentiate between students' unacceptable actions and who they are as people.			
I plan opportunities for my students to showcase their strengths to others and practise public performance.			
I have realistic but high expectations for every student.			
TOTAL SCORE			
Supporting students			
I identify areas where students need extra academic or emotional support and then try to provide it.			

	Satisfied (3)	OK (2)	Under-developed (1)
I persist in trying to support difficult and challenging students even when I feel discouraged and don't seem to be getting anywhere.			
I am approachable and available for students to talk to about their personal concerns. I know a lot about each student's background details, interests and learning needs.			
I structure opportunities to talk to students when I know they have a problem.			
I keep ongoing records and notes on each student, apart from formal records.			
TOTAL SCORE			
Teaching initiative, goal setting and problem-solving skills			
I provide many opportunities for students to show initiative, that is, to take responsibility for thinking of ideas, planning and completing a project.			
I provide many opportunities for students to make decisions and have choices about their work.			
I stress the importance of persistence and effort.			
I teach the skills of creative thinking and problem solving using many real-life problems.			
I encourage students to work with me to solve any problems that arise in the classroom.			
I encourage students to set specific goals and monitor their progress.			
TOTAL SCORE			
Developing optimistic and helpful thinking			
I make it clear that I see mistakes as necessary learning experiences.			
I model being optimistic about situations that affect both my students and myself.			
When things go wrong, I stress the temporary nature of the problem.			
I model not expecting perfection from myself or others.			
I communicate a hopeful attitude in regards to global issues that we discuss.			
I use humour as much as I can in my classroom.			
TOTAL SCORE			

	Satisfied (3)	OK (2)	Under-developed (1)
Developing a prosocial classroom culture			
I make it clear that I expect students to be kind, friendly, respectful and supportive towards each other and I model this in my interactions with them.			
I directly teach social skills and don't just hope they will happen in group work. I provide opportunities for students to practise social skills in planned class activities and group work.			
I consistently enforce fair consequences if students break the class rules but not in a negative way.			
I give students the opportunity to offer constructive and positive feedback and affirmation in response to the contributions of other students.			
I highlight and model the importance of understanding and accepting differences between people.			
TOTAL SCORE			
Encouraging cooperation			
I use cooperative learning structures on a regular basis.			
I use table teams.			
I review the skills of cooperation before I set tasks for students that require these skills.			
I use mostly random grouping to mix students up and break down 'cliques' that might exclude others.			
I have some assignment tasks which are completed cooperatively.			
I model the process of negotiation by negotiating whatever I can with students.			
TOTAL SCORE			
Building relationships			
I organise structured opportunities so that my students can get to know each other at the start of the year.			
I share part of myself with my students so they get to know me as a person.			
I make sure that I have fun activities and educational games in my classroom where they enjoy each other's company.			
I make sure that students who have been away know that they have been missed.			
I make sure that all students get a chance to work with all other students as much as possible.			
I take the time to talk to students socially, not just about their work or their behaviour.			
TOTAL SCORE			

TARFIC: Scoring my personal profile—Secondary

A score can be calculated for each section as well as for the overall checklist.
• Each response of SATISFIED is given a score of 3.
• Each response of OK is given a score of 2.
• Each response of UNDERDEVELOPED is given a score of 1.
　The profile sheet below gives you a quick picture of your results on the TARFIC.

	Total possible score	My score
Creating a safe classroom environment	18	
Building healthy self-esteem	18	
Supporting students	18	
Developing initiative, goal setting and problem-solving skills	18	
Developing helpful and optimistic thinking	18	
Developing a prosocial classroom culture	18	
Encouraging cooperation	18	
Building relationships	18	
TOTAL SCORE	144	

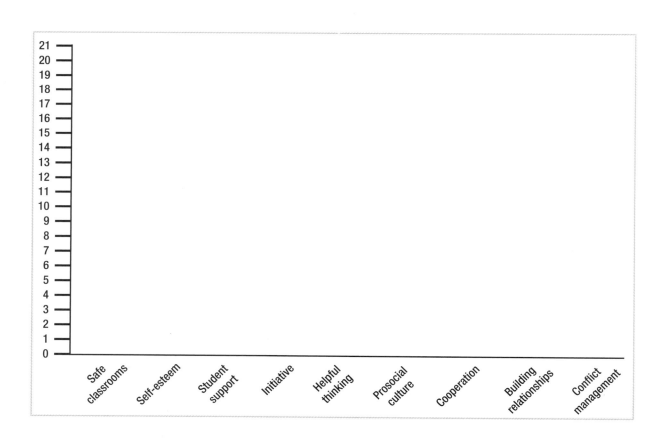

Assessing changes in aspects of resilience

Changes in individual students' resilient behaviour

It can be difficult in a school context to directly observe an increase in student resilience. A 'sleeper' effect often occurs in regard to learning social and personal skills; many students understand and learn new coping skills and attitudes but they often lie 'dormant' for a while until the students either:

- Are more mature
- Feel confident about actually using the skills, or
- Encounter a situation that urgently requires their use.

Nonetheless there are some indicators of increases in individual student resilience, such as:

- Making more references during student discussions or in other contexts to the kinds of statements used in the BOUNCE BACK! acronym
- Having a higher overall score on the PRASE (or higher scores in specific sub-sections) when it is readministered at a later point
- Having a higher score on the SPOCC, indicating that the student perceives improvement in class connectedness
- Demonstating more effective coping behaviour under challenging conditions such as being embarrassed, making a mistake, losing a friendship
- Achieving better learning outcomes
- Demonstrating improved peer relations and higher levels of social acceptance (see *Friendly Kids, Friendly Classrooms* for primary classroom measures of social acceptance).

Changes in the bigger picture

Some of the assessment instruments can be used to gauge the bigger picture of changes that are happening in the school. Documenting progress and improvements is not only important to justify the inclusion and continuation of the BOUNCE BACK program but can also provide a 'positive feedback loop' to sustain the implementation of the program.

Possible indicators that the program is having a positive effect on the bigger picture of student resilience and student behaviour across the school might be:

- Improved frequency of scores on the SPOCC for a class, a year level, or across the school
- Improved frequency of scores on specific items of the SPOCC for a class, a year level, or across the school
- Improved frequency of scores on the PRASE for a class, a year level or across the school
- Improved frequency of scores on specific aspects of the PRASE for a class, a year level or across the school
- An increase in observations of classmates' acts of cooperation, kindness and support for each other
- Fewer student absences from school
- Fewer sick-leave days taken by staff across a year
- Lower rates of playground disputes and misbehaviour as reported by the teachers on yard duty
- Lower rates of senior staff involvement with student misbehaviour
- Lower rates of students being suspended from school
- Reductions in the number of bullying incidents reported
- Reductions in the numbers of students changing schools for unclear reasons
- Increase in parent involvement in school
- Positive feedback from parents about student behaviour at home and at school
- Improved learning outcomes because students are no longer distracted from learning.

REFERENCES

McGrath, H. and Francey, S., 1991, *Friendly Kids, Friendly Classrooms*, Longman, Melbourne.

COOPERATIVE GROUP STRATEGIES

Teaching aids for cooperative learning groups

Role cards

Assigning roles to students is an efficient way to ensure group members work productively together. Make some cards that go around the neck on a cord or make badges. Role cards remind students of their role and the social skills associated with that role. One side of the card has the name of the role. On the other side write phrases that the person fulfilling that role might say. For example, checker might say 'explain to me . . .', 'give an example . . .', 'how did we get that answer?'; an encourager might say 'good try', 'have another go', 'great idea'. You will need one set of cards per group.

Talking prompts

Talking prompts remind students whose turn it is to speak, as only the person who holds the prompt is allowed to talk. Other group members' jobs are to actively listen. Use novel talking prompts or work as a class to make an official 'class talking prompt'. Younger students love using small soft animals or small toys. Older children like wrap wristbands or soft balls like koosh balls or other novelty balls. There are even squashy balls with plastic 'spiders' and 'maggots' inside them available from supermarkets. All ages like using a torch with cellophane over the light so it glows when it's turned on in a dim room. Use talking prompts in circle time and Throw the dice. Also use the prompts in cooperative group work if you feel that students are not having an equal say.

Group cooperative learning strategies

These group cooperative learning strategies are described below:
- Before or after?
- Bundling
- Circuit brainstorm
- Cooperative controversy
- Information scavenger hunt
- Jigsaw teaching
- Multiply and merge
- Pairs rally and pairs compare
- Paper plate quiz
- Partner retell
- Postbox

- Predictor cards
- Round table
- Smiley ball
- TEAM coaching
- Think–Pair–Share
- Thirty-word summary
- Throw the dice.

Before or after?

Groups of four compete with each other to be the first to work out the mystery word selected by the teacher from a list of topic-related words.

1 Put students into groups of four and give each of them a role as follows:
   - The writer, who keeps information
   - The decision coordinator, who helps the group to decide
   - The information seeker, who says the group's chosen 'information probe word'
   - The guess coordinator, who directs the group in making their signal to let the teacher know that they want to make their one and only guess.

2 Every group has the right to make only *one* guess as to the word and they can do so at any stage of the game. They signal to the teacher that they want to make their one guess by having all members of the group put both hands in the air and wave them (or any other signal the class agrees on). No person in a group can make a guess unless the entire group agrees.

3 If the group does not correctly guess the word, say 'I'm sorry but your guess is incorrect'. Do not give any feedback on the alphabetical position of this incorrect word.

4 An 'information probe word' is *not* a guess. Each group takes it in turn to choose an 'information probe word' to give to the teacher (e.g. 'We would like some information on the word "bushranger"'). The teacher then gives feedback as to whether that word is before or after their mystery word in alphabetical order (e.g. 'Your word "bushranger" is after/before my word in the alphabet').

5 If at any point in the game the word chosen by a group as its 'information word' is actually the word the teacher has selected, then the game is over and the teacher wins!

6 When a group *guesses* correctly, say 'Your word is the same as mine and you win!'

   Note: You'll need about ten words for years K–2, 20 words for years 3–4, and 40–50 for older students. For younger students have only one word for most of the letters of the alphabet so that they don't have to worry about the order of the second letter. To make the game easier, you can alphabetise the words in an A–Z format. For years K–2 choose a simple category such as Animals. Go through the words on the list. Pair an advanced reader with a less able reader. Ask each pair to make a guess about the word you are thinking of. Give feedback on whether the word is before or after the one you have selected, and write their word under the appropriate letter of the alphabet.

Bundling

Students each have five strips of paper. On each one, they write a different example or answer, according to what is asked for. For example:
- Write down five things about (e.g. the desert/hope/spiders).
- Write down five ways in which we can protect our environment.
- Write down five ways in which people can be honest.

   Students work in a group of 3–5. They pool their pieces of paper and then sort the responses into categories. One person reports their categories to the class. They can also write a paragraph about each category. Use three responses with younger students rather than five.

Circuit brainstorm

Groups of students move around a circuit of question sheets attached to a wall. They write down answers, giving a different response to each sheet from that of the groups that have gone before them.

1 Prepare one large sheet of paper for each group of four students. Give each group a different coloured texta. Attach the sheets to the wall around the room. Now you have a circuit of stations for each group to visit.

2 Think of one question to write in large print on the top of each sheet (called 'stations'). The success of this strategy depends on the quality of the questions. The best questions lead to deeper understanding of the topic and bring out the experiences and perceptions of the group. Good questions have at least six to eight possible answers because each group must be able to give a different answer to that of the other five groups. For example:
   • List one good way to increase exercise levels (theme: health).
   • Name one well-known Aboriginal person and say why they are famous (theme: Aboriginal studies).
   • Give one example of people not treating the environment with respect (theme: the Environment).

3 Note again that all of these questions can be answered in many different ways. They are not just questions with one correct answer.

4 Organise students into groups of three or four using these roles:
   • Writer: writes the group's answer
   • Sheep dog: moves the group efficiently and kindly between stations
   • Spokesperson: reads out the group's 'home station' answers
   • Decision coordinator: helps the group make quick negotiated decisions (optional role).

5 Each group initially starts at one 'station' which becomes their 'home station'. Students quickly brainstorm possible responses to the posted question. Then the group decides which response will be their *one* different answer to the question and the writer writes it on the sheet. Allow 2–3 minutes.

6 Then signal groups to move clockwise to the next station. It is important that they don't go to the next station until all teams are instructed to do so or chaos will reign!

7 They read the responses generated by the previous group and then decide on an additional and different response and add it to the sheet in their own coloured pen.

8 Rotations continue until teams are back to their 'home station'. They then read out the responses on their home sheet to the rest of the class.

Variation

Use the same format with a group of four. Each member of the group has a different question to answer on one sheet each. Then, on the signal, they all pass their sheet to the person next to them until they have responded to all four sheets.

Cooperative controversy

This activity is based on the work of David and Roger Johnson (Johnson, D. & Johnson, R., 1992, *Creative Controversy: Intellectual Challenge in the Classroom*. Interaction Books, Edina: Minnesota). Students argue for one side of a controversial question and then switch and argue for the opposite side.

• Allocate students to groups of four. Each group of four divides into two pairs. These pairs are called Pair A (person 1 and 2) and Pair B (persons 3 and 4).

• The groups are given a proposition such as 'Children should not watch TV during the week and should be limited to a total of three hours on the weekend'. They could also be asked to evaluate a concept or product such as the new cinema complex in the town.

• Then Pair A in each group moves away from pair B a little and discusses the arguments *in support of* this proposition in order to come up with two strong arguments *for* the proposition. At the same time, Pair B discusses the arguments *against* the proposition in order to come up with two strong arguments against the proposition. Arguments should be written down by person 1 in pair A and person 3 in pair B.

- The two pairs return to re-form their group of four. Then person 2 in Pair A summarises their two arguments in favour of the idea. Next person 4 in Pair B summarises their two arguments against the idea.
- Pair A then returns to their working space to come up with one more argument *against* the proposition that Pair B hadn't proposed in their two arguments against.
- Pair B meanwhile tries to come up with one more argument *in favour* of the proposition that Pair A didn't think of. The aim of this stage is to get students to switch their perspective.
- The pairs return to their group and Pair A report their one extra argument against and Pair B their one extra argument for.
- Then all four negotiate to decide on the one strongest argument in favour and the one strongest argument against the proposition. Then they negotiate as a group of four on whether they are in favour of the proposition or against it and they write up their arguments for and against. Each group of 4 appoints one spokesperson who reports to the class on their decision and their strongest argument for and their strongest argument against.

Variation

Students can be asked to undertake research or reading on a topic before they participate in a Cooperative controversy and present a final written project.

Information scavenger hunt

Students work in groups. Post a list of questions about the current theme to which answers are needed. For example:
- What was the name of the inventor of television and in what year was this person born?
- Why do we need a TV aerial?
- What does CIC on a video stand for?

Choose questions that require some research. The first person to give you the correct answer in writing gets a point for their group. The group that has the most points at the end of the week wins.

Jigsaw teaching

Students work in a home group of three, each learning one different sheet of information about a topic. They work with one other student from a different home group who has the same sheet of information so that they are sure they understand their material. Then they return to their home group and teach what they have learned to the others.

1 Prepare a set of three information sheets. Do not put too much information on each sheet. Use a large font. Use different coloured paper for each sheet. Make enough copies so that each group of three can have one set of the three sheets.

2 Organise students into home groups of three. Hand out one sheet from each set of three to each student.

3 Students then form 'expert learning pairs' by pairing up with someone else in the class who has the same coloured sheet. The pairs spend five to ten minutes together to learn the information and make written and visual summaries (e.g. mindmaps) to teach the information to the others in their home group when they return.

4 Each student now pairs up with *another* person in the class who has the same coloured sheet as 'expert teaching pairs'. They show each other their visual summary and practise their teaching of what they have learned. Encourage each student to take ideas from each other.

5 Then each person returns to their home group. In turns they teach the information to the other group members.

6 Make sure each student is given a normal-size copy of all the information at this point.

Variations

- The home group could then make a group mindmap that summarises all of it.
- Follow up with an individual test to show how well home group members have taught each other.
- Use the jigsaw strategy with a group project and research tasks. Students research one of the three topics/people with a partner from another group who has the same task but each student then returns to their home group. Then all home group members pool their information and the group puts together a group assignment.

Multiply and merge

Individually each student makes a list of five 'things' (e.g. the five best snack foods). Then each student pairs up with a second student and they negotiate to merge their lists so they still only have five between them. Then that pair joins another pair to make a group of four and they negotiate to merge their lists so that the group of four has only a list of five. Each group then writes its final five choices on the board. You will need to work out whether the numbers 'fit' the model; that is, you need multiples of four or some adaptations.

Pairs rally and pairs compare

Students sit in pairs with one paper between two students. They take turns at passing the paper to each other and brainstorming and writing responses (e.g. what are dairy foods?). Then they join another pair. One pair reads their list and the other pair ticks their list if they have the same idea. The other pair reads new ideas from their list that the first pair did not mention. The two pairs then write ideas for a combined list.

Paper plate quiz

Each group of four students makes an answering device using a white paper plate held up by a paddle pop stick and sticky tape. One side says 'true' and the other side says 'false'. Students answer questions by showing one side of their paper plate.

1 Prepare a sheet of 8–12 theme-related questions for each group. The questions should be either true or false.
2 In each group allocate roles as follows:
   - Engineer: makes the answering device under the group's direction
   - Mediator: helps the group to make decisions about answers fairly so that everyone feels included and heard; this person needs to be a good listener
   - Time manager: lets people know how time is going but isn't bossy or critical
   - Go-for: collects and returns materials as required.
3 Give each group the sheet of questions and five minutes to decide on their answers.
4 Then read out each question one at a time. After each question, the group member responsible for answering that question holds up the answering device high above their head with their answer facing the teacher.
5 Count the number of 'true' and 'false' responses for each question. Keep them in suspense. Then give the correct response.
6 Repeat the process with the other questions.

Variations

Use questions that have multiple choice (four) answers. Each group can make four cards (A, B, C and D) and a plastic 'pouch' on one side of the plate made from a plastic ringbinder insert.

For younger students use questions which can be answered with 'Yes' or 'No' and read out one question at a time.

Partner retell

Students interview each other in pairs about a specific theme-related area and then summarise what their partner said for another pair or for the class.

1   Select a theme-related question. Organise students into pairs. Tell them that they will be asked to give a summary of what their partner says.
2   One person interviews the other for one or two minutes. Remind them to make 'listening checks' as they listen, that is, stop every now and then and summarise what they have heard so far. No written notes can be used.
3   Partners then swap and the other person becomes the interviewer.
4   Remind them to mentally prepare a 'simple summary', that is, a brief recap of what the person said that does not include small details.
5   Pairs join to form groups of four. Each student then takes turns to summarise their partner's response for the other two people.

Postbox

Students complete a theme-related survey. Then they work in groups to collate the responses and group them into categories. They give a report to the class. This provides information for the teacher as to what the students know or think they know already, how they feel about certain aspects of a topic and the experiences they have had. You will need a sheet of questions per student, scissors to share, and one postbox for each question (e.g. small desktop garbage bins or shoeboxes with slots).

1   Prepare one postbox per group of four. Label them with a number, one for each question asked.
2   Prepare a sheet of questions (one question for each postbox). Give one sheet to each student. The questions should be completed individually without discussion. Questions should have a personal aspect, for example a personal opinion, preference or experience: 'What colour do you most associate with summer?' 'What is your favourite dairy food?' 'Who comes to mind when you think about a politician who has made a big difference to Australia in the last fifty years?' 'In your opinion, what is the best argument for restricting immigration?'
3   They answer the question using as few words as possible and then cut out the question strips and post each one into the appropriately numbered boxes. You may need some crowd control procedures here!
4   Place students in groups of four. Number each group to correspond to the number of questions/boxes. Allocate students in each group to one of four roles:
    •   The 'Go-for': collects the postbox that contains the answers to the question that is the same as their group number; and puts the paper in the recycle bin at the end
    •   Sorter: takes charge of organising the group to sort the answers into categories
    •   Counter: counts and then records the statistics
    •   Mediator: helps the group to make decisions about categories.
5   The task for each group is to sort the answers into no more than four categories and then report to the class. Make sure they are reminded not to lose the 'richness' of their data by oversimplifying the categories. They should also record some typical answers given in each category. Encourage groups to accompany each oral presentation with a diagram or chart on an overhead transparency. Give each group a one- or two-minute time limit for their presentation.

Variation

Write the questions on an overhead transparency. Students write the numbers on their answer strips.

Predictor cards

Students predict the results of a survey based around a single theme-related question with three response options. Each group needs three blank cards.

1 Decide on a topic-related survey question that has three alternative responses. For example, 'Which of these three characteristics is the most important in a friend—keeping their secrets, being fun, or standing up for them?'

2 Ask each student to write their own personal answer on a scrap of paper without talking about their choice to anyone else. Collect their responses.

3 Organise students into groups of four. Tell them that the task of each group is to predict the order of results of the responses you have collected from the whole class. Which of the three responses do they predict will be the most popular response chosen by the class? Which will be the second most often chosen? Which will be the least chosen? Each group will also be asked to give their one strongest reason for their prediction of what they think will be the most common response. During their group discussion they must not mention their own individual answers to the survey question.

4 Allocate roles as follows:
   • Card manager: writes each choice on a card and is the only person allowed to move the cards around to reflect what is being discussed
   • Mediator: listens well and helps the group negotiate their decision by summing up what is agreed and where decisions still have to be made
   • Time manager: lets people know how time is going but does this in a positive way, not in a bossy or critical way
   • Spokesperson: reports the group's predictions and reason to the class.

5 While the groups work together to make their decisions about ranking, the teacher counts the responses to ascertain the correct ranking of responses to the survey question.

6 Each group writes up their ranking decisions plus their reason on paper or card for the bulletin board and reads them out to the class. Then the teacher announces the correct ranking to the class.

Variations

Instead of predicting the results of a survey in which they take part, students can predict:
• The results of a survey question they ask their parents, teachers, or other students in the school.
• The order of known facts, for example predict the rankings of these countries in terms of how many public holidays they have per year (Australia (10), Japan (17), UK (8)).
• The results of future scientific experiments, for example predict the order in which these three growing conditions for carrot tops will be effective (wet cotton wool in the sun; wet cotton wool in the shade; wet cotton wool under glass).
• The results of future measurements, for example predict the order of these places in terms of how far they are from the principal's office (canteen; library; art room).

Round table

Students categorise in a group.
• Groups of three students are each given one A3 sheet, and a set of pictures that represent three categories (e.g. for transport the three categories could be land, sea and air).
• Students paste the picture on their A3 sheet into the correct (category), then they pass the sheet onto the next student who does the same with another picture.

Smiley ball

Use a medium-sized plastic ball with a smiley face drawn on it. Throw or roll the ball to specific children and ask them a question.

TEAM coaching (TEAM = Together Everyone Achieves More)

Students learn basic concepts, facts, spelling or vocabulary in a group. They have a pre-test as individuals, then form groups and pool their scores. They set a group goal and help each other learn for a second test. The aim is to improve and achieve the team's goal, not to do better than other teams.

1 Select ten facts, words or concepts which you want your students to learn to master (e.g. spelling of topic words, definitions of terms, foreign language vocabulary, countries and their landmarks, chemical symbols, scientific concepts).

2 Give all students a pre-test (completed individually) on the facts to be learned. They mark their tests and give themselves a score out of ten.

3 Organise students into groups of four. Ask them to select a group name that reflects something they all have in common. Then allocate the following roles:
   • Statistician/board writer: works out the team's pre-test and post-test total scores, and writes up the team's data on the board
   • Positive tracker: comments on the things that are going well in their team
   • Mediator: helps the team to make decisions about the name of the group and the goal the team sets for the second test
   • Checker/recorder: checks individual and team progress along the way and notes down good ways for remembering particular facts.

4 Draw the following chart on the board:

Team name	Team score on 1st test	Team goal	Team score on 2nd test	Team improvement score

5 Students pool their individual results. The statistician works out the average or the total. The group then decide on their goal for the next test (test completed individually, not as a team) in 15–20 minutes time.

6 The board writer from each team then writes their team name up on the board, their team score on the first test and their team goal *before* each team starts learning the content.

7 Then they spend 15–20 minutes helping each other to find effective ways to learn and remember the facts, concepts, vocabulary or spelling.

8 At the end of the learning period, students individually do the test again with no help from their fellow team members.

9 The statistician works out the team's second average or total test score, and calculates their team's improvement score. The board writer writes this up.

Think–Pair–Share

Students individually reflect on a question and then share their reflections with a partner. Then the pair report the main points of their discussion to the class.

1 Ask a theme-related question or raise an issue (e.g. why do people choose not to vote in elections?).

2 Each student has a minute or two to think of their own ideas.

3 Each student pairs up with another student and they share their ideas.

4 Each pair then shares their main ideas with the whole class.
   You can add a time for each step.

Thirty-word summary

Students work in a group of three to produce a 30-word summary (exactly).

1 Students work in their groups to write a 30-word summary of a lesson, part of a lesson, a chapter, a book or a video.

2 Suggest that the groups start by identifying key words that focus on major concepts presented in the lesson. They then work these key concepts into sentences to make up 30 words.

3 When the summaries are completed, they can write them on visually attractive posters to be displayed around the room for everyone to read.

Throw the dice

Students throw a dice and answer the theme-related but personal question which corresponds to the number thrown.

1 Prepare a sheet of six questions and print a copy for each student. Use questions which require a personal view about or reaction to the topic, a recall of a personal experience related to the topic or a personal preference related to the topic.

2 Give students the sheet of questions the day before the activity so that they can think about their responses to all of them or discuss them with family and friends. This is especially important for socially anxious or shy students.

3 Students sit in groups of four and take turns to throw a dice. The person who throws the dice answers the question on the sheet that corresponds to the number they have thrown. They hold a talking prompt while they answer the question. They then pass the 'talking prompt' to the person on their left, who, having listened carefully, asks them one good question about what they have said. Then anyone else can use the talking prompt and ask the dice thrower a question based on what has been said.

4 Then the second person throws the dice and answers a question that corresponds to the number on the dice and so on until everyone has answered twice.

5 If a person throws the same number again, they should have another throw. However, if a student throws a number that someone else has already thrown, it's OK for them to answer the same question. If the same question keeps coming up they can throw again.

Variations

• For younger students, have a shoe hanger with six compartments (or six separate boxes or containers). Number the compartments 1–6 and put a simple question in each. The student throws the dice, collects the question from the compartment and reads it (or the teacher can do this).

• Consider using two dice and eleven questions.

• Use playing cards instead. Each group of six gets an Ace, a King, a Queen, a Jack, a Ten and a Nine. They are dealt out. Each card corresponds to a question on an OH transparency.

Whole-class cooperative learning strategies

These whole-class cooperative learning strategies are described below:
• Collective classroom research
• Four corners
• Inside–outside circle
• Movers and shakers
• Musical stop and share
• People pie
• People scavenger hunt.

Collective classroom research

Put up a large poster or set aside a large area of the bulletin board. Tell students that everyone will be researching the question asked. All students then look for, research and bring along answers and material on the designated question(s). For example:
• What examples can you find of charitable organisations in Australia and what do they do?
• Where are the rainforests in Australia?

- What are some good kinds of sports or gym equipment for building muscles?
- What are some of the laws relating to . . .
- Who are people famous for their inventions?

Keep a ring binder folder full of empty plastic document envelopes for students to insert any printed or drawn material. Remind students to correctly acknowledge the source of their information.

Four corners

Students go to the corner of the room which reflects their opinion and discuss with the other students in the same corner.

1 Designate the four corners of the room as A, B, C and D. Then draw a diagram on the board with each corner named.
2 Prepare a number of theme-related questions about personal preferences and experiences. Each should have four choices to select from. Here are some examples:
    - Which of these four characters from our book do you most dislike and why?
    - Which of these four reasons for having the Olympics in our home city do you think is the strongest and why?
3 Then ask students to choose the corner which best represents their response and go to it. When they get there, they should discuss why they chose that corner. If there are more than three or four students, they should break into two groups.

Variation
With a larger group, you may need a fifth choice in the middle of the room.

Inside–outside circle

Students answer or discuss a question with the person they pair up with.

1 Students form two concentric circles so each student has a partner. They face each other.
2 The teacher poses a question or issue. One person answers and then they swap.
3 On a signal the outer circle moves two or three spaces and the process is repeated with a new partner and a new question.
4 The questions can be prepared by the teacher and shown on an OH transparency or printed on individual sheets.

Movers and shakers

This is a personal survey in which students give their responses by making specific movements rather than verbally.

Prepare some questions which students can answer with YES or NO and then attach some movement options to each. For example:
- Pretend to bounce a ball with your right hand if you play competition netball or basketball.
- Put your left hand on your hip if you have a moveable toy with elastic bands.

Musical stop and share

When the music stops, students discuss a question with the person nearest to them.

1 Prepare some interesting and personal questions related to your topic. Play music. Ask students to mill around.
2 Start the music. Then turn it off a short time later. Students walk around the room until the music stops and then they take turns to discuss a question posed by the teacher with the person nearest (use an OH projector or a question sheet for each student).
3 Repeat the procedure for each question.

People pie

Students make a pie graph by sitting in a circle in the same spot as the other students who answered the same way they did.

1 Each student has a paper plate.
2 They colour one side blue and add a smiley face. This represents YES. They leave the other side white and add a frowning face. This represents NO. They add a paddle-pop stick for the handle.
3 Ask the whole class a question that requires a 'yes' or 'no' answer, for example 'Do you have a pet?' 'Have you had the mumps?' 'Have you travelled overseas?'
4 All the YES people sit together in the circle, as do all the NO people.
5 Stand in the centre of the circle with a piece of wool and pass it to the people at the ends of the two sections of the circle to make a visual pie graph.

Variation

Students can predict how many will answer 'Yes' and 'No' each time.

People scavenger hunt

Students have a sheet of categories and they walk around and interview classmates to find people who fit those categories.
1 Make a 'Find someone who' sheet with about eight different questions. For example, in a unit on Media they might be asked to find someone who:
  • can sing their favourite commercial and ask them to sing a couple of lines to you
  • likes the same TV show as you and ask them one thing they like about it and write down their name.
2 Students are instructed not to use the same person for a category more than twice and to sit down when they have found someone for each category.

Variations

Have fewer items for younger students and use picture cues.

Grouping strategies

Table teams

A table team stays together for a period of time such as a month or a term. The benefits are that each table team provides an opportunity for connection and the practising of a social skill such as cooperation. To ensure a mixed group consider mixing genders (two boys, two girls), ability (one highly able, two average, one struggling), and races and cultures. Spend some time at the beginning on fun team-building activities to help the group 'gel' and work well together. Take photos of table teams, laminate and display the team photos, and encourage teams to devise a group name. Make the rule that the only way 'off' a table team is to work at the teacher's desk.

Fun ways to form groups

Here are some fun ways to form groups that ensure random allocation. Using different ways means everyone works with different classmates over time, and this helps to build class connectedness. Many use the format of a set of four cards which are the same, which go together or which have a theme in common. You can also write numbers from 1 to 4 on the back of each frame to allocate roles.

Acting or actions

Use sets of four cards with the same sports written on them. Students act out the sport till they find their team members with the same sport written on their card. You could also use actions such as wink, hop, clap hands, skip, take long steps.

Cartoons

Many cartoons have four frames. Find different four-frame cartoons in the newspaper, photocopy them on to card and cut them out. Students match up the cartoon pieces to find their team members.

Categories

Choose a number of different categories such as sea, land and air transport, or animals such as monotremes, marsupials, mammals. Use sets of the same cards (e.g. all kangaroos) or sets of animals in the same category (e.g. all marsupials).

Countries

Make sets of cards about a number of countries. A set should contain four facts (e.g. name of country, its leader, its major river, its capital city, famous monument).

Dictionary cards

Use topic words and write out three or four different forms of the same word family (e.g. bounce, bouncing, bounced or bouncily).

   You could also use sets of cards which contain definitions of the same word (e.g. four different definitions of the word DUCK or HARD or ROUND). Write the words used on the board and let students use a dictionary.

Fact cards

Make question and answer cards, such as an author's name and three books they have written or four facts about a topic such as the first settlement or Egypt.

Humming

Make sets of well-known tunes such as nursery rhymes like 'Baa Baa Black Sheep', 'Twinkle, Twinkle Little Star' or tunes of songs you have been singing in class. Students hum (not sing) the tune to find their team-mates.

Jigsaws

Use postcards, old birthday/Christmas cards or pictures from magazines and make jigsaws. Make sets of four pieces.

Line-ups

Students line up without speaking on the basis of one criterion such as:
• Heights
• Name order in the alphabet (first name, surname)
• Birthdays (month first, then day).
Then count off each group.

Value line-ups

Students line up on the basis of where they stand on an issue that is likely to generate a range of opinions. Possible topics are wearing school uniforms or moral issues such as euthanasia or cloning. The line represents strongly agree at one end to uncertain to strongly disagree at the other end. For younger children the line can represent 'yes' to 'maybe' to 'no'. Form groups by cutting the line in half and getting one half to move along and pair up with people in the other half so you get a range of opinions in each group.

Maths cards

Make sets of cards which contain number facts which all have a total of the same number (e.g. $2 + 4$, $12 - 6$, 2×3 and $5 + 1$). Each team member has to work out the answer to their sum before they can look for their team members with the same answer. They can show their answer without speaking by holding up the correct number of fingers.

Name cards

Write everyone's first name on a card, shuffle the cards and then draw 4 out to get different group combinations.

Playing cards

Use a pack of cards to sort out your groups so all the Fours go together, all the Jacks go together and so on. Use the suits to allocate roles.

Pictures or words of things starting with the same letter

Make sets of cards with pictures of objects that begin with the same letter (or blend or ending) (e.g. a boat, a bee, a balloon and a belt).

RESOURCES AND OTHER TEACHING STRATEGIES

This section provides step-by-step instructions on how students can make the resources that have been referred to in different BOUNCE BACK! units of work. Older students may like to adapt the ideas and design and make their own versions of some of these resources. The second half of the chapter includes other teaching strategies that are not cooperative learning. Like cooperative learning these teaching strategies also actively engage students in learning.

Resources

A–Z of emotions
Balls that bounce
Bounce-backers
Class books
Cube pattern
Electronic matching pairs quiz
Flappers and lift-up circles
Flip book
Fridge magnet frame

Library resources
Mobiles
Music resources
Pop-up toaster: How it works
Puppets and masks
Responsibility pie charts
Things with Springs
Wallet card
Wax-resist badges

A–Z of Emotions

An A–Z list of emotions appears in BLM 11:1. It can be used for writing, drama or categorisation activities.

Balls that bounce—make your own

Students can make their own bouncing balls and then test out the bounciness of their own productions. For a class of 28 students, working in pairs and each making one ball, you will need (approximately):
- Two 2-litre bottles of distilled water (one 2-litre bottle costs $2 in large hardware shops or discount department stores)
- Six bottles of good quality squeeze-bottle PVA glue
- One packet of powdered borax, a water softener available from hardwares (a 500-gm box costs about $6 and goes a long way)
- Fourteen coffee mugs (or similar), teaspoons, metal dessertspoons and ice-cream containers
- Two rolls of paper towel
- Timers or an accurate clock or reliable watches
- Large ice-cream containers and a supply of cold water
- Lots of plastic shopping bags

- A roll of cling wrap
- 28 copies of the instructions (BLM 11:2).

This is a good activity for procedural writing. Since it can take a while for the process to work, it is also a good activity for stressing the need to be persistent. The borax needs to be handled with care and not consumed. Warn students not to leave their creation in the fridge at home in a way which lets smaller children get to it.

None of the containers and tools should sustain any damage from the materials used, but they need to be thoroughly washed afterwards.

This can get a bit sticky so it is best done near a wet area.

Students must wash their hands thoroughly afterwards as borax can dry out the skin.

The mixture can be difficult to get out of hair if students are careless, so it is a good idea to ask students to bring caps to wear on the day or tie back their hair to avoid the possibility of the sticky substance getting stuck in their hair. Keep some De-solvit (or similar) handy in case of disaster. Consider some paper hats like the ones worn by food preparation staff.

When the sticky stuff dries, it can be scraped off most surfaces. But don't flush it down the drain because it will cause blockages. Wait till it dries and then scrape it into the bin.

Students can be asked to devise a method for measuring, timing and graphing the change in the material from a liquid to a solid.

Ask: Why does the mixture change shape again if it is left sitting in the warm air without glad wrap around it? (Answer: Because gravity sucks! The liquid had temporarily become a solid. When left in a warm spot, it returns to its liquid state (as happens with ice to water and margarine to oil).) Students could draw the area of the material as it changes to a different state.

Bounce-backers

For each young child you will need:
- A hollow plastic playpen ball already cut in half. These can be bought in packs of 50 cheaply from discount department stores
- One paddle-pop stick for the body and extra paddle-pop sticks for the arms and legs
- Thick paper or cardboard to make a circle for the face
- Plasticine or play-dough
- Textas, scissors, sticky tape and glue to share.

Steps

- Students fill the half-ball with play-dough or plasticine.
- They stick the paddle-pop stick in the middle, draw a face on the cardboard circle (or add their own photo) and then paste it onto the paddle-pop stick.
- They can make arms and legs from paddle-pop sticks and then draw and cut out clothes for the bounce-backer.

Variations and follow-ups

- Older students can fill the half-ball with plaster of Paris and, when half set, stick a small wooden kebab skewer in the centre of the ball with the pointy end up. When the plaster has set, they stick a table tennis ball or a small polystyrene ball (available from craft shops) onto the skewer. Then they draw eyes and mouth or use googly eyes.
- Add a costume to the bounce-backer. Draw a 21 cm diameter circle onto light card. Divide into thirds and draw lines to show each third. Cut one of the lines to the centre of the circle. Draw and colour/paint the costume for the bounce-backer in one of the sections of the circle next to the cut line. Then make the circle into a cone shape by overlapping the paper until only the costume part of the cone can be seen.
- *Understanding the motion of the bounce-backer.* The main reason that the bounce-backer comes back after being tipped over is that the centre of gravity shifts. Comparisons can be made with seesaws.

• Upper primary/junior secondary students can design, draw and make their own version of the bounce-backer using a range of different materials. This drawing should be to scale. The drawing could be by hand or they can use computer drawing software. Students then make their bounce-backer and test its capacity to bounce back. The class then devise criteria to judge each design.

Class books

Class books can be made in shapes that reflect the contents (e.g. a frog book shape for a book on frogs). Cut out the cardboard to make the shaped covers. Then cut out a page for each student who is contributing to the book in exactly the same shape and size.

Cube pattern (see BLM 11:3)

This cube pattern can be made into a dice (e.g. a feelings dice) or suspended on a string as a cube to display information (e.g. six positive things in my life).

Electronic matching pairs quiz

Students can make a reusable electrical

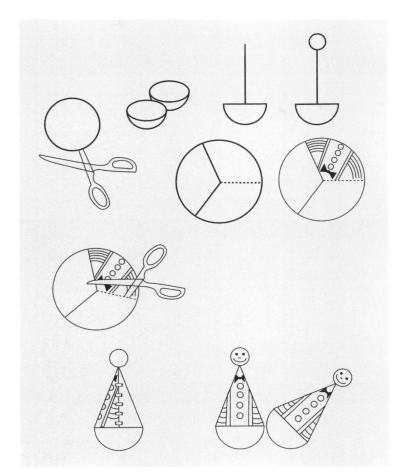

circuit quiz board game with questions and answers. You will need:
• Two copies of A4 template (BLM 11:4) made on light card
• One stiff backing card 25 cm by 35 cm
• 16 split pins
• Insulated wire
• 4.5 V battery
• 3.5 V bulb or buzzer (buzzer can be bought from electrical shops or hardware stores)
• Bulb holder (optional)
• 2 paper clips
• Scissors and sticky tape to share.

Steps

1 Cut out the windows of one of the A4 templates.
2 Tape the window template to the cardboard backing. Tape down both sides and along the bottom of the window template to make a pocket for the answer sheet.
3 Fix a split pin to the outside edge of each window. Make sure the pin is on the cardboard backing and not on the A4 window sheet so you can still slide your Q & A sheet into the pocket. You may need to cut a little off the edges of your answer sheet so it smoothly slides into the pocket.
4 Turn the card over and number the split pins on the left 1 to 8, then number the split pins on the right 1 to 8 but jumble up the number order.
5 Use short pieces of insulated wire to join the two '1's, the two '2's, and so on.
6 On a scrap piece of paper write 8 questions and answers. Then write the questions on the left side and the corresponding answers on the right side of your second A4 card template in a jumbled up number order.

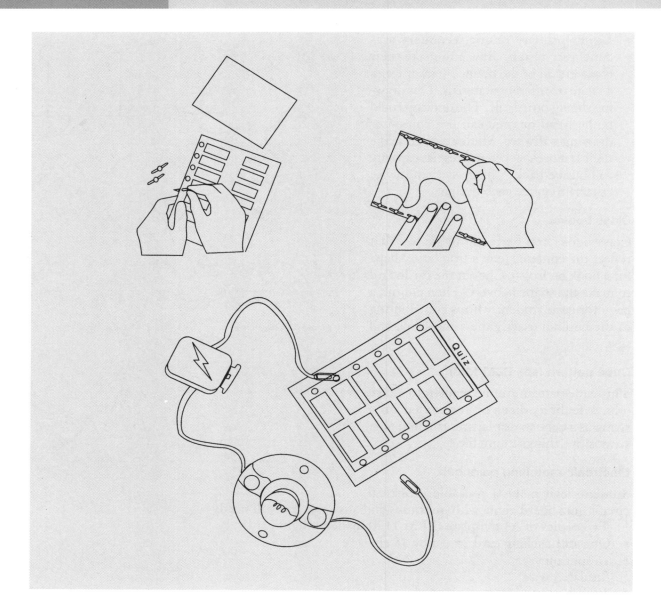

7 To make your quiz tester cut three pieces of wire. Attach one wire to a battery terminal, one from the other battery terminal to the bulb holder or buzzer and one to the free side of the bulb holder or buzzer. Attach a paper clip to the two free ends of wire.

8 Classmates try to match each question with the right answer. To check if their answer is correct they place the two paper clips on the two split pins beside their choices. A correct answer will light up the bulb or make the buzzer go.

Flappers and lift-up circles

Flappers and lift-up circles offer students a chance to invite classmates to interact with their work. They write a question on the front of the flapper or circle (e.g. why did dinosaurs become extinct?). The answer is found when you lift up the flapper to see what is written underneath.

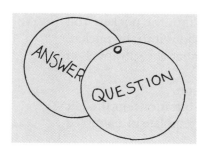

Little flappers are attached to a very large sheet of cardboard, along with those by other people, or they are attached to a bulletin board. To make a little flapper, fold a small piece of card in two (like a place card or a small birthday card) and paste it onto cardboard, or attach it with a drawing pin (in the bottom part) to a bulletin board.

Big flappers sit on a benchtop or desk. To make a big flapper, you will need:
- An empty shoe box cut to half size (you'll need the lid too)
- A plastic document sleeve
- Coloured cardboard
- Something to make a handle to lift up the top with (e.g. a champagne cork attached with a screw and washer underneath).

The question is written on a piece of cardboard that sits in the plastic sleeve (cut in half) taped to the outside of the lid of the box. The lid sits on the upturned base of the box. There is another plastic sleeve on the base which gives the answer. Using masking tape, attach the lid to the base of the box at the opposite end to the handle. An optional step is to cover the box and lid with birthday/christmas paper.

Lift-up circles are attached to a very large sheet of cardboard, along with those of other people, or they are attached to a bulletin board. To make lift-up circles, make two identical cardboard circles. Join them together and attach them to the larger sheet of cardboard or to the bulletin board with a split pin (cardboard) or drawing pin (bulletin board). The top circle should be able to be swung to either side. You can also have three sets of these. The middle set contains a single circle with a question. The other two have different answers written on the top circle. On the bottom circle of the right answer is a smiley face and the words 'Well done! You are correct'. On the bottom circle of the wrong answer is a frowning face and the words 'Sorry, you are wrong. Try again'.

Flappers/circles class project

Students could work in groups of four to research a specific area of a topic such as Ancient Egypt (work, architecture, fashion, art, etc.). They present their project as a class flapper display. They use all forms of flappers and lift-up circles. For example, 'Lift up the lid to find out why Ancient Egyptians mummified some of their dead'.

Flip book

For each child you will need:
- Two A4 sheets of the same coloured paper or thin card
- Three white sheets of A4 paper
- A hole puncher to share with other members of the class
- Textas or crayons
- Coloured wool.

Steps

1 Fold the three sheets of white paper in half and cut along the fold to make six half sheets.
2 Place them together to make a smaller book of six pages. These sheets of paper make the bottom half of the A4 book.
3 Use two A4 sheets of same-coloured paper to make the front and back cover of the book.
4 Use a hole puncher to make two holes in the top half and two holes in the bottom half of the book (the six half pages and two covers).
5 Use wool to tie the covers and pages together.
6 On the top half of the book (inside back cover) the children write the main statement (e.g. 'At Christmas time I like to . . .'). On each of the six sheets of the 'book' they write and illustrate six endings that complete the main statement (e.g. open presents; eat pudding; give presents).

Fridge magnet frame

The fridge magnet is designed to serve as a memory jogger for key messages such as the BOUNCE or BOUNCE BACK! acronyms, the acronyms for STAR, CHAMP and WINNERS for the 'Success' unit of work, or a prompt for goals they have set themselves.

You will need:
• Ruler
• Coloured paper (for inserts)
• A piece of thick cardboard (150 cm × 100 cm) for the base of the frame
• Paint and paintbrush/textas
• Very small flat magnets (available at hardware stores and some newsagents or toy shops)
• PVA glue and scissors to share
• Marker pen.

Steps

1 Measure and draw a frame 1 cm from the edge of the cardboard.
2 Draw a second frame 1 cm inside the first frame you have just drawn.
3 Use a marker pen to draw a picture which extends into the outer frame (see picture).
4 Cut out the parts of the outer frame which are not needed for the picture.
5 Cut out the inside rectangle.
6 Glue a small magnet to each of the four corners.
7 Insert the coloured paper with the message behind the frame.

Library resources

If you find that a book used in a unit is hard to buy, try borrowing from your local library or ask them to borrow it for you from another public library. The following sites help you to identify which libraries hold the books.

National Library of Australia Gateway to all libraries in Australia
www.nla.gov.au/libraries

University libraries in Australia
www.anu.edu.au/caul/unilibs/

Northern Territory libraries
www.ntlib.nt.gov.au/pcl

Queensland libraries
www.slq.qld.gov.au/ROADS/librp.htm

Victorian libraries
www.librariesvictoria.net
www.coolcat.edu.au (universities)
www.libraries.vic.gov.au

Western Australian libraries
wwwlib.murdoch.edu.au/catalogue/walib.html

Mobiles

A mobile is a sculpture with parts that move. Mobiles have two parts:
- The structure or base you hang things from, and
- The things you hang.

    Bases can be made from skewers, a cork with two skewers inserted through it, bits of wood (cane, bamboo, driftwood, thin dowel, balsa wood), fine wire, cardboard, cardboard cylinders, drinking straws, string, fishing line.

    Things to hang can be drawings, cards or cardboard shapes, things made out of paper, small boxes, tissue, papier-mâché items, small toys and objects such as balls, wooden people (from craft shops), paper cut-out people, or small stones.

Standard wire mobile

1 First cut your wire to lengths.
- Make one wire twice as long as the rest.

- Use pliers to make hooks at each end.
- Find the centre and form a twist.
- Cut smaller lengths of wire.
2 Shape your 'hangers'..
3 Use strong cotton or fine string to tie to the end of each wire and attach your shape at the other end.

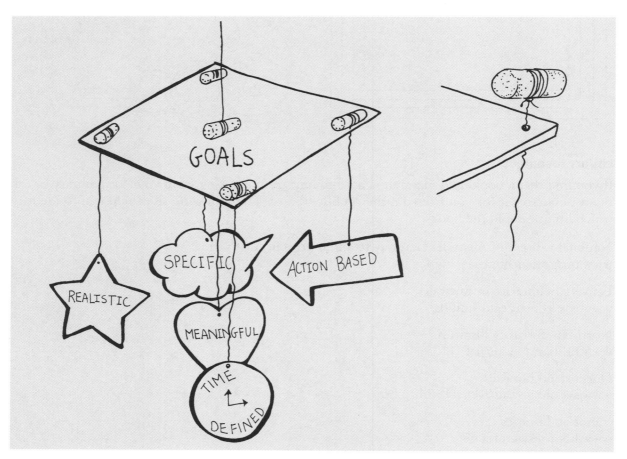

Music resources

Throughout all units of work there are references to songs that convey key messages in regard to the resilience themes. Most songs are linked to websites that provide the lyrics and the music (usually separately). You can use the web addresses that are given for specific songs in the units of work. You can also access sites by using the general web addresses below. If you are trying to find the lyrics of a specific song, you can do so by using the following steps:
- Use GOOGLE as your search engine.
- Find the SEARCH box and type in the name of the song and then add 'midi' (to hear just the music) or 'lyrics' to get just the words of the song. The music and lyrics may be in the same site or in different sites. Do not type in AND before 'midi' or 'lyrics'.
  Sites can also be accessed by your students to find the suggested songs or other songs that are congruent with the resilience themes.
  The two best current sites are <www.niehs.nih.gov/kids/music.htm/> and <www.kididdles.com/mouseum. Another useful site is <www.geocities.com/EnchantedForest/Glade/7438.

Pop-up toaster: How it works

What happens when you put your bread in the toaster and press the handle down? The handle you push down catches on a special switch and connects the house current to the heating elements.

The elements on each side of the toast glow red hot as the current runs through them, and they toast the bread. The toaster's thermostat and the timer control how brown the toast gets. The current runs through a bimetallic strip on its way to the heating elements. When the elements have warmed up to the toasting temperature the bimetallic strip has warmed up enough to curl over and push a button that starts the timer. You set the timer when you decide how dark you want your toast. The timer ticks away for a certain amount of time and then releases the handle when that time is up. A spring pops the handle and the toast up.

The heating elements go off because the handle no longer connects them to the source of the electric current. Then you get your toast just the way you like to eat it!

Puppets and masks

There are references to using puppets throughout the Teacher's Resource Books 1 and 2. Here is a list of lots of different kinds of puppets. Masks can also be used in lieu of puppets.

Masks

Glue pictures of faces from magazines onto cardboard and add a paddle-pop stick to hold it with. You can use just eyes, or just the mouth or use the whole face. Cut out small eyeholes. Similarly, you could make paper plate masks to hold. Cut out eyeholes and add wool for hair.

Finger puppets

Version one: Use felt finger covers as illustrated

Version two: Make hand strappers by making a long paper watch with an animal shape or person's face in the position that the watch face would be. Strap them over the back of the hand and use fingers as legs.

Version three: Cut out a circle on stiff card with two holes in the base for fingers. Children draw on the card or paste their drawings on the card as illustrated.

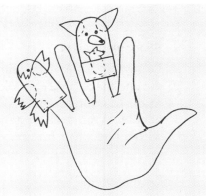

Balloon puppets

Add a balloon to a cardboard cylinder. Thread the string which ties the end of the balloon through the cylinder and tape to the side. Add a face and other features.

Brown paper bag puppets

Draw a face and hair on a paper bag. Stuff the bag with crumpled paper. Attach to a stick with a rubber band.

Glove puppets

Use a woollen or rubber glove. Staple an image such as a picture of a lion to the top of the glove. Or make the glove into the animal by stitching on ears out of fabric such as furry fabric for animals and buttons for eyes. On a rubber glove you can draw features with a permanent pen. Add buttons for eyes.

Paper plate puppets

Add wool for hair, and draw in the face.

Paper spring puppets

Draw a body and then make legs and arms out of paper springs.

To make the springs children cut out two long strips of paper. Paste the paper at right angles to each other and then fold one on top of the other until all the paper is folded. Glue to the body of the puppet. Paste a long stick or paddle-pop sticks to the back of the puppet.

Self photo puppets

Use digital photos of children's faces and glue them onto cardboard. Make a cardboard body. Add paddle-pop sticks or a wire coat hanger (straightened and then doubled) for a handle.

Shadow puppets

Draw the shape of an animal or person on cardboard. Cut it out and make large eye holes. Straighten out a wire coathanger to make a long handle. Tape the puppet to the end of the handle. Wrap masking tape on the other end. Make a screen with a bed sheet hung over a rope. Put a light source such as a lamp between the puppet and the sheet.

Sock puppets

Cut a cardboard rectangle about 7 cm × 20 cm and curve the corners. Cut the sock at the toe. Fold the cardboard

rectangle in half to form the inside of the mouth. Place the cardboard inside the slit of the sock and glue in place. Add features.

Split pin puppets on strings

Cut the shape of the character or animal from cardboard. Join legs, arms and head to the body with split pins. Add string to the head and arms and legs so that different parts of the puppet can move.

Soft toy/animal puppets

Use children's old soft toys or animals as puppets. Make a hole in the base and insert dowelling to serve as a handle.

Wooden spoon puppets/paddle-pop sticks

Draw features on the spoon or the top of a paddle-pop stick.

Responsibility pie charts (RPCs)

See BLMs 11:5–6. An RPC is a concrete way for students to understand that all negative situations can be said to occur as a result of a combination of three factors:

- Their own actions: How much did their own behaviour contribute to the situation (me)?
- The actions of others: How much did the behaviour of others contribute to the situation (others)?
- Random unpredictable factors: How much did bad luck or circumstances (e.g. weather, timing, coincidences, lack of knowledge, illness) contribute to the situation (random factors)?

Students can individually make the simple RPC, a moveable device that allows them to change the amounts of responsibility they attribute to each of the three factors as they think about the situation. When using the RPC it is possible for students to attribute no responsibility to 'random or bad luck' and no responsibility to 'others', but there must always be at least 10% responsibility attributed to their 'own actions' (me).

Some students allocate too much responsibility to their own actions or characteristics. Point this out when you are working with them. Some allocate too much blame to external factors. They need to be made aware that they are not seeing their own behaviour accurately.

Alternatively, the teacher can make an RPC to use when talking one-on-one with a student. Try to avoid the use of the words 'blame' and 'fault' and instead use terms such as:

- How much was . . . responsible for what happened?
- How much was what happened due to . . .?
- How much did this happen because of . . .?
- How much does . . . explain what happened?

Steps

1. Draw a circle on a rough piece of paper.
2. Think about your situation and identify the details of the three factors: your actions, the actions of other people, bad luck.
3. Then allocate what you see as an honest percentage of responsibility due to each of the three categories, that is, 'me', 'others' and 'bad luck'.
4. Draw these in on the circle to make a 'responsibility pie chart' (RPC).
5. Look carefully at the RPC you have made and re-think the percentages in case you misjudged the first time.
6. Identify what you can learn from each of the three categories so that the negative situation is less likely to happen again.

BLM 11:5 can be used by students to make their own RPC from their own templates. However, the three templates are also already drawn (BLM 11:6) for faster creation.

Things with springs

These are some of the more common things which use springs:

analogue timers	bungy rope
analogue watches	car accelerator
any item which requires AA or AAA batteries	car doors
bathroom scales	car suspension systems
bike pump	certain toys
bridges	click pens
bulldog clips	clipboards

diving board
hair clips
jack-in-the-boxes
light bulb socket (when BC light bulbs are used)
light switches
mattresses
measuring scales (e.g. greengrocers' scales)
mousetraps
music boxes
oven doors
phone indexes
pillows (some)
pogo sticks

pop-up toasters
pumps (e.g. in soap dispensers and shampoo bottles)
screen doors (some)
self closing windows (some)
shears or secateurs (not all of them)
shock absorbers
slinkies
sofas
springboard
staplers
torches
trampolines
washing machine timers

Wallet card

Wallet cards can be single-sided or double-sided. They can feature 9, 12 or 16 squares. For example, if an A4 sheet is folded four times, it folds down into a single square but can open up to display 16 statements, one in each of the 16 squares.

Two squares of harder card are stuck on the ends, as illustrated. The hard ends can be laminated. Use colourful paper.

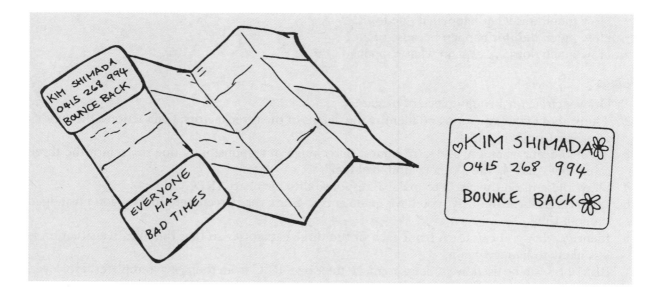

Wax-resist badges

You will need:
• Wax crayons
• White card
• Paintbrush
• Double-sided tape
• Scissors
• Safety pins
• Dark coloured paint.

Steps

1 Children draw a shape for the badge with wax crayons. They colour in the drawing in bright colours. For example a pot and sunflowers for 'Bright side', a funny face for 'Humour', a medal for 'STAR' and 'CHAMP'.

2 Paint over the wax drawing with poster paint.

3 When the paint is dry, the crayon will shine through.

4 Cut out around the drawing for the badge.

5 Turn the badge over.

6 Use a piece of double-sided tape to attach the safety pin.

Other classroom activities

- Balloon burst quotes and balloon burst sentences
- Classroom stroll
- Data chart
- Freeze frame and rewind
- Good fairy, bad fairy or Good wizard, bad wizard
- Lightning writing
- Literature prompts
- Quick quotes
- Venn diagram

Balloon burst quotes and balloon burst sentences

Buy enough balloons to have one for each student. Buy them in different colours so you have enough of the same colour to form groups of three or four. Place a different quote in each uninflated balloon. Each student takes a balloon and goes to the group with that colour. Students blow up their balloons. Taking turns, each student pops their balloon and then reads the quote, explains what they think it means and makes a personal comment on it. Others can respond by asking for the talking prompt. The quote could then serve as the basis of a writing activity.

For younger students, cut up sentences photocopied onto card. Place several words in each balloon of the same colour so that the whole sentence is contained in the three balloons. Students burst their balloon and then work with two other people with the same colour balloon to put their whole sentence together. This is then written down.

Classroom stroll

Use this activity when students are working on a project or problem that is presented visually. During the project provide the option for two out of a group of four to go on a classroom stroll to silently check what other groups are doing. When they return to their group they talk to their partner and then they write down two things that surprised them and two things they want to know more about. Alternatively, students can take a stroll to view displayed work or news items in their own class or another class.

Data chart

Purpose: providing a structure for students to organise information they research on a topic.

Children work with a partner to think of some questions to ask about a topic. For example, in the topic of bushrangers, they might ask:
- What is a bushranger?
- What are some of their names?
- What were they before they were bushrangers?
- Did they get caught?
- What happened to them?

Then they research several sources and fill in the answers on the data chart.

Questions decided as basis of research	Book title . . .	INFORMATION SOURCES		
		Notes in the museum at . . .	A relative who is an historian	Internet site called . . .
What is a bushranger?				
Some names?				
What did they do?				
What happened to them?				

Freeze frame and rewind

Use freeze frame when students are acting out a scenario such as a conflict situation or a story. At a vital point in the story ask the actors to stop and freeze. This gives the participants and the audience time to reflect on what has happened, what effect this has had on the characters in the story, and what might happen next. Rewind creates the opportunity for the students to rewind a scene and do it with a different ending. This can also be used with puppet plays.

Good fairy, bad fairy or Good wizard, bad wizard

This strategy can be used as a puppet play or drama in conjunction with the freeze frame strategy. The good fairy or wizard whispers positive messages to the main character about choices they can make (e.g. be brave because . . ., be honest because . . ., be strong because . . .). The bad fairy or wizard whispers negative messages (e.g. give up because . . ., tell a lie because . . ., just walk away and don't do anything because . . .). Provide costumes. The good fairy wears traditional fairy colours and sparkles and wings, the wizard wears a sparkly cloak or wizard hat. The bad fairy or wizard wears black! Wooden wands are available to paint and decorate from fabric or craft shops or children can make their own.

Lightning writing

Students write down all the things they can think of on a topic in a specific time frame, such as three minutes. For example:
- Write down what you think of when I say the word 'elastic' (words and phrases).
- What do you think is meant by the expression 'bounce back'?
- How could we make people better at recycling? (problems)
  Give students sheets of paper already printed with an interesting border or graphics plus the heading 'Lightning writing' with a lightning bolt somewhere nearby.

Literature prompts

Picture books and simple novels are used throughout BOUNCE BACK! as a starting point or to reinforce key messages. The picture books incorporated in the level 3 book are suitable for work with older students. The best feature of good picture books is that they provide a quick, succinct entry into a topic and often multi-layered meanings. The following questions can be used to guide student reading and reflection on texts. These questions can be used for discussion in a whole class, a cooperative pair or a group. They can be used with Partner Retell, Think–Pair–Share etc.

Prompts to help students understand the text
- What do you already know about this topic?
- What do you think this book might be about?
- Who are the characters?
- What are the main events?
- Where is it set?
- When did . . . happen?
- How/why did it happen?
- What happened in the beginning . . . middle . . . end?
- What text type do you think it might be?
- What text features might be used?
- What does the cover/title tell us about the text?
- What effect do the illustrations have on the reader?
- What do you think might happen next? Why?

Prompts to help students to think critically about the text
- What is the subject matter or topic?
- What is this story about? How do we know?
- Are there gaps or absences or silences in this text? If so what are they? For example, is there a group of people missing who logically should be included? Are different groups talked about as though they belong to the same group? Does the author write about a group without including their perspective on things or events?
- Do you like what the author is saying?
- How could we re-write this story so that it matches more closely all our experiences and fits more effectively with what we know about the world and about people?

- How do the characters relate to one another? What if they behaved differently? How would it affect the story?
- How has the illustrator made us feel or think in this way?
- How is the reader positioned in relation to the author: as a friend, an opponent, as someone who needs to be persuaded, as invisible, as someone who agrees with the author's views?
- Is there any group of people here who are under-represented or represented in a demeaning or stereotyped way (e.g. fathers, women, older people, members of ethnic groups, professions)?
- What clues do the words or pictures give us about how the characters are feeling?
- What do the pictures/illustrations tell us? Do they support the text or convey the same message?
- What do you think the writer wants the reader to think about?
- What does the author want us to believe about the world and the people in it? What suggests this to us? Does this 'fit' with what you believe about the world and about people? Why/why not?
- What is the message/moral of the text? Do you agree with the author's message? How does the message relate to your life?
- What knowledge do you, the reader, need to bring to this text in order to understand it?
- What might this character be thinking right now?
- What point is the writer trying to make?
- What world view and values does the author assume that the reader holds? How do you know?
- Who do you think it was written for? Why?
- Why was the story ended in this way?
- What does the ending mean?
- Who would feel 'left out' in this text and why—is it a problem? Who would find that the claims made in this text clash with their own values, beliefs or experiences?
- Why did the writer/illustrator . . .?
- Why might the author have written this text?
- What is the tone or mood of this book?
- In what ways is this book the same as/different to your favourite book?
- How powerful would this book be if it had no illustrations?
- What literary conventions are used in this picture book (anti-hero, metaphor, parody humour, circular story structure, linear story structure, irony, suspense, fable, legend, folk tale, fairy tale, atmosphere, parallel story structure)?

Questions which can be used with books/poems/songs and videos in the BOUNCE BACK! Resilience Program.

General literature prompts are found above. The questions on the following page can be used with all of the books, poems, songs and videos in the program. Some questions will be suitable for some books more than others. Students can be given the questions as a basis for book reviews.

- *Question focusing on predicting likelihood*
  —How likely is it (was it) that what this person is (was) worried about will (would) happen?
- *Questions focusing on courage*
  —Who showed courage in this story? What fear did they overcome?
  —What risks had to be taken? Were they thoughtful or foolhardy risks?
- *Questions focusing on resourcefulness*
  —Who was resourceful in looking for different ways in which to solve problems?
  —Where in the story did someone refuse to give up?
  —What goals were set in this story and who set them? What plans did they make?
  —Did anyone in this story learn from the mistakes they made?
  —Was hard work and effort a factor in the successful outcome?
- *Question focusing on 'Bad times don't last. Things always get better.'*
  —Was there any part of this story where a character found that their bad times were only temporary and things got better?

- *Questions focusing on 'Other people can help if you talk to them. Get a reality check.'*
  —Was there any part in this story where a character coped better because they talked to someone else about their problem and their feelings?
  —How did this character do a reality check?
- *Questions focusing on 'Unhelpful thinking makes you feel more upset.'*
  —What feelings did the different people in this story have? (Stress accurate naming of the feeling and its intensity, as described in the 'Emotions' unit.)
  —Did anyone in this story jump to conclusions without good evidence?
  —Did anyone in this story change the way they were thinking so that their thinking was more helpful (that is, helped them not to exaggerate, to look for facts and to find a solution)?
- *Question focusing on 'Nobody is perfect—not you and not others.'*
  —How was this character 'not perfect'?
- *Questions focusing on 'Concentrate on the good bits no matter how small and use laughter.'*
  —Did any character in this story use humour as one of the ways in which they coped?
  —Where were people in this story looking on the bright side and concentrating on the positive aspects?
- *Question focusing on 'Everybody experiences sadness, hurt, failure, rejection and setbacks sometimes, not just you.'*
  —What were the 'hard times' in this story? Which ones are the sorts of hard times that everyone faces at some time in their life? Which ones were the sorts of hard times that many people your age experience? Which ones were very rare?
- *Question focusing on 'Blame fairly—how much was due to you, others and bad luck?'*
  —How much of what happened was because of what this character did? How much was because of what another person in the story did? How much was due to bad luck or circumstances (what was happening at the time)?
- *Question focusing on 'Accept the things you can't change, but try to change what you can first.'*
  —What did this character have to accept that couldn't be changed by them?
- *Question focusing on 'Catastrophising exaggerates your worries. Don't believe the worst possible picture.'*
  —Was there any catastrophising in this story?
- *Question focusing on 'Keep things in perspective. It's not the end of the world. It's only one part of your life.'*
  —When one unhappy time happened for this character, which parts of the rest of their life were still OK?
- *Question focusing on empathy*
  —What would this character have felt like? How would this character have described what was going on? Is it possible to find some understanding of why this character behaved this way?

Quick quotes

Students use the digital camera to make a photo of themselves. The whole class places their photos on a section of the bulletin board. Then each time a new topic comes up, they type one of their thoughts about the topic into a speech balloon and paste it next to their mouth. Many computer programs have speech bubbles.

Venn diagram

In two overlapping ovals or circles students compare the similarities of and differences between two things such as two characters in their book or two different books on the theme of resilience, or students work in pairs to compare how they are the same and different.

BLACK LINE MASTERS

When you feel unhappy, you can BOUNCE back again and feel better

Bad feelings always go away again.

Other people can help you to feel better if you talk to them.

Unhelpful thinking makes you feel more upset.

Nobody is perfect. Mistakes help you learn.

Concentrate on the good things and have a laugh.

Everybody feels sad and worried sometimes, not just you.

BOUNCE BACK ACRONYM

When things go wrong for you, or you get 'knocked down' by what happens in your life, remember that you can decide to BOUNCE BACK! and be yourself again

Bad times don't last. Things always get better. Stay optimistic.

Other people can help if you talk to them. Get a reality check.

Unhelpful thinking makes you feel more upset.

Nobody is perfect—not you and not others.

Concentrate on the positives (no matter how small) and use laughter.

Everybody experiences sadness, hurt, failure, rejection and setbacks sometimes. They are a normal part of life. Try not to personalise them.

Blame fairly—how much of what happened was because of you, how much was because of others and how much was because of bad luck or circumstances?

Accept the things you can't change, but try to change what you can first.

Catastrophising exaggerates your worries. Don't believe the worst possible picture.

Keep things in perspective. It's only one part of your life.

RULES FOR CLASSROOM DISCUSSIONS

- Think carefully about saying something that is highly personal or private.

- If you talk about somebody you know, and if the information is personal, do not give any information that identifies them to others. Use the 'no names' rule to protect other people. Say something less specific, such as:

   I know/knew someone who . . .
   I know of a situation where . . .

- You have the option to 'pass', but try not to make a habit of it.

- You can choose to talk at a less personal level by leaving out some details in a story or making the story simpler than it really was.

- There is a 'no put-down' rule in place at all times. Don't judge others. They have a right to their own opinion.

- Remember to listen well when someone else is talking. Don't interrupt.

RULES FOR CLASSROOM DISCUSSIONS (CONT.)

- Remember to use the skill of 'respectful disagreeing'. Don't start by saying things like:

  No, that's wrong because . . .
  I don't agree . . .

First say the exact part of what has been said by someone else that you can agree with. Then add the bit where you think differently. This is a good example:

> *I can see what Emma means about parachuting being dangerous because the parachute might fail, but I don't think it would be as dangerous as bungey jumping.*

> This is a bad example:

> *That's ridiculous because there are hardly any deaths from parachuting.*

- Please respect each other's confidentiality. Anything said in this room should stay in this room. We hope that everyone will honour this agreement, but you need to be aware that confidentiality cannot be *guaranteed.*

SURVEY ON BULLYING

Bullying is when one or more people deliberately give someone a hard time by trying to make them feel miserable, left out or humiliated. They do this often, not just once.

Write down the names of any students in this class or school who you know are bullying another student in this way.

Person 1 _____

The class they are in is _____

Person 2 _____

The class they are in is _____

Person 3 _____

The class they are in is _____

Can you name any people in this school who are often given a hard time by one student or several students together?

Person 1 _____

The class they are in is _____

Person 2 _____

The class they are in is _____

Person 3 _____

The class they are in is _____

A-Z OF EMOTIONS

Affectionate
Afraid
Aggressive
Agitated
Alarmed
Alive
Amazed
Amused
Angry
Anguished
Annoyed
Anxious
Apathetic
Appalled
Apprehensive
Arrogant
Ashamed
Awe-struck
Baffled
Bashful
Bereft
Betrayed
Bewildered
Bitter
Blase
Blissful
Blue
Bold
Bored
Brave
Calm
Cheated
Cheerful
Compassionate
Concerned
Confident
Confused
Conspicuous
Contemptuous
Contented
Contrite
Cool
Cornered
Courageous
Cranky
Cross
Curious
Dazed
Defeated
Defenceless
Deflated
Dejected

Delighted
Depressed
Deprived
Despairing
Despondent
Determined
Devastated
Disappointed
Disapproving
Disconcerted
Discouraged
Disgruntled
Disgusted
Disheartened
Dismayed
Disoriented
Dissatisfied
Distracted
Distraught
Distressed
Distrustful
Disturbed
Doubtful
Down
Downcast
Dumbfounded
Ecstatic
Elated
Embarrassed
Empathic
Empty
Enchanted
Energetic
Enraged
Enthusiastic
Envious
Euphoric
Exasperated
Excited
Excluded
Fearful
Fed-up
Flabbergasted
Flat
Flustered
Fond
Forsaken
Fortunate
Fragile
Frenetic
Frenzied
Friendly

Frightened
Frustrated
Furious
Gentle
Glad
Gloomy
Glum
Grateful
Gratified
Grief stricken
Grumpy
Guilty
Happy
Hassled
Hateful
Helpless
Hopeful
Hopeless
Horrified
Hostile
Humiliated
Hurt
Ignored
Impatient
Important
Inadequate
Incensed
Indignant
Infuriated
Insecure
Interested
Intimidated
Irate
Irritated
Isolated
Jealous
Jittery
Joyful
Joyous
Jubilant
Jumpy
Keen
Left-out
Let-down
Livid
Lonely
Lost
Loved
Loving
Low
Mad
Mediocre

Melancholy
Mellow
Miffed
Miserable
Mistrusting
Misunderstood
Nonplussed
Nostalgic
Offended
On-edge
Optimistic
Ordinary
Outraged
Overwhelmed
Panicky
Mortified
Muddled
Mystified
Nauseated
Negative
Nervous
Paralysed
Passionate
Passive
Pathetic
Peaceful
Peeved
Perplexed
Petrified
Petulant
Pitying
Pleased
Positive
Powerful
Powerless
Proud
Provoked
Put-out
Puzzled
Quarrelsome
Rattled
Regretful
Rejected
Relieved
Remorseful
Repulsed
Resentful
Resigned
Revengeful
Revolted
Riled
Sad
Satisfied

Scared
Scornful
Seething
Self-conscious
Self-pitying
Shattered
Sheepish
Shocked
Shy
Silly
Slighted
Smug
Snubbed
Sorrowful
Sorry
Spooked
Stubborn
Stunned
Successful
Superior
Surprised
Suspicious
Sympathetic
Taken-aback
Tearful
Tender
Tense
Terrified
Threatened
Thrilled
Timid
Trapped
Troubled
Uncertain
Uncomfortable
Uneasy
Unhappy
Unloved
Unnerved
Unsure
Unwanted
Upset
Used
Vengeful
Victorious
Vindictive
Vulnerable
Warm
Wary
Wistful
Worried
Worthless

HOW TO MAKE A BALL THAT BOUNCES

You will be working with a partner.

1. Prepare an ice-cream container half full of cold water. It must be COLD water.

2. Lay out an old plastic shopping bag.

3. Have paper towels ready.

4. To make the ball you will need:
   - Distilled water
   - One glass or crockery container (approx 250 mL) such as a coffee mug
   - A teaspoon and a measuring jug
   - One metal dessertspoon
   - PVA white glue in a squeeze bottle with a pouring tip (to be shared)
   - Powdered borax (to be shared)

5. Measure out and pour 200 mL of distilled water into your 250 mL container.

6. Add one and a quarter teaspoons of powdered borax to the 200 mL of water.

7. Stir the mixture and then let it stand for 5 minutes (use the timer) until all the undissolved borax has sunk to the bottom of the jug. Do not stir the mixture again during this 5-minute period.

8. Using the metal dessertspoon, one of you should then stir the mixture slowly but continuously.

9. At the same time, the other person should hold the glue bottle upside down over the mixture, squeeze it and pour a steady stream into the mixture. Stop pouring when the spoon has become thickly coated with the glue. A chemical reaction has occurred between the PVA (which is a polymer) and the borax.

HOW TO MAKE A BALL THAT BOUNCES (CONT.)

10. Using your hands, pull the material off the spoon and quickly place it into the ice-cream container of cold water. At this stage what you will have will look like a long stringy and sticky mess! Leave it in the water for 30 seconds. Then remove it and place it onto the plastic bag.

11. Dry your hands on the paper towel.

12. Using your hands, pick up the wet stringy material and squeeze and press it and shape it until the water begins to disappear and it begins to dry a bit and turn into a ball. Then, when it feels a bit dry, roll it in your hands to give it a round shape. As it dries and is shaped, it gets more bouncy. The palms of your hand will do a better job than your fingers. It may take a few minutes to work, but don't give up—it *does* work!

13. You may need to dry your hands several times during this stage. While you do this, your partner can continue with the moulding and squeezing.

14. Now, while it is rounded, try gently bouncing the ball on a table.

15. Wrap it in clingwrap and store it in the fridge for future use. When you want to use it again, remove it from the fridge for a few minutes beforehand so that it warms up and is more pliable and bouncy.

16. Write up a report or wall flow chart on what you did.

CUBE PATTERN

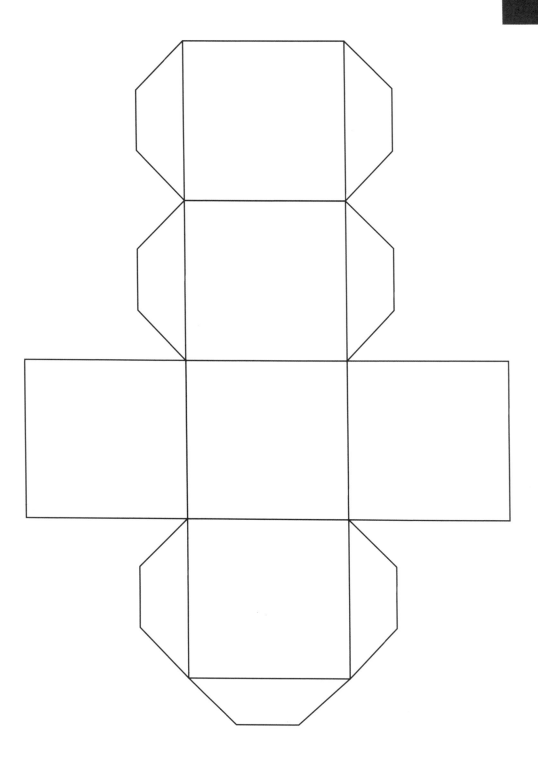

TEMPLATE FOR ELECTRONIC MATCHING PAIRS QUIZ

INSTRUCTIONS FOR MAKING A MOVEABLE RESPONSIBILITY PIE CHART

You will need:
- An A4 piece of fairly heavy white cardboard
- Two A4 sheets of light red cardboard
- Two A4 sheets of light blue cardboard
- A split pin with 3 or 4 cm ends
- The three pattern sheets (A, B and C).

Making the base: random and bad luck (sheet A)
Cut out and paste sheet A on heavy white cardboard for the base.

Making the second layer: others (sheet B)
Photocopy two copies of sheet B on light blue cardboard. Cut out 5 segments.

Making the top layer: me (sheet C)
Photocopy two copies of sheet C on red cardboard. Cut out the 10 segments.

Assembly
Assemble the device with the white base at the bottom, followed by the light blue layer (5 segments) and then the red layer on the top (10 segments). Insert the split pin through the middle.

TEMPLATES FOR MAKING A MOVEABLE RESPONSIBILITY PIE CHART

Sheet A

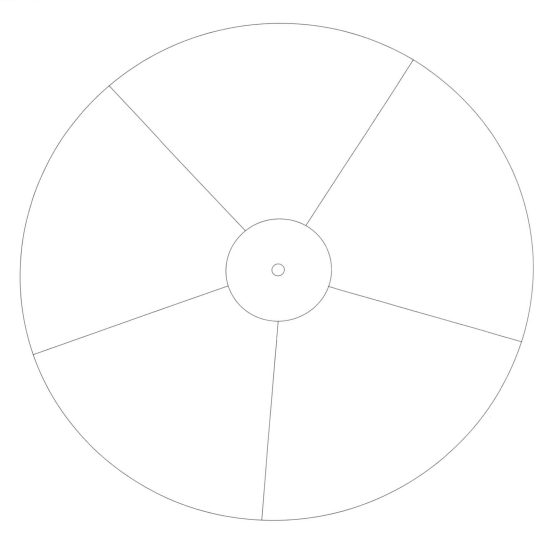

TEMPLATES FOR MAKING A MOVEABLE RESPONSIBILITY PIE CHART (CONT.)

Sheet B

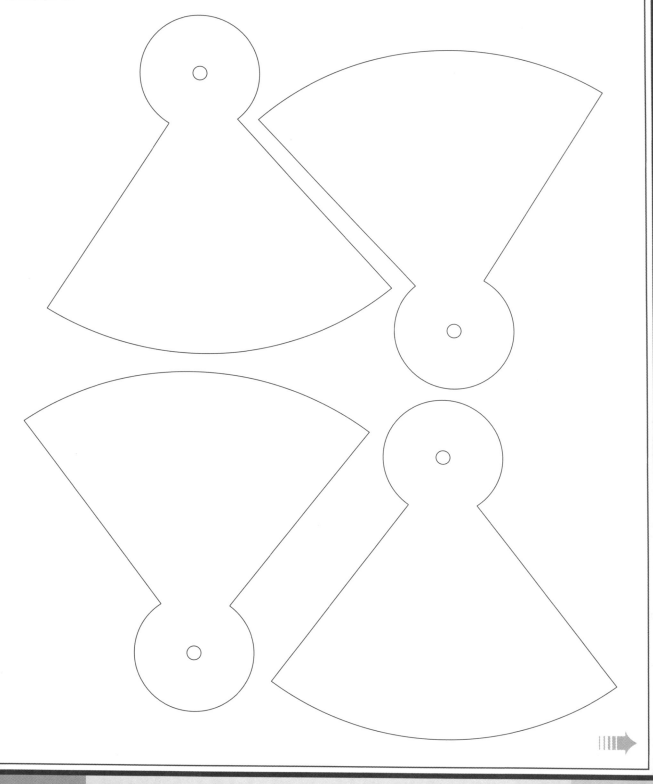

TEMPLATES FOR MAKING A MOVEABLE RESPONSIBILITY PIE CHART (CONT.)

Sheet C

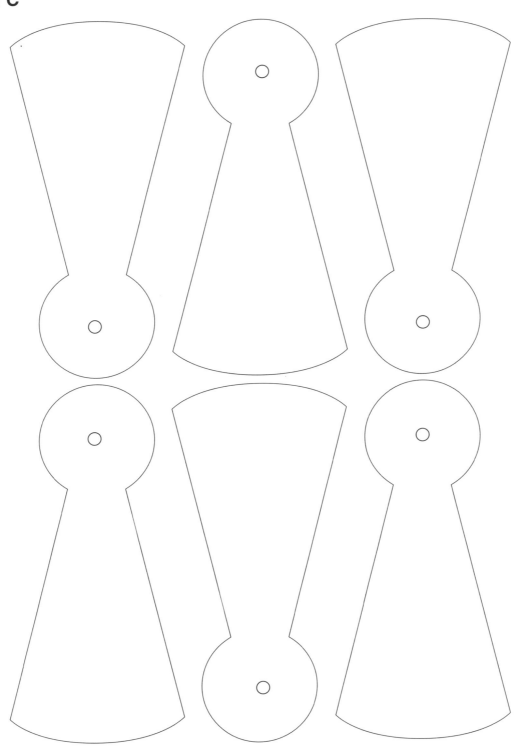

HOW ANIMALS AND PLANTS PROTECT AND DEFEND THEMSELVES

	Self protection	Warning the predator to go away	Escaping	Self-defence (counterattack)
	How does it stay safe and keep out of trouble? Examples: • Avoids predators' territory • Uses camouflage • Safety in numbers • Has protective covering • Plays tricks • Has 'Danger' colours or sounds	How does it warn predators to leave it alone when confronted? Examples: • Makes loud angry noises • Squirts unpleasant smells or fluids • Bluffs by making itself look larger and more dangerous than it really is	How does it get away fast from the predator and out of trouble?	If attacked, how does it act in self defence to try to drive the predator away or outsmart it?
Frilled Neck Lizard	Its colours are similar to the trees it lives in.	Opens its mouth to erect its frill. Then it stands tall on its two back legs and hisses.	Runs on its two back legs so it looks faster Climbs a tree	Scratches and bites
Chameleon	Changes colour so it is harder to see. Eyes can move separately to see better		Runs fast	
Zebra	Its black and white stripes makes it hard to see where one zebra finishes and another starts. Travels in a herd. Keeps moving from place to place	Snorts, and paws the ground, and lowers and raises its head as if it is going to charge	Runs fast	Kicks and bites
Grass Snake	Changes colour Stays in the same-coloured grass	Hisses	Slithers away into a hole	Bites

Opossum	Plays dead' for 40 minutes to 4 hours (Many predators won't eat carrion.)			
Armadillo	Has nine protective bony plates.			Bites and scratches
Monkey	Lives in a community group	Screeches loudly to other community members, glares, and shows its teeth	Swings through the trees	
Echidna	Has a spiny covering which is hard to grasp. Spines are normally flat to the skin.	Erects its spines so that it looks larger and more dangerous	Rolls into a ball and burrows into the ground	
Domestic Cat	Stays inside with its human protector Sleeps up high or in enclosed spaces so it can't be surprised	Raises its fur, hisses, raises the back part of its body, shows its teeth and glares	Runs fast and climbs trees and fences	Bites and scratches
Domestic Dog	Stays inside a lot with its human protector	Growls, shows its teeth, raises the back part of its body and its neck hairs and glares	Runs fast	Bites and scratches
Meerkat	Stays in a family group. All take turns as the 'watch guard' on a high spot.	Raises its tail. Advances on a predator in a group to deter them.	Runs into pre-built tunnels	Has long sharp claws to scratch with
Leopard	Its spots make it harder to see	Growls, roars, and glares	Runs fast, climbs trees	Bites and scratches

HOW ANIMALS AND PLANTS PROTECT AND DEFEND THEMSELVES (CONT.)

	Self protection	Warning the predator to go away	Escaping	Self-defence (counterattack)
Ape	Its size is protective	Beats its chest, screeches, shows its teeth and glares	Swings through the trees	Bites and scratches
Skunk		Stands on its two back legs, raises its tail and sprays a foul-smelling liquid	Smell allows a fast escape Runs fast	
Tortoise	Has a shell		Pulls head into shell as it can't travel fast	
Antelope	Travels in a herd. Doesn't stay in the same place for long		Runs very fast	Attacks with head and antlers if it has any
Stick Insect	Looks like a stick and stays very still		Some can lose a leg (and regrow it) to distract predators	
Caterpillar	Bright 'danger' colours	Bluffs by looking fierce Has stinging hairs		
Snail	Has a shell like a 'caravan'		Goes into its shell	
Earwig		Bluffs by raising its pincers over its head so that it looks like a poisonous scorpion		

Puss Moth Caterpillar	Has a tail which looks like the forked tongue of a snake which it waves it in the air	Rears its head and reveals a bright red frill with large blank spots which look like the staring eyes of a larger insect, and squirts a stinging acid substance	
Bee	Buzzes and has yellow and black stripes which signal 'danger—I sting!'		Stings
Harlequin bugs	Bright 'danger' colours	Gives off a nasty-smelling chemical if touched	
Puffer Fish	Has spines lying flat against its body	Swallows a great deal of water to make its spines erect	
Hermit Crab	Borrows the discarded shells of other creatures		
Sea Anemone		Grabs onto the predator	Disappears into its shell
Octopus	Changes colour	Squirts ink	Swims away very fast
Leafy Sea Dragon	Looks like a piece of seaweed so it can't be easily seen		Strangles with tentacles

HOW HUMANS PROTECT AND DEFEND THEMSELVES

Using self protection: staying safe and keeping out of trouble	Warning them to go away	Escaping from danger	Fighting back (e.g. defending oneself or outsmarting them)
We stay away from places and people that are dangerous	We stand tall, stare firmly and say 'leave me alone'	We quickly leave places when we realise that there is danger and go to a safer place	We ask someone else to help us
We don't draw attention to ourselves if there are dangerous people around	We tell them we will call the police if they don't go away	We know where some safe places are (e.g. police stations, family, neighbourhood watch houses). We move fast and go immediately.	We ask the people who have the job of looking after us (police, teachers) to help us
We stay together or near safe people			We try not to let them hurt us by putting up our hands to stop them
We pretend we aren't upset or scared			Sometimes we have to fight back, but not very often
We lock up things that are important to us			
We don't let people think it would be easy to rob or hurt us			
At school We don't try to attract attention to ourselves	**At school** We look angrily at them and say 'leave me alone' in a strong voice	**At school** If someone is tormenting us, we leave fast and go to a safer place	**At school** We ask a teacher or parent to help us fix the problem
We look for signs of danger and avoid people and places that are threatening or have been dangerous before	We say 'if you don't stop annoying me I will have to speak to the teacher about it'	We remember where the safe places at school are (e.g. near a teacher, in the library, near the older students)	
We stay near safe people and in company			
We don't bring things to school that are important to us			
We put on 'armour' by pretending we aren't upset if teased			